THE ROMANCE OF AFRICAN METHODISM

THE ROMANCE OF
AFRICAN METHODISM

*A Study of the African
Methodist Episcopal Church*

GEORGE A. SINGLETON

EXPOSITION PRESS · NEW YORK

To Monnaie

Preface

It is hoped that readers of this monograph will get at least a sympathetic view of a Church founded by erstwhile bondsmen, the majority of whom could not write their names, and whose backs bore lasting brands of slave ownership. Their stiffened and hardened fingers made cross-marks as they touched the pen, as Charles the Great had once impressed his signet ring. This is the story of a Church which existed seventy-eight years under the slave regime and eighty-odd years of freedom without liberty. The writer, whose grandparents were slaves, will feel amply rewarded should just one reader experience somewhat of the heart-tug and thrill of exultation which he had from time to time over a period of fifteen years while trying to prepare that story for the press. It was begun at Springfield, Illinois, while he was serving St. Paul as Pastor. It was continued at St. Paul, Lexington, Kentucky, and Philadelphia, where for eight years he served the Church as Editor of the *Christian Recorder*; then at Paul Quinn College, Waco, Texas; Jackson Theological Seminary, North Little Rock, Arkansas; St. Paul, Des Moines, Iowa; and finally at Philadelphia again where he was a displaced preacher, a supernumerary, for fifteen months. Often the economic shoe pinched but our faith was never diminished.

This volume is the outgrowth of love for the Church which began before I was born. In early childhood I often sat beside my father on the front steps of our Conway, South Carolina, home as he read the *Christian Recorder*, the *Richmond Planet*, the *Indiana Freemen*, the *Voice of Missions*, the *Boston Guardian*, and the *Sunday School Monitor*. The pictures of colored men inspired me before I learned my letters. In the chimney corner on wintry evenings and rainy I devoured these, in addition to the "library" of about a dozen books which my father, "Uncle" George C. Singleton, prized highly. He was the sage of Conway, and the mentor who lived "on the hill."

Early in life I saw and could distinguish the pictures of Richard

Allen and the other Bishops. Father was not an educated man. He never went to school a day in his life, and my mother was unlettered, but he believed in education and always wanted to write the history of Bethel, our local church. He had collected some material for the task. Finally he desired me to do the work, but his zeal outran his and my collective abilities. However, fate decreed that I should be elected to edit the *Christian Recorder* for two terms of four years each. First I had learned to read its pages by kerosene-oil lamps in the Conway home; when elected I was in my thirties. While editor, I traveled the Church widely and was always questing for historical material. A few valuable out-of-print books were added to my collection. Today they are of inestimable value for this work.

Interest in the study of history was heightened by a four-year sojourn with the lamented George Croft Cell, Ph.D., Professor of Historical Christianity in Boston University School of Theology, Dean Shirley Jackson Case, Professors William Warren Sweet and William E. Dodd of the University of Chicago, and Dr. James Moffatt, eminent scholar in the history of the Early Church.

While the book is written for the general reader, sources have been indicated for the benefit of those who may desire to make more extensive investigation.

It would be impossible to mention the names of the large number of friends and interested persons who have uttered words of encouragement along this way. Many have long since crossed the Great Divide, such as Bishops Henry Blanton Parks, John Albert Johnson, William H. Heard, and Joseph Simeon Flipper. Incidentally, their class of Bishops, elected at Norfolk in 1908, established a scholarship for graduate study in Divinity in 1916, and the second of these was awarded to the writer. He used it in the University of Chicago.

Drs. L. Ruffin Nichols, George Brown of Illinois, John M. Henderson, R. R. Downs, who was once Secretary of Missions, J. Campbell Beckett and H. P. Jones gave valuable information about Bishop D. A. Payne. Dr. J. P. Q. Wallace of Indianapolis gave many helpful incidents in the life of Bishop Wm. Paul Quinn. The rich storehouse of knowledge and the library of Bishop Reverdy C. Ransom, the Historiographer of the Church, aided materially. Portions of the manuscript were read by Bishop R. R. Wright, Jr., A. Wayman Ward, and the late Dr. John R. Hawkins, Financial Secretary. Most encouraging has been Mrs. Edna Dredden Gullins of Philadelphia. The Free Library of Philadelphia put at my disposal their invaluable resources of books and photographs, which aided in completing this work. The Presbyterian Historical Society, the Methodist Historical Society, the Princeton University Library, Dr. Francis Tees, retired Pastor of St. George in Philadelphia, Dr. George Conner, editor of *The Autobiography of Dr. Benjamin Rush,* aided by making available photographs of historical value. Especially do I owe a debt of gratitude to Dr. John Bright for having directed me to the engraving of the woman who walked with Richard Allen from St. George to Sixth and Lombard Streets. Bishops D. Ormonde Walker and Joseph Gomez assisted in checking the matter on "Radicalism and Reform." Bishop George W. Baber encouraged me to work. My thanks to those who have crossed the flood. And to Ettie Ruth, my wife, for inspiration and comfort from childhood days until now in the work of the ministry of reconciliation.

GEORGE A. SINGLETON

Philadelphia
February, 1952

Contents

INTRODUCTION   XV

CHAPTER I   Background and Early Environment   1
CHAPTER II   The Beginning — Richard Allen   12
               The Organization   20
CHAPTER III   Growth and Expansion   25
CHAPTER IV   An Eventful Period   33
               Divorce   41
CHAPTER V   The Church and Slavery   45
CHAPTER VI   Meeting a Vital Issue   57
CHAPTER VII   The Missionary Enterprise   68
CHAPTER VIII   An Adventure in Education   80
CHAPTER IX   Advancing Frontiers   100
CHAPTER X   Unsung Heroes   110
               Daniel Coker   113
               Morris Brown and Associates   114
               A Glorious Company   115
               William Paul Quinn   116
               T. M. D. Ward   116
               John Mifflin Brown   121
               Daniel Alexander Payne   122
               Henry McNeal Turner   123
               Other Leaders   126
CHAPTER XI   Following the Trail of the Fathers   137
CHAPTER XII   The General Conference of 1936   144
CHAPTER XIII   Radicalism and Reform   162
CHAPTER XIV   Years of Trial   170
CHAPTER XV   The Department and System of Finance   183
CHAPTER XVI   The Forward Look   189

APPENDIX A   Letter of Dr. Benjamin Rush to His Wife   199

APPENDIX B   Reproduction of "Speech on the Eligibility of Colored Members to Seats in the Georgia Legislature," by the Honorable H. M. Turner, September 3, 1868   201

APPENDIX C   Opinion in the District Court of the Honorable George A. Welsh Dismissing the Bill of Complaint, David H. Sims *vs.* S. L. Greene, July 1, 1947   219

BIBLIOGRAPHY   241

INDEX   247

List of Illustrations

RICHARD ALLEN, Founder and First Bishop of the African M. E. Church. (*By courtesy of the Free Library, Philadelphia, Penn.*)

BENJAMIN RUSH, M.D., Signer—Declaration of Independence; celebrated physician; close friend of R. Allen. (*By courtesy of the Free Library, Philadelphia, Penn.*)

ROBERT RALSTON, Philadelphia merchant; trustee of Princeton U.; Treasurer, Building Fund, first Bethel, Philadelphia. (*By courtesy of the Presbyterian Historical Society.*)

JANE ANN MURRAY, Contemporary of R. Allen. Left Old St. George Methodist Church with him in 1787. (*This photograph was found by Dr. John D. Bright, now Pastor of Mother Bethel. The copy was made by G. Marshall Wilson.*)

STEPHEN HILL, Wealthy lumber merchant; pioneer in the Church. Founded Old Folks Home and Zion in Philadelphia. (*Photograph copied by G. Marshall Wilson.*)

DANIEL ALEXANDER PAYNE, Educator; Church historian; editor; musician. Founded Wilberforce U. (*Photograph by courtesy of Mother Bethel, Philadelphia. Copied by G. Marshall Wilson.*)

T. M. D. WARD, "The old man eloquent." A powerful preacher-orator. Trail-blazer of the Church to the Pacific.

HENRY McNEAL TURNER, Ex-slave; first colored Chaplain in U. S. Army; orator; Georgia Legislator; Bishop in 1880.

Introduction

The story of the rise, expansion, and development of the African M. E. Church in the United States of America is a romance and constitutes another thrilling chapter in *The Acts of the Apostles*. The Church is a true offspring of the Methodist Church, until a few years ago known as the Methodist Episcopal Church, founded as a result of the Wesleyan movement in England and America in the eighteenth century. In the analogous sense that the true beginning of American history is in Europe, the African M. E. Church stemmed from the Methodist Episcopal Church. John Wesley was a member of the Episcopal Church until his death. Richard Allen, the founder of the African M. E. Church, was a bona fide member of the Methodist Society, licensed and ordained to preach by Francis Asbury.

Events in history do not occur adventitiously. Back of them always lie a series of related and interblended causes. The rise of African Methodism is no isolated phenomenon. It must be regarded in the light of revolutionary ideas in the realm of religious, politicial and social philosophy which were current in England and on the Continent. The philosophy of emancipation was in the air. The doctrine of the Rights of Man had triumphed in France following the Revolution. Royalty was dethroned and the common people came into their own with the magic words, *"Liberté, Égalité, Fraternité!"*

A great Frenchman once said, "An idea is irresistible." It may be added that ideas cannot be isolated or shut up in watertight compartments. The immediate backdrop of the American scene was the struggle of the colonies to free themselves from the Mercantilist policy of the mother country. A series of exploitative measures such as the Stamp Act of March 23, 1765, the bill to tax tea in 1767, the Molasses Act, and the Writs of Assistance were stubbornly and bitterly resented by the merchants and traders of Boston, New York, and Philadelphia who entered into nonimportation agreements. Meetings of protest were held in Boston and in the Quaker City. Eloquent and fiery speeches were made. Faneuil Hall became the Cradle of Liberty. Twenty years earlier, Crispus Attucks, a runaway slave of William Brouno of Framingham, Massachusetts, was no doubt an eager listener to many of these speeches; and he was so deeply impressed that on the night of March 5, 1770, when the ill feeling between the mother country and her colonial subjects had been rapidly gaining ground, with her troops concentrating at Boston, the torch of liberty was lighted by this black man. He led his white compatriots against the red coats, exclaiming: "These rebels have no business here; let's drive them away." As the people became enthusiastic he grew more daring. The soldiers under Captain Preston appeared to give way. "Come on! Don't be afraid! They dare not shoot, and if they dare, let them do it! Don't hesitate! Come on! We'll drive the rebels out of Boston!" These were his last words, for the soldiers volley-fired and brave Attucks fell, the first to bathe the American soil in his precious lifeblood for independence.[1]

Richard Allen was then ten years old. Even though communication and transportation were slow, he must have heard with mounting zeal of brave Attucks' supreme sacrifice. The eloquent Patrick Henry, who had been a failure as a merchant and was now a lawyer, had stirred the Virginia House of Burgesses with a moving address which many regarded as treasonable. He concluded: "I care not what course others may take; but as for me, give me liberty or give me death!" The ether waves were still carrying the voices of James Otis, John Hancock, and Samuel Adams. The stage was being set definitely for the mighty drama of freedom. Paradoxical as it may seem, the Colonial Fathers were struggling for self-determination against England, and at the same time held in bondage people represented by the first man who died for their liberty. Benjamin Franklin had declared that "slaves rather weaken than strengthen a state." The Sage of Monticello, Thomas Jefferson, expected to see "An entire stop forever put to such a wretched, cruel and unnatural trade."[2]

Richard Allen was born in time to be a strong young man during the American Revolution. He was a teamster for the army of

1. William Wells Brown, *The Rising Son*, 420 f.
2. Charles H. Wesley, *Richard Allen, Apostle of Freedom*, 46.

George Washington and hauled salt from Rehoboth, Delaware. He was thus a noncombatant with the army of supply. It is not difficult to see how one participating in such a conflict would be overmastered by the same spirit which fired the breasts of the leaders. For such is not limited by skin-color or hair-texture. The love of liberty and passion for equal human rights may be found burning in any man's heart. Just one year after Allen's birth, Phillis Wheatley was brought to this country from the shores of Africa, a slave girl of twelve. She was purchased by Mr. John Wheatley of Boston, and reared in an atmosphere of culture and refinement. She became a brilliant poetess and twenty years later wrote:

> Negroes black as Cain
> May be refined, and join the angelic train.

Allen was a slave owned by Benjamin Chew of Germantown in Philadelphia. Chew was a foremost citizen and was trained for the legal profession at the Middle Temple in London. He was distinguished not only for his legal attainments, for purity, and for his ability as a judge, but for a general literary culture, private worth and the accomplishments of a gentleman.[3] His city residence was at 110 South Third Street, and Seventh and Market, not far from the homes of Benjamin Franklin and Robert Morris, who lived on Market Street near Sixth. The Indian Queen, a popular tavern where the elite gathered to talk politics as they quaffed their refreshing beverages, was not far distant on Fourth Street near Chestnut. Chew's country estate was "Cliveden" in Germantown. Here Richard Allen was born. The name "Allen" was popular, for the mayor of the city was William Allen.

Many social affairs were held at "Cliveden" on week ends, to which important people came. The conversation and "table talk" was of great import and lasting value. Within this social environment Allen lived until sold to a Mr. Stokely who lived on his place in Delaware near Dover. No one will ever be able to measure the extent of the impression made upon Allen during these early formative years by these incidental contacts.[4]

---

3. John F. *Watson, Annals of Philadelphia,* III, 166, 460.
4. Wesley, *op. cit.* 10; Brown, *op. cit.,* 336 ff.; *Life of Lorenzo Dow,* 545 f.; Abel Stevens, *History of the M. E. Church,* IV, 259 f.

Proscription and segregation in Old St. George Methodist Episcopal Church constituted the concrete situation which gave rise to the beginning of African Methodism; but deeper than that was the desire and determination on the part of Allen and his associates to be clothed with the full panoply of manhood. One of the greatest and most eventful days in the history of Christian civilization dawned when they left that church and went out, not knowing whither, but sustained by an unconquerable faith, and faced an untried future. The very idea of former slaves resenting social injustice to the extent that they break with the old organization is startling. They were indeed daring and heroic. By this act Allen's greatness towers above that of John Wesley, the father of Methodism, or Martin Luther, the Monk of Erfurt. True, the leader of the Protestant revolt struck a blow against an intrenched autarchic papacy and gained the right of private judgment, the universal priesthood of all believers, and the freedom of a Christian man. Wesley was the spearhead of a great revival movement which reached the poor, neglected classes, and shot a decadent, formalistic religion through with emotion. With him religion was a heartfelt experience, the work of God in the soul of a man. But Richard Allen transcends them both and becomes the first since Jesus walked the ways and climbed the hills of Judea, and Galilee, to interpret religion as the Fatherhood of God, and the Brotherhood of Man. In this he is a vitalist. Religion is deeply concerned with human personality, which is of supreme worth. God is the Father of all, and all men are brothers. In this philosophy there is no room for color discrimination or segregation. In the church of God it is unthinkable. Allen believed this and did something about it. He is the religious pioneer incomparable, and stands ahead of Cephas and Paul. Religion with Allen rises above caste and proscription. He is thus a prophet of the new day.

It has been alleged that the African M. E. Church came into existence as a result of jealousy on the part of Francis Asbury, who envied Allen because of his power and popularity as a preacher. This insight has been questioned since it was made by Lorenzo Dow, regarded by such historians as Abel Stevens as "eccentric." However, Allen was located in Philadelphia when there were only five persons of color as members of St. George Church. By 1787 Allen had gathered around him forty-two persons, and formed a Prayer Band, the real beginning of the Church. In 1793 he built a church for his people at Sixth and Lombard Streets. It was an old, abandoned blacksmith shop, which he hauled from in front of the Walnut Street Prison at Sixth and Walnut Streets. He removed it with his own team of six horses.[5]

Dr. W. E. B. DuBois has well said that the test of American Christianity is the test of the color line. That has been patent from the very beginning of the American Colonies, the period of the Confederation, the formation of the Union, and the adoption of the Constitution, so vividly portrayed by Carl Van Doren in his *The Great Rehearsal*. It was evident in the slavery controversy, division and reunion, the Reconstruction Era, and down to the present with President Truman's Civil Rights Program. The African M. E. Church is a protest as were Sempach, Runnymede, and Harper's Ferry. It believes steadfastly with the Apostle unto the Gentiles that out of one blood God created all people to dwell together on the face of the earth. It holds with Cephas at Joppa that God is no respecter of persons. It makes bold to accept the findings of modern natural and social science, and asserts that there are no fundamental and inescapable differences among men, except as a result of geographical and environmental factors and forces. The Church believes in an open road to talent, the abundant life for all. At the same time it is not a Jim Crow church. Shortly after the organization of the Church in Philadelphia, one of the societies had on its roll 1,196 white persons and 96 colored persons. Many whites have joined it, and many are members of it today.

While Allen's Church was a separate one, his religion was comprehensive, and his pastoral services to all men. He risked his life and spent himself in sacrificial service nursing yellow-fever patients in Philadelphia in 1793. The victims were mostly whites; Negroes seem to have been largely immune to the malignant scourge which decimated the city. The separatist movement came in the sheer logic of events, and Allen was a child of his age.

The Church of Allen feels that it has a sacred duty to perform for the Kingdom of God. Its unique task is to preach a whole Gospel, to interpret Jesus in terms of human relations, to preach Christ

5. *The Autobiography of Benjamin Rush*, 95-102, 244, 308; *Life, Experience, Gospel Labors of the Right Reverend Richard Allen*, 21 f.

in all of His offices — as Prophet, Priest, and King — and at the
same time to maximize the social emphasis, with due regard to the
mystical element. The Church will teach racial self-esteem and
self-help. It will regard the world as its parish, and all as spiritual
descendants of John Wesley. It will not be a stickler for non-es-
sentials, but sees in the word *African* an historical significance,
stemming from the period when all movements by people of African descent were denominated thus, e.g., the "Free African
Society."

THE ROMANCE OF AFRICAN METHODISM

CHAPTER I

Background and Early Environment

Look at the rock whence ye were hewn, the quarry you were dug from. — ISAIAH 51:1

The growth of the A. M. E. Church is a splendid tribute to the Negro genius. Of all the denominations under the name of "Methodist," white or black, it has seemed to touch the heart of the Negro and make him a man of power. Its institutions and laws are the result of Negro genius, and also are the exhibition of his executive ability and abundant wisdom. — AFRO-AMERICAN PROGRESS

The rise of African Methodism in the United States during the latter part of the eighteenth century was no mere accident. It grew out of the spirit of the times and represents in a concrete way the doctrine of the Rights of Man — a social and political philosophy then current in England and Europe, and whose influence was felt in America. The Independent African Church movement was led by such men as Richard Allen of Philadelphia, Daniel Coker of Baltimore, and Morris Brown of South Carolina. The social milieu out of which the Church rose was characterized on the one hand by slavery, on the other by an effort on the part of the Colonists to free themselves from Great Britain, which resulted in the Revolutionary War.

The spiritual antecedents of African Methodism have their roots deep in the soil of the past. The very genius of the Christian religion is Brotherhood. Jesus, through whose veins coursed the blood of diverse peoples, was not circumscribed by lines of color or caste. His Gospel and personal attitude cut directly across lines of racial distinction. Dr. Shirley Jackson Case of the University of Chicago Divinity School holds that Jesus' probable con-

1

tact in Sephoris was seen in the breadth of His social outlook. He was a universalist.

The Church during the early centuries in the Mediterranean world and down through the Middle Ages, did not base membership upon pigmentation of skin. Color-Christianity is very largely American. Here it reaches untenable heights of illogicality. Present-day findings in the various fields of scientific investigation do not leave race prejudice a leg on which to stand. But in spite of science, the Church, and religion, it persists — the supreme test of our social and religious institutions.

One of the greatest interpreters of Jesus, one of the most outstanding protagonists of the faith once delivered unto the saints, teaches that "there is no distinction of Jew, and Greek, the same Lord is the Lord of them all." In another place he says: "There is no room for Jew or Greek, there is no room for slave or freeman, there is no room for male or female. You are all *one* in Christ Jesus." Once more he says: "In it there is no room for Greek or Jew, circumcision or uncircumcision, barbarian, Scythian, slave or freeman. Christ is everything, and everywhere." Another great Apostle who preceded him in time caught the vision that God is no respecter of persons, shows no partiality, but welcomes the man of any nation who reveres Him and does what is right. The attitude of these Christians was that out of one blood the Father had created all peoples to live together as brothers, and children of a common heavenly Father. When Christianity is genuine and moves upon its highest levels, it regards all men as centers of value, of intrinsic worth, and in terms of their highest possibilities. There is nothing in all the world of more value in the view of God than a human person. A newly born babe of African parents on the banks of the Zambezi River is worth more in the sight of God than all the wealth on Wall Street and the armed might of the nations of the world.

In the latter part of the eighteenth century, Europe saw the travail of her soul. Those upsetting and transforming ideas and ideals of democracy which had smoldered with scarcely a spark through the period of Feudalism and the Middle Ages were blown into a burning flame in the Renaissance. They moved with atomic power under the leadership of Martin Luther, the hero-prophet. His pamphlet, *The Universal Priesthood of All Believ-*

ers, The Freedom of a Christian Man, The Right of Private Judgment, unfurled the banner of Christian liberty in the sphere of conscience and patterns of Christian behavior. Brave and daring souls spoke and wrote about equality of all men. Gradually it dawned upon those who led the advance along the thought frontier, and who like the loftiest mountain peaks catch the first golden tints of the dawn, that men are persons, endowed with certain innate, inalienable rights, among which are life, liberty and the pursuit of happiness. Man — "Noble in reason! infinite in faculty! in action like an angel! in apprehension like a God! the beauty of the world! the paragon of animals!" Human beings became invested with sacredness.

The Protestant Revolt resulted in the spiritual emancipation of the Church in Europe. The Counter Reformation sought to regain what had been lost. Too late! The revolters won a priceless victory. It was but a short step from Luther's defiance of a religious and ecclesiastical monarchy to the people's defiance of a secular and political monarchy. They are of the same piece. A little more than two hundred years later the common people in France were on the move. Intrenched power was challenged; the French Revolution was on, and on July 14, 1789, the Bastille fell. Like a comet, Napoléon Bonaparte flashed across the European sky and caused the Continent to tremble until one day he met Wellington at Waterloo.

Allen and his liberty-loving co-workers learned lessons of religious manhood from the very people who held them in the house of bondage. They must have caught snatches of the stories that make up the early Christian history of the country, of the "Mayflower" and its heroic band which braved the perils of the Atlantic Ocean and the greater hazards on land, that they might enjoy freedom of conscience and freedom of worship. Roger Williams in Rhode Island, William Penn in Pennsylvania, certainly appealed to many of the leading men who held slaves. Methodism itself is a phase of reaction and revolution.

For three hundred years or more the world had been emerging into a new order as a result of discovery, exploration, and invention. Europe had passed through a series of upheavals, phases of a larger one, commercial, industrial and intellectual. The machine age had begun, which tended increasingly to break up rural

communities and create urban centers. Vice and crime went hand
in hand as the people embraced the new mores. Drunkenness was
the means of trying to drown out the dreary existence and weari-
ness from excessively long hours in mill and factory. Gambling,
licentiousness, and rowdyism held undisputed sway. The clergy,
in too many instances, were grossly corrupt. The people patterned
themselves after their spiritual leaders. There was little real, vital
religion. The Church had become callous, cold, and indifferent.
Some deadening influence was upon it. Religious ceremony was
an empty form and hollow mockery. Genuine content was wanting. The poor common people constituted a neglected class as in
the days when Jesus came preaching.

Into this situation, with his "heart beating strangely warm,"
came John Wesley, the founder of Methodism in England, whence
it spread to the American Colonies. Methodism may be rightly
thought of as a reaction against the acute secularization of religion in the Church of England, a militant protest against a decadent faith and a launching-out into the deep of a personal, heartfelt religion as experience.

This, then, is to say that the story of African Methodism must
of necessity begin with the Wesleyan movement. John Wesley
was born on June 14, 1703, in the parish of Epworth, Lincolnshire.
It was exactly fifty-six years and eight months before Allen saw
the light of day. Many volumes have been written about Wesley
and his work. It is our present interest to state that Methodism is
a natural event in the steady trek of the human race down the
ages, a gradual unfolding of the process of emancipation. Revo-
lutions never move backwards, and Methodism was no exception
to the general rule. Wesley loved his Church and was a member of
it until his noble spirit passed. His was a religious purpose and
ideal. "This one thing I do" might be very aptly applied to him.
His evangel reached the poor, unconsidered, neglected people. To
thousands he preached in the broad open spaces in God's great
out-of-doors. He was an itinerant field preacher and went everywhere; constantly on the go, a figure astride a horse, and with a
Bible under his arm. Wesley's method and approach were new.
Such had not happened since Jesus entered His home-town syna-
gogue one day and proclaimed: "The poor have the Gospel
preached unto them," and since St. Francis ministered unto the

sick and indigent in Italy. As strong men were convicted of sin and became conscious of their condition, one could often trace on greasy, sooty faces the paths made by tears which met beneath their chins. Wesley was adept at organizing. Associated with him was his brother Charles, and George Whitefield. The former was a writer of hymns, and the latter an effective and powerful preacher.

Methodism had its rise in England at a time when the religious and moral tone of the people had reached very low levels. Authors like Lea, Dickens, and Lecky give vivid and lurid portraits of the prevalent social life. This is augmented by the works of E. G. Coulter. The interested reader might peruse these books and be amply rewarded. However nauseating, they enable one to behold the evolution of religion on its moral side and to see how necessary Methodism was to cleanse and purify the stagnant ecclesiastical waters which flowed through the eighteenth century. Methodism was a necessity in the long perspective and revealing logic of events. It pointed the people to the lofty ideals of holiness, Christian perfection, and religion as an inner experience. John Wesley himself was a mystical pragmatist. His subjective experience was tested on the level of performance. He has been regarded as the "true center of a century."

Professor George Croft Cell says: "His life spans the eighteenth century; his constructive influence, the Western world. He is an epitome of the last two centuries. He tried out and transcended the humanized Christianity of the Age of the Enlightenment. He summed up in his thought and experiments in religion a thorough trial of its decadent Christianity, the evangelical reaction against the superficial liberalism, and the origin and progress of the Revival for half a century."

From the outset Methodism was no chauvinistic religion or esoteric cult. The periphery of its circle was the rim of the universe, and the most far-distant horizon. "I look upon the world as my parish" was expressive of its goal. This was a way of paraphrasing the words of the Greatest Religious Genius of all time. He had said eighteen hundred years previously: "Go ye into all the world, and preach the Gospel to every creature."

In 1735 Wesley came to Georgia with James Oglethorpe as chaplain. The colony was formed as a haven for the poor of Eng-

land and persecuted Protestants in Europe. Slavery was absolutely
prohibited.

> Slavery, the misfortune, if not the dishonor, of other
> plantations, is absolutely proscribed. . . . The name of
> slavery is here unheard, and every inhabitant is free from
> unchosen masters and oppression.[1]

Wesley's dream was not only to be a missionary to the members
of the colony, but an apostle to the native Indians as well.

Savannah was the locale of his labors, and down the coast on
St. Simon Island. The ruins of Oglethorpe's old fort are still visible about seven or eight feet out from the sandy shore-line and
partly covered with water. One may stand beneath the old moss-
bearded oak where Wesley preached to the Indians. He did not
remain long in the colony. His method and technique failed to
work among the colonists and natives. He was a High Church-
man.

After his return to England, he had a religious experience that
altered the course and emphasis of his life. Feeling had a place
definite in religion. His work bore abundant fruit, and the common people heard him gladly. Wesley never lost sight of his
world-girdling evangel. In 1784 he ordained Thomas Coke for the
American work, which had been started about twenty years earlier in New York by Barbara Heck, Phil Embury, and Captain
Thomas Webb, who had lost the sight of his right eye and wore
a green shade over it. Robert Strawbridge, a local preacher from
Ireland, came to the Colonies about 1760 and preached at Sam's
Creek, Frederick County, Maryland. There is a question of priority, whether Methodism began in New York first or in Baltimore. The preponderance of opinion and evidence is in favor of
New York.[2]

From the beginning of Methodism in America, Negroes were
admitted to membership in the various societies. "Aunt Annie,"
a servant in the Sweitzer family in Frederick County, was one of
the first members of the Log Meeting House on Sam's Creek,

---

1.   James M. Buckley, *History of Methodism*, I, 75.
2.   *Ibid.*, 113, 141 f.; James A. Handy, *Scraps of A. M. E. Church History*,
22 f.

"Lovely-Lane Meeting House," and old Strawberry Alley. Richard Allen, and Harry Hoosier, called "Black Harry," were members of the Christmas Conference which met in Baltimore, December 24, 1784, and organized Methodism in America. This "General Conference" also elected and ordained Asbury a Deacon one day, an Elder the next, and elected him and set him apart as a Bishop the next. Methodism met the needs of the times, and history has fully justified the action taken. Asbury was a true son of God, and he endured hardship as a good soldier of Jesus Christ.

Harry Hoosier was a powerful preacher. Bishop Coke used him freely and writes that "he really believes him one of the best preachers in the world." Hoosier traveled with Jesse Lee through New England, and helped lay the foundation of Methodism in that region.[3] He frequently traveled with Asbury. On one occasion the Bishop was ill and could not preach. Instead, Harry delivered the sermon to an immense crowd. Many were on the outside and could not get in, but they heard. When the sermon was over, one remarked that the Bishop certainly preached a great sermon. Another brother who was on the inside told him that the message was not brought by the Bishop but by his servant. The man who heard but did not see rejoined that if the servant could do that well, what must the Bishop himself be able to do! In 1787, of the 21,949 members in the Methodist Church, 3,893 were Negroes.[4] The 1784 General Conference failed to order the ordination of its colored members. An ordaining resolution was not passed until 1800.[5]

Methodism grew as heralds of the Cross went from point to point, from settlement to settlement, and from plantation to plantation, and told the story of salvation to the people, masters and slaves. At the same time England's commercial policy met with increasing disfavor in the Colonies. The ancestors of the Colonists had come to America seeking religious liberty. With several thousands of miles between them and the mother country, the Colonists felt strongly the ties that bound them to their motherland. But they were in a new world, a new environment, and imbued with a new spirit. To be sure, there were some Royalists

---

3. Buckley, *op.cit.*, I, 320.
4. *Ibid.*, 304, 374.
5. Joseph T. Wilson, *The Black Phalanx*, 29 f., 51.

and Tories, and a large segment thought of selfish interests and
were swayed by the fortunes of the conflict. More and more the
exploitative economic and commercial policy was felt. The policy of taxation was very unpopular. Events followed fast, and
finally blood was shed. The Boston Massacre stirred the country.
The death of Attucks aroused the people. He was regarded as a
martyr, and his funeral was one of state. He was buried with three
white comrades. Today his resting-place is visited with reverence.
On the marker which stands at the head of the common grave are
these words:

> Long as in freedom's cause the wise contend,
> Dear to your country shall your fame extend;
> While to the world the lettered stone shall tell,
> Where Caldwell, Attucks, Gray, and Maverick fell.[6]

For a few years, March Fifth was observed as our national
birthday. Later July Fourth was substituted, following the sign-
ing of the Declaration of Independence and victory in the Revolutionary War. The country was yet to take due notice of its
first martyr for freedom. But the voice of justice will not forever
remain silent. Crispus Attucks awaits the unbiased and unpreju-
diced historian to accord him his rightful place in the American
chronicle.

With such an ideological background of struggle for independence, liberty and equality; with the thoughts of Rousseau,
Hume, Locke, Adam Smith, and Kant taking root in the minds
of men; with William Wilberforce, Granville Sharp, and Thomas
Clarkson waging a relentless campaign for the abolition of the
slave trade in England; with patriots in the Colonies voicing the
spirit of the times; with Attucks dying in Boston and George
Washington taking command of the Continental Army and leading it through seven years of intense suffering; with Tom Paine,
the unkempt who never trimmed his fingernails but was a soldier
par excellence and pamphleteer superb, rallying the soldiers and
stirring the people with his *Common Sense*, and *Crisis* — there
appeared a restlessness among the members of the Methodist
Church. There was a growing antipathy on the part of the whites,

---

6. B. T. Tanner, *Apology for African Methodism,* 291.

and a corresponding desire on the part of the Negroes for manhood rights. If they were good enough to fight for freedom in the land, they were good enough to enjoy it in the Church of God. They were admitted to membership in the Methodist Church but were compelled to occupy the gallery, the outer fringe, or some other designated place during the service. In some instances the slaves sat in the rear, which was partitioned off by a wooden screen. They observed the services by peeping through eyeholes cut for the purpose. They were admitted to the Communion Table after the whites had been served. When these colored Christians met together from time to time, it was only natural that they should discuss events in their little world which meant most to themselves — the manner of their treatment in the religious service. And perhaps many of them had served in the Continental Army. Certainly Richard Allen had served as a noncombatant. He had risked his life to serve the citizenry during the malignant fever of 1793. His associates and close friends were among the leading white people of Philadelphia. He had entertained them in his Spruce Street home, including Bishop Thomas Coke, Dr. Benjamin Rush, Robert Ralston, and their friends.[7]

Prayer meetings were organized in Philadelphia and Baltimore. Out of these groups independent societies were formed. For the first time in the history of the world, the color of a man's skin was the badge by which he would be welcomed or discriminated against in the Church of Jesus Christ. Thus, the African Methodist Episcopal Church was organized because of racial discrimination. White Methodists did not care to associate with their colored brethren. In Philadelphia the situation was becoming acute. Richard Allen's popularity as a preacher was increasing. By industry and thrift he had grown wealthy. Dow says:

> Francis (Asbury), being jealous of his power, noticed Allen with a watchful eye — and finally embargoed him to locate and become stationary. He accordingly, after looking around, fixed upon the city of Philadelphia, where there were but five colored people in society at that time.

---

7. *The Autobiography of Benjamin Rush*, 202, 221, 250; Matthew Carey, *The Malignant Fever in Philadelphia in* 1793, 77.

However, he turned in to hold meetings in season and out of season, here and there, and wherever he could find an opening and gain access — so that the society soon increased to forty-two. This mode of conduct raised a "dust," and gathered him some opposition. . . . The colored people were considered by some persons as being in the way: they were resolved to have them removed, and placed around the walls, corners, etc. — which to execute, the above expelled and restored man, at prayer time, did attempt to pull Absalom Jones from his knees — which procedure, with its concomitants, gave rise to the building of an "African Meeting House," the first ever built in these Middle or Northern States.

This raised a "dust" — the colored people were commanded to desist, and make acknowledgment within a limited period, or somebody would know the reaşon why! Upon this they sent in their resignation and went on with the building.[8]

The final test of history is that of outcomes. It is the testing ground for all values. Time will place its stamp of approval or disapproval upon the acts of Allen and his associates. In the short perspective of a century and threescore years, the Church has carved a niche of lasting value for itself. Members of an enslaved race, while most of their brethren and many of their kindred were in chains, boldly struck out for themselves and blazed a new highway of Gospel grace. When the tides of opposition surged around Allen, he stood like a rock. He might not have heard of his African forebear and kinsman Athanasius at the Council of Nicea. But he stood!

The Church which Allen founded is not a Jim Crow organization. Whosoever will, may unite with it. Anyone, except a *Slaveholder*. It believes and holds with John Wesley: "If thy heart be as my heart, then give me thy hand." The restriction and prohibition against slaveholders joining the Church remains in the Discipline as a reminder of the struggle through which the Church has passed. The motto of the African M. E. Church is the Father-

———————
8. Lorenzo Dow's *Journal,* quoted in B. W. Arnett, *The Budget of 1885,* 156.

BENJAMIN RUSH, M.D.

Signer—Declaration of Independence; celebrated physician; close friend of R. Allen

RICHARD ALLEN

Founder and First Bishop of the African M. E. Church

ROBERT RALSTON

Wealthy Philadelphia merchant; trustee of Princeton University; Treasurer of Building Fund, first Bethel, Philadelphia

JANE ANN MURRAY

Contemporary of R. Allen. Left Old St. George Methodist Church with him in 1787

hood of God, the redemptive work of Jesus Christ, and the Brotherhood of Man. "God our Father, Christ our Redeemer, Man our Brother." There is nothing beyond that. It expresses the essence of the teaching of Jesus.

Every great movement is to be thought of in terms of a personality of distinction. The birth of Christianity goes back to the Jesus of history; the expansion of the Church from Palestine into the Graeco-Mediterranean world was largely the work of a small, slightly hunchbacked, weak-eyed Jew, Paul; orthodox Christological thinking will move for a long time in Augustinian paths; the Protestant Reformation will be forever thought of as the personality of Martin Luther thrown into the logic of events; John Wesley cannot be dissociated from the Eighteenth Century Revival in England and the rise of Methodism. His organizing genius and constructive influence stand as an imperishable monument to his never-fading memory. So the beginning of African Methodism stems from and centers in Richard Allen, the Apostle of Freedom and spiritual emancipator of his people. The chapters which follow will attempt to relate the story of the Church which he founded.

CHAPTER II

The Beginning — Richard Allen

I called to the Eternal in my plight, I cried to my God
for aid ... he heard my voice. — PSALM 18:6

I met with opposition. — ʼALLEN

Truly the world is never the same after a great man has
lived and wrought in it. The appearance of Richard Allen within
the area of humanity is one of the most significant events in the
long sweep of humanity through the centuries, and one of the
most important in the two millennia history of the Christian
Church. Looking backward at his life, it seems as if he were a
child of destiny, born from his mother's womb, like Jeremiah,
for some high task. His very life is a thrilling romance. As John
Wesley stands upon the shoulders of Martin Luther and the Protestant reformers who in turn stand upon the shoulders of Augustine, Richard Allen stands upon the broad shoulders of the father
of Methodism.

All great men in the annals of the race's history are to be
thought of in connection with the age which produces them, and
with the preceding events. The situation was ready for such a
man and such a movement. The fullness of time had come. Had
Richard Allen not appeared, some character like unto him would
have been oncoming to defy the hydra-headed monster of race
prejudice and segregation in the Church of Christ. The time was
ripe for a move in the direction of spiritual emancipation of the
race. Of this movement Richard Allen became the spearhead. He
overtowers as a matchless leader all of those sincere and brave men
who rallied around his banner, most of whom could not write
their names. Richard Allen is the lengthened shadow of African
Methodist Episcopalianism: "as monachism, of the Hermit Anthony; the Reformation, of Luther; Quakerism, of Fox; Metho-

dism, of Wesley; abolition, of Clarkson. Scipio, Milton called 'the height of Rome'; and all history resolves itself very easily into the biography of a few stout and earnest persons." The observation of Emerson applied by Buckley to Methodism is quite apropos of Richard Allen and the Church which is the offspring of his heart and brain.[1]

Shortly after the birth of Allen, his parents and four children were sold as slaves into Delaware, near Dover. There he was awakened as a result of the preaching of Freeborn Garretson, who did not know that slavery was wrong, since he had never read a book on the subject and no one had ever told him of the evil.[2] However, when he saw that the iniquitous system was not consonant with Christianity, he liberated his slaves.[3] The religious experience in which Richard Allen came to a saving knowledge of the Lord Jesus Christ was similar in content to that of John Wesley who said that he felt his "heart beating strangely warm." There was a deep searching of heart, and self-examination, repentance and godly sorrow. The outcome was a happy conversion. He experienced what E. Stanley Jones calls, "The gradual or sudden changing from the Kingdom of Self to the Kingdom of God through the grace and power of Christ." Allen was a new creature in the Lord. He describes it himself: "All of a sudden my dungeon shook, my chains flew off and, glory to God, I cried. My soul was filled. I cried, enough for me — the Saviour died!" Allen went from house to house exhorting his old companions and telling all with whom he came in contact of the newly found joy and peace.[4] Paul, Augustine, and a goodly fellowship of saints in many ages had traversed the road before him, the strait and narrow way of the truly converted.

The validity of a conversion experience is always found in the changed life which follows. There come into the center of one's life new loyalties and new ideals to motivate and impel. Old things pass away, and all things become new. Allen was dependable, honest, and industrious. His was a "religion worth having."

1. James M. Buckley, *History of Methodism*, I, 1.
2. *Ibid.*, 375.
3. Halford E. Luccock and Paul Hutchinson, *Story of Methodism*, 328.
4. Richard Allen, *Life*, 10.

His master could rely upon and trust him to do his work at all times. This master was a man with a good heart. Allen's industry and thrift are to be seen in his having saved sufficient money to purchase his and his brother's freedom. The price was two thousand dollars in gold and silver. The kindness of Allen's master, Stokely, who was deeply moved by the preaching of Garretson, held no charm for him. Allen said: "Slavery is a bitter pill."

He left the house of bondage and went out like Abraham not knowing whither but looking for a city that hath foundations whose maker and builder is God. And like Paul, he worked with his hands, and earned a living by cutting cord wood, doing a day's work in a brickyard, and hauling salt from Rehoba, Sussex County, in Delaware, during the Revolutionary War. He had regular places where he would stop and preach. After peace was declared, Allen traveled extensively and preached the Word. In 1783 he went to New Jersey; in 1784 he returned to Pennsylvania. "I walked until my feet became so sore and blistered the first day that I scarcely could bear them to the ground."[5] He stopped with one Caesar Waters at Radnor about twelve miles from Philadelphia and was invited to eat supper with the family. His feet were so sore that he could not go to the table. They bore it to him. After supper the good wife bathed his feet with warm water and bran.

The Organizing Conference of the Methodist Church, called the Christmas Conference, met in Baltimore on December 24, 1784. Garretson was sent "like an arrow over North and South" summoning the preachers. Dr. Thomas Coke had already been set apart by Wesley for the American work. Francis Asbury was ordained a Deacon on one day by Whatcoat and Vasey. On the next day he was ordained an Elder. And on the next day he was set apart as a Bishop in the Methodist Church, the first in a long line of Episcopates. About sixty ministers were present, of whom two were men of color — Richard Allen and Harry Hoosier, or "Black Harry," the great preacher — and they accompanied Thomas Coke on the first route of about a thousand miles.[6] An old picture of the conference shows Harry. This session plainly revealed the position of the colored members in the church; it

---

5. *Ibid.,* 15.
6. Buckley, *op. cit.,* 287 f.

failed to order the ordination of its colored preachers, as in every subsequent General Conference up to 1800, when a special resolution, under certain regulations, allowed the Bishop to ordain the colored preachers.[7]

After the General Conference Richard Allen traveled with Richard Whatcoat, a "man of God." Bishop Francis Asbury requested Allen to travel with him, but he told Allen that in the slave states he must not mingle with the slaves, and that on many occasions he would have to sleep in the carriage. His allowance was to be his victuals and clothes. The offer was directly and positively refused. Richard Allen's manifest destiny was to be a Bishop himself, the first of his race, and not a Bishop's servant — to mingle with whomsoever he wished, to sleep in his own home, and not in someone's carriage.

The year 1786 saw Richard Allen again in Philadelphia, where he preached at five o'clock in the morning at St. George's Church. He soon saw a large field open in seeking and instructing his African brethren, who long had been a forgotten and neglected people. He often preached five times a day. He gathered his people and established prayer meetings. His prayer group of forty-two members was the beginning of the African M. E. Church in 1787. An open and effectual door was before him, but there were many adversaries. When he proposed erecting a place of worship, he met with strong opposition from among his own people. When he left St. George's Church, he was accompanied by Absalom Jones, whom the officers had attempted to drag from his knees while in the act of prayer with William White and Dorus Ginnings. They were also opposed by the white ministers of the Church.[8] But Allen continued, having obtained help of God, and the work of his hands prospered.

Richard Allen was a preacher of might and power. He felt the "woe is me, if I preach not the Gospel" and "held meetings in season and out of season, here and there, and wherever he could find an opening and gain access — so that the society soon increased to forty-two."[9] Like one who had turned the world upside

---

7.   James A. Handy, *Scraps of A. M. E. Church History,* 23 f.
8.   Richard Allen, *op. cit.,* 21 f.; Lorenzo Dow, *Strictures on Church Government,* 545 f.
9.   Dow in B. W. Arnett, *Budget for 1885,* 156 f.

down he came, he saw, he wrought. No power could stop him.

A contrary reaction was the result. He says: "*I met with opposition.*" But Richard Allen was one of those rare spirits whom opposition could not quell. Some thought that the colored people were in the way and were determined to have them removed. When the attempt was made to pull Absalom Jones from his knees, Allen and his friends walked out. This action was greater and entailed more personal sacrifice than that of the man who nailed his ninety-five theses to the church door at Wittenberg, or when he stood before the Diet of Worms. On that day and by that deed Richard Allen broke down the partition-wall of racial proscription and segregation in the Christian Church, not only in America but throughout the world. For until this hour the supreme test of Christianity, and especially the American brand, is that of color. Abstruse questions of theology and philosophy are not so engaging to the best Christian minds and leaders of the Church as those of social problems. The creation of a social order dominated by the ideals of Jesus, in which all men shall live together as brothers, is more to be desired than some discussion of "how many angels can dance on the point of a needle." It has been remarked that the Negro is not theologically minded. At the same time it must be remembered that neither was Jesus. He was a vitalist. Human persons were his chiefest concern. In spite of the Patristics in the formative period of the Church, it will capture and enshrine more of the spirit of Jesus when it can say in a new creedal formulation: "*I believe in the brotherhood of man.*"

When the colored people began to attend St. George's in large numbers, they were removed from their original seats and placed around the wall. One Sabbath morning they were sent to the gallery. The sexton at the door so informed them. They went to the gallery and occupied seats generally as they had formerly done on the main floor. The meeting had begun and the prayer was about to be offered. Allen had not been on his knees long before he heard "Considerable scuffling and low talking." One of the trustees had hold of the Rev. Absalom Jones and was trying to pull him up off his knees, and saying, "You must get up — you must not kneel here." Mr. Jones replied: "Wait until the prayer is over, and I will get up and trouble you no more." The trustee beckoned to another trustee to come to his assistance. He came, and went to William White, to pull him up. "By this time prayer was over, and *we all went out of the church in a body, and they were no more plagued with us in the church.*"[10]

The colonies had been engaged in a struggle for independence from England. The doctrine of the Rights of Man had inspired the people to line up in embattled array for a new order, and the way to personal martyrdom was led by the Negro, Crispus Attucks, on the streets of Boston, the night of March 5, 1770. Richard Allen was ten years old at the time. When he made his advent into the world, George III came to the throne of England. He was three years old when the French and Indian War ended. He was fifteen when Tom Paine started *The Pennsylvanian*, and sixteen when by the light of campfires Paine wrote, "These are times which try men's souls."

Even though communication of news was poor in those days, it is quite certain that in due course of time information concerning the Boston Massacre, and the death of Attucks trickled through. But Allen was a soldier in the army of the Lord. His zeal was canalized in another direction. When he and his friends met for prayer and exhortation, the air was vibrant with upsetting revolutionary ideas of alarming proportions. Consequently they must have discussed things other than their religious experience. They could not fail to see and feel the rising tide of apathy and intolerance on the part of their white Christian brethren. It was natural for them to have said that upon the first overt act on their part, "We will go out, and trouble you no more."

Finding themselves without a church home, the next logical step was for Allen and his friends to secure a place of worship as soon as possible. This they did with celerity. They hired a store-room and held worship by themselves.[11] This move met with strong opposition from the Elders of St. George. On the other hand, the celebrated Dr. Benjamin Rush and Mr. Robert Ralston espoused their cause and aided them materially. Dr. Rush headed the subscription list for the new venture, and wrote a letter to

10. Allen, *op. cit.*, 22 f.; *The Autobiography of Benjamin Rush*, 228.
11. Allen, *op. cit.*, 24.

Granville Sharp, the leading antislavery agitator and leader in England, for help. Dr. Rush and Allen were fast friends, and the former often dined at Allen's table and attended his church services. When the roof on Bethel was raised, Dr. Rush and fifty of his prominent white friends were present. They were served a sumptuous dinner by the colored people. Afterwards the colored people took places at the table and in turn were served by the whites, among them Dr. Rush, one of the signers of the Declaration of Independence, professor in the University of Pennsylvania, and founder of Dickinson College at Carlisle, Pennsylvania. Mr. Robert Ralston was a wealthy Philadelphia merchant, and trustee of Princeton University. He was Treasurer of the Building Fund.

At the corner of Sixth and Lombard Streets a house of worship was built — the beginning of African Methodism in a concrete way.[12] According to Dow, the building would accommodate three thousand persons. Richard Allen dug the first spadeful of dirt for the basement, or cellar. The excavated earth was hauled by his own three teams. He was the first to propose the African M. E. Church, and was the spearhead of the movement. Of the persons who left St. George with him and accompanied Allen to the Sixth-and-Lombard-Streets site was Mrs. Jane Ann Murray. She saw him when he put his spade into the ground, and her eyes followed his every movement as he brought it up full of earth. Mrs. Murray's great-granddaughter lives in South Philadelphia at the ripe age of eighty-six years, and remembers vividly the great Dr. W. D. W. Schureman and men of other days of whom the world was not worthy.

In 1793 Allen was called to be the Pastor of the Congregation, but he still considered himself a Methodist. Like John Wesley, he never did purpose to leave the Church of his spiritual nativity. The new meeting house was called "Bethel."[13] The name was suggested by John Dickens, a white clergyman, in his prayer of

---

12.   *Ibid.,* 31; Thomas Scharf and Thompson Westcott, *History of Philadelphia,* I, 551, 585 f.; 589, 599, 634; *Autobiography of Benjamin Rush,* 202.

13.   B. W. Arnett, *op. cit.,* 157.

Mrs. Jane Ann Trusty of Tuckerton, New Jersey, died at the age of seventy-seven. Her daughter was Jane Ann Murray, the mother of Pauline Trusty Haydon. She was the mother of Mrs. Jennie Trusty McMullen, 769 South Twentieth Street, Philadelphia, who is a member of Allen A. M. E. Church. The author was introduced to her by her pastor, the Reverend John D. Bright, and obtained a picture of Mrs. Ann Trusty from an old steel engraving.

dedication, *"That it might be a Bethel to the gathering in of thousands of souls."* The meeting house was opened in 1794 by Francis Asbury, the prophet of the long trail, as designated by Ezra Tipple. And John Dickens is the same who made the motion to form the Methodist Episcopal Church at the Christmas Conference of 1784 in Baltimore.[14]

Opposition broke out afresh. Some of the Mother Church desired Allen to make the new Bethel over to the conference. He absolutely refused. The Bethelites, as they were called, were inveigled into having their church incorporated, and when they came to themselves they discovered that the paper had been drawn in favor of the conference. This continued for ten years, when the Bethelites voted unanimously to change it. The Elders of St. George then tried to extort six-hundred dollars yearly from them for their preaching service. They dropped to four-hundred dollars, then to two-hundred dollars. Finally they came to one-hundred dollars. They were determined to control the new Church, but in the end failed. Allen would not sell his birthright for a mess of pottage. Thus the movement of 1787, when the people of color met and considered their lot and withdrew, began to take shape in an eventful way. It was the guiding hand of Richard Allen that enabled it to move steadily forward, overcome the opposing forces, and unfurl the flag of religious freedom to the breeze. In many respects he was the greatest man of religion in two centuries — his life spans the last part of the eighteenth, and the first part of the nineteenth.

It is noteworthy that in the same year that Richard Allen and his associates decided to withdraw from Old St. George and begin a chapel, the Founding Fathers of the Republic were in session in the State House at Sixth and Chestnut Streets. The site is on a straight line from north to south from the church to Sixth Street between Pine and Lombard. So, when Allen left Mother Church he walked straight ahead. He was twenty-seven years old, full of fire, vigor, and manhood. He must have walked along Market Street at Fourth, and seen the aged, beloved, bewigged, and respected philosopher, Benjamin Franklin, sitting in his garden, beneath a mulberry tree in pleasant weather, resting in a rocking chair — invented by himself — and drinking tea. About

---

14. Luccock and Hutchinson, *op. cit.,* 160.

him were several men of renown, whose names were destined to adorn the hallowed pages of American history: the opulent, wealthy one-legged Gouverneur Morris, the banker Robert Morris, the dashing John Hancock, the acrid John Adams, the radical Samuel Adams, "Mad Anthony Wayne" with his plumed hat at a rakish angle. He certainly saw with awe and respect the great General himself, George Washington, President of the Assembly. He was present no doubt when he entered the city, and was met at Gray's Ferry by a troop of cavalry. Bells chimed, and citizens cheered as he was escorted to Mrs. House's house at Fifth and Market. Richard Allen saw his General with his ill-fitting dentures and an arm in a sling. As Allen moved about Philadelphia his eyes saw the Pinckneys of South Carolina, Madison and Randolph from Virginia, Alexander Hamilton from New York, and the other framers of the Constitution. With others he passed by The Indian Queen, the unofficial headquarters, watched the great men, makers of history who came and went. They were perhaps unconscious of the seriousness of the parts they were playing in the greatest drama of Independence.

Perhaps Allen was also unconscious of the epochal role he was beginning to play upon the world stage of religious freedom. To be sure, Allen moved about with ears open, and absorbed information like a sponge. There was talk about the large states against the small, the strong against the weak, how the government should be constituted, how the Negro should be counted, compromise here and compromise there, the "three-fifths rule," and curbing the power of the President. Even though the sessions were secret, these things leaked out. All the while the liberty notes of the State House bell continued to ring in his ears. "Liberty and freedom for all." How his heart within him must have burned as he mused on these things, along the streets, on his way to church, and his Spruce Street home near the water front.

THE ORGANIZATION

The colored people in Baltimore had an experience similar to that of their Philadelphia brethren. There were the class and prayer meetings and preaching services from which they were excluded. "Aunt Annie" was one of the first colored persons in America to embrace Methodism. There were scores of them as members of the "Log Meeting House," on Sam's Creek, Lovely Lane, and Old Strawberry Alley. Bishop Francis Asbury passed through Baltimore in 1790 and was requested to preach to the colored Methodists in Fish Street, but the recent ordination of Richard Allen in the city of Philadelphia had caused such a discussion that he had to pass them by. In 1812 there was a congregation of about 633 persons, neither in nor out of the Methodist Church. Steps were taken to purchase a piece of property. The news spread like wildfire that a church for colored persons had been organized. Early in 1816 an invitation came from Richard Allen in Philadelphia to meet them in General Society. It was accepted, and history has recorded the results.[15]

The General Convention met in Philadelphia, April 1816. Baltimore, Philadelphia, Wilmington, Attlebourough, Penna., and Salem, New Jersey were represented:

Baltimore: Daniel Coker, Richard Williams, Henry Harden, Edward Williamson, Stephen Hill, and Nicholas Gilliard;

Philadelphia: Richard Allen, Clayton Durham, Jacob Tapsico, James Champion, and Thomas Webster;

Wilmington: Peter Spencer;

Attlebourough: Jacob March, William Anderson, and Edward Jackson;

Salem: Reuben Cuff.

Total, 16.

The organization was perfected on the ninth of April with Daniel Coker as Chairman, and Richard Allen, Jr., a lad of fourteen, as Secretary.

He was not a member of the group but he was chosen because of his ability to write. A resolution was offered by Stephen Hill of Baltimore, and adopted:

That the people of Philadelphia, Baltimore, and all other places, who should unite with them, shall become one body under the name and style of the African Methodist Episcopal Church of the United States of

15.   James A. Handy, *op. cit.,* 22-26.

North America, and that the book of Discipline of the Methodist Episcopal Church be adopted as our Discipline until further orders, excepting that portion relating to Presiding Elders.

On the ninth of April, and under the new government of the newly formed Church, an election of Bishops resulted in the elevation of Richard Allen of Philadelphia and Daniel Coker of Baltimore. Richard Allen was not present just at this juncture. Business had called him to his country estate. The next morning when he returned and the journal was read, he rose and thanked the delegates for having so signally honored him with their suffrage. He informed them that he was conscious of the great responsibility which the office imposed, as well as of the duties that would be expected of him. But with a sense of his duty to the Church, and the fitness of things, he was of the opinion that two Bishops were too many for the organization to start with. One Bishop was enough at this time, he said. He stated that he would resign his office, and let the Convention say who would hold over.

Allen's speech at this juncture caused some hard feeling on the part of the Baltimore delegation, who were in favor of Coker. Since the Philadelphians were strong for Allen, the whole matter of Bishops was reconsidered, and a new election held. On the eleventh day of April, 1816, Richard Allen was set apart by the imposition of the hands of five ordained Elders in the Church of God, one of whom was Absalom Jones, a priest in the Episcopal Church in the diocese of the Reverend Bishop White of Pennsylvania.[16]

There is a strong tradition that the reason Daniel Coker was not chosen as Bishop was on account of his color. His mother was an Englishwoman, and his father a Negro slave. This was told the writer by several old men of a former generation, including the Reverend John M. Henderson, secretary to the late Bishop W. B. Derrick.

Thus the Convention finished its work in great power,

---

16. John M. Brown, (ed.), *Repository of Religion and Literature,* III, 1-4.

and commends it to you, through us, for your favorable
consideration and reception.

[*signed*:]

DANIEL COKER
RICHARD WILLIAMS
EDWARD WILLIAMS
HENRY HARDEN
STEPHEN HILL
NICHOLAS GILLIARD

The report was made to the Baltimore Conference in 1817 by
Coker, and upon a motion by Stephen Hill it was adopted. The
entire Committee and the assembly arose and sang: "Praise God
from whom all blessings flow."

William Paul Quinn was present at the Organizing Convention of 1816, but took no part in the deliberations. He was a
young man of about eighteen years. No one dreamed of the wonderful contribution that this young prophet was destined to make
to African Methodism. Within a few brief years he would cross
the Alleghenies as the first pioneering circuit rider, and become
one of the world's greatest missionaries in that period of American
frontier days. The most distinguished men in the Convention were
Richard Allen, Daniel Coker, and Stephen Hill.[17] Allen was a far-
sighted, aggressive leader. Coker was way above the average in
mental preparation. When he ran away from slavery in Maryland
he went to New York City and attended school. He was a
teacher and author of a book *A Dialogue Between a Virginian and
an African Minister*. He was the first antislavery writer of color
whose productions survive. Coker was a financier of no mean
ability. He was to the Negroes in Baltimore what Richard Allen
was to his people in Philadelphia. He organized African Methodism in Maryland. The fact that he was elected to the Episcopacy
attests to the high esteem in which he was held by his brethren.
Stephen Hill was outstanding because of his counsels and wisdom.
He was regarded as the "lawyer." The Church is indebted to him
for the form which it took.[18]

A public statement was given out, and the next year, 1817,
the first Book of Discipline was published, following in the main

---

17. Payne, writing in Brown, *op. cit.,* III, 97-100.
18. Daniel A. Payne, *History of the A. M. E. Church,* 14.

that of the Methodist Episcopal Church. The book bears the names of Richard Allen and Jacob Tapisco as Book Stewards.[19] A hymnal was also prepared. The work of organizing completed, "The African M. E. Church, the child of many trials, was born in a hurricane, and cradled in a storm, in the year of our Lord 1786. It was formally organized in April 1816," and like a Divine youth made its way in the world.

> Mountains shall sink to plains,
> And hell in vain oppose;
> The cause is God's, and must prevail,
> In spite of all its foes.

---

19.   C. M. Tanner, *Reprint of the First Edition of the Discipline of The African M. E. Church.*

CHAPTER III

Growth and Expansion

First the blade, and then the ear. . . . — MARK 4:28

*The Church like a Divine youth made its way in
the world.* — CLEMENT

The strategic centers of African Methodism in the first two decades of the nineteenth century were Charleston, Philadelphia, and Baltimore. From these cities the Church was extended under the aggressive leadership of God-intoxicated men with hearts full of zeal and unconquerable determination. They cast themselves literally into the work with utter abandon and consuming passion. About the same time that Richard Allen began corresponding with Daniel Coker of Baltimore, he entered into negotiations with Morris Brown of Charleston, and with other colored Methodists who were aggrieved over the treatment they were receiving from their white fellow-communicants.

In Charleston the colored Methodists outnumbered the whites by a ratio of ten to one. They had a Quarterly Conference of their own and increased rapidly. Two of their number went to Philadelphia and received ordination for the work in Charleston.[1] By 1818 the society in Charleston stood next in size to that of Philadelphia. A dispute arose over the custody of a burial ground. Nearly all the Class Leaders gave up their papers and more than three-quarters of their six thousand members withdrew. "The galleries, hitherto crowded, were almost completely deserted, and it was a vacancy that could be *felt*. The absence of their responses and hearty songs were really felt to be a loss to those so long accustomed to hear them. . . . The schismatics combined, and after great exertion succeeded in erecting a neat church building. . . . Their organization was called the African Church."[2] The venture was doomed to a short life because of opposition by the

---

1. Ulrich B. Phillips, *American Negro Slavery*, 421.
2. *Ibid.*, 421.

slave authorities, who held that their conduct violated a statute of 1800 which prohibited the assemblage of slaves with free Negroes for mental instruction without the presence of white persons; a plea by the colored preachers for a special dispensation was refused; attendants at meetings were seized; the head of the church and a dozen exhorters were imprisoned; some were sentenced to leave the city, others to ten lashes or ten dollars' fine. In spite of this hostile attitude on the part of the constituted authority, the Church continued in existence until 1822, when the Denmark Vassey and Gullak Jack insurrection plot was discovered by the government. The leaders of the church were not implicated. There was such a hostile feeling engendered by this abortive attempt to secure freedom that Morris Brown removed to Philadelphia. Evidence of a fine spirit of co-operation and love for the cause is evidenced by his having joined in heartily with Richard Allen and the movement in Philadelphia. The name of Morris Brown appears on the Philadelphia Conference roll of 1818. After 1822 he renewed old acquaintances and made new contacts. Six years afterwards, in the city where the African M. E. Church was born, Morris Brown was elected and set apart as the second Bishop.

The bulk of the colored people in Charleston returned to the white congregations, where they soon crowded out the whites. They overflowed the galleries and even the "boxes." A crisis soon came when protests were sent to the minister by the whites who complained that they did not have sufficient room. On one occasion more whites came than could be accommodated; the forward-sitting Negroes refused to yield their seats. A committee of young white men attempted to eject them forcibly. At a subsequent "love feast" the young men were criticized. They took offense. The affair could not be adjusted and nine of the young men were expelled. A hundred and fifty of the membership followed them and united with the Methodist Protestant Church.[3] Strange paradox. The color question in Philadelphia and Baltimore caused the withdrawal of Negroes and the formation of a separate Church, but in Charleston it caused not only the withdrawal of

---

3. *Ibid.*

the people of color, but that of the whites as well. The growth of the Church in Charleston was for the time being halted.[4]

African Methodism was known to have existed in the city of Mobile as early as 1820, but its growth was hindered by "the walls of slavery," therefore "the little band had to bow low again."[5] The traffic in slaves caused them to be sold into various parts of the South. Those who had been exposed to Christianity and African Methodism in Baltimore and Charleston and were sold into Alabama would take their faith with them. In the new home those of kindred spirit came together and found a common bond. In this way the Church in Alabama must have had its rise. Very soon it was forced to give way to slavery.

From Philadelphia the Church grew eastward into New York and New England and westward into Ohio. South Carolina was for the present lost. The power of slavery was rapidly rising toward its zenith. At the close of the first decade there were 98 appointments, and 4,087 members in the Church. The preachers' salaries for the three circuits and Baltimore City amounted to $448.30. Many of the ministers had entered the ranks from the early days of the existence of the Church and played well their parts in laying its foundations. At this early date there was a vision of providing for itinerant ministers. In 1828 a resolution was passed that a sinking fund be created for the aid of traveling preachers. Support for the Book Concern was provided. The Fathers saw the need of dissemination of knowledge in books, pamphlets, and literature.

Hedged in by the walls of slavery in the South, the expansion of the Church was westward into the free territory of Ohio, Indiana, and Illinois. These states were virgin soil in the territory of the West, an empire that was to be won. It was the day of the covered wagon. Through the wilderness, across mountains and prairies, the men with long rifles threaded their irresistible way. Taking their lives in their hands they staked them on winning the frontier. And onward came the backwoodsman and circuit-riding preacher. William Paul Quinn, who was a lad in 1816 and present when the Church was organized, and whose name appears on the

---

4. *Ibid.*
5. Wesley J. Gaines, *African Methodism in the South,* 225.

Philadelphia Conference Roll of 1818, was the first African Methodist preacher to mount a horse and enter the western country.

The Reverend Moses Freeman organized Allen Temple in Cincinnati in the year 1824. Shortly after its organization, Reverend Philip Broadie came and took charge as its first pastor. It was then the Cincinnati Circuit. Broadie was a Virginian by birth. He was not a man of scientific or theological training, but a serious Bible student. He applied himself diligently. His travels were many, and wherever he went revivals broke out. He was a blessing to the Church in the wilderness. When his strength began to fail and disease had wasted his frame, it was his great delight to call young members together at his house to instruct and counsel them. The nearer his life drew to a close the more fervent he became in his final service of prayer and advice, "a living proof of his firm belief in the Gospel which he preached; his death — peaceful and calm, yet triumphant, a striking demonstration of the glorious victory of a dying man."[6]

John Charleston, another Virginian, by his evangelistic and pioneering endeavors, entered the Ohio country and left a record of heroic Christian service that will stand out more gloriously with the flight of time. He was the first convert of an American Sunday school, organized by Francis Asbury in Hanover County, Virginia. This was in 1786. As a boy, Charleston came to Ohio and lived at Chillicothe, where he was a local preacher in the Methodist Episcopal Church. When the missionaries entered the territory to establish the African M. E. Church, he was one of the first to join, and was commissioned to work. He co-labored with John Boggs, Noah Cannon, and William Miller.

The *Christian Advocate* of February 22, 1828 copied the following from the *Zion's Herald:*

> The Reverend John Charleston is now in his sixty-first year, jet-black, between six and seven feet in height, weighing two hundred and thirty pounds; his short hair inclined to be gray. During eighteen years of his life he would walk thirty miles in a day and preach three times. He could not be stopped by trifles; would wade to his

---

6.   Daniel A. Payne, *History of the A. M. E. Church,* 42.

neck through streams of water. He had taught his dog
to swim rivers and brooks, and carry his hymn book
and Bible in his mouth without getting them wet. He
is a correct and powerful preacher. Hundreds and
thousands have, I doubt not, been converted through
his instrumentality. During his ministry he had been
severely persecuted but out of all the Lord delivered
him. The earliest Sunday school in the United States of
which any record is known was abundantly fruitful,
even if it achieved no other result than the conversion
of that colored youth.[7]

Once Charleston was en route in a storm of sleet and snow to keep
a preaching engagement. He had to ford a stream, and when he
arrived at his destination his feet were frozen to the stirrups. He
knocked his feet loose, dismounted and preached the gospel with
power and telling effect. No more thrilling story of Gospel romance is to be found anywhere in the history of the Christian
Church.

Having remained at the head of the Church as Bishop for a
period of fifteen years, Richard Allen passed away in 1831. This
year saw the uprising of slaves under Nat Turner at Southampton,
Virginia. The passion for freedom and manhood rights lingered
in the breasts of the colored people. It is remarkable that this insurrection was in the state where years previously a great orator
had declared, "Give me liberty, or give me death!" Such a passion might burn and consume the heart of any man regardless of
his skin-color. It has been remarked that people of color did not
rise up all over the South and strike for freedom. The slaves represented several groups and tribes. The system of chattelism broke
up and disintegrated these groups so that social cohesion and
unanimity of opinion and unity of thought were impossible. On
the other hand there was the ever-present police power, and
watchful eye of the owner. However, the number of attempts
for freedom was much larger than is generally known. Many escaped to free territory. Some preferred to die free men rather
than live slaves.

---

7. B. W. Arnett, *Colored Sunday Schools,* 5.

> Before I'd be a slave
> I'd be buried in my grave
> And go home to my God
> And be free.

Richard Allen died, but he had lighted a torch, which by the grace of God would never go out.

In 1828 General Andrew Jackson of Tennessee was elected to the Presidency of the United States. The common people thought they had come into their own. They trampled the beautiful carpets of the White House during the inauguration ceremony and jostled each other in their scramble for cakes and lemonade. In the same year Morris Brown was elected to the Episcopacy. He had come from Charleston because of slave efforts for freedom in his native city. When he reached Philadelphia, he joined in with the Allen movement. He was not a brilliant man, though an ardent advocate of education in a day when that was very, very unpopular. Until he came to the end of his ministerial life he was a tower of strength in the young Church and projected the ideals of Richard Allen. Before Morris Brown's death he was assisted by Edward Waters, who was elected to the Bishopric in 1836. The assistant Bishop never held an Annual Conference, or ordained a single minister, not even a deacon, though he sat in the episcopal seat for eight years, from 1836 to 1844, when he resigned. He was appointed annually like other ministers. He is the only Bishop in the long history of the Church who ever resigned his Bishopric. Following his resignation, Edward Waters returned to the ranks of the itineracy and served Ellicott Mills Circuit, and sometimes Bethel, Baltimore.[8] He finished his course in 1847, after having been run over by a horse and buggy. The team was driven by some rude white men. Edward Waters was born a slave, but bought his freedom of Duvall, his master.

The membership of the Church was 6,904 in the year 1826. Ten years later it had grown to 7,594. Salaries had increased to $926.39. The work in Philadelphia and Baltimore had slumped somewhat, but there were unmistakable signs of advance in the western territory. The Book Concern was removed to New York,

---

8. Payne, *op. cit.*, 112 f.

where George Hogarth, the Book Steward, resided. Interest in literary development and education was evidenced by the Baltimore Annual Conference having adopted a resolution authorizing the publication of a quarterly magazine. At about the same time the Ohio Annual Conference went on record commending education. These are early indications of interest in mental improvement. The Baltimore Annual Conference passed a resolution in 1838 making it the duty of the ministers to deliver an address on education once a quarter, so great was the need. Christianity thrives on the soil of intelligence. No one realized it more than the Fathers of African Methodism. While many of them were not men of the schools, they appreciated training and saw its value. The next move was to take steps toward the education of the ministry. The Fathers of the Church did not desire to leave their posterity in the hands of an ignorant clergy, after they themselves slumbered in the dust. In the same year, 1838, the first official document relative to ministerial preparation appeared over the signatures of Morris Brown, Edward Waters, and George Hogarth, Book Steward. Morris Brown was a Charlestonian, and spoke with a decided accent that betrayed his nativity. He was limited in his mental attainments, but his early interest in education gave evidence of the major role he was to play a few years later when by an impassioned plea to the General Conference he was able to have that body reverse itself on the day following that in which it had howled down Daniel Alexander Payne's resolution calling for a Conference Course of Studies for men entering the ministry. This incident occurred at Brooklyn, August 1, 1839.

The church was planted in Malden, Boston, Providence, Lockport, Toronto, and Upper Canada. The following table shows its numerical growth from 1836 to 1839.

	Ohio	Philadelphia	Baltimore	New York	Total
1836	1,131	3,344	2,052	713	7,240
1837	1,507	3,443	2,345	810	8,105
1838	1,817	4,044	2,794	1,053	9,708
1839	*	4,479	2,300	1,222	8,001

*Ohio lacking.

Willis Nazrey united with the New York Conference in 1840. No one present that day even dimly conceived the thought that twelve years from the day he would be elected and set apart as Bishop, and in the very house where he joined the Annual Conference. This was the first and only such coincidence in the history of the Church. He led the ticket in the episcopal election in 1852, but was set apart second to Alexander Payne. Nazrey was a man of rare ability; he was methodical and possessed great capacity for hard work. He made one of the most efficient Bishops the Church has ever had. He stood full six feet two inches tall. He was very active, prompt, and had irresistible force of character.

The General Conference of 1840 saw the organization of the Upper Canada and Indiana Conferences. By this time there was intense interest in education, and the Church was soon to commit itself to a program of racial self-help and mental enlightenment. In 1841 another stalwart defender of the faith and herald of the flame joined the New York Annual Conference, a man who was destined for the Episcopacy, Jabez Pitt Campbell. There was a falling-off in Church finances; however, pledges were secured for the publication of a "quarterly or monthly magazine," for the benefit of the Connection, instead of the "minutes." The Book Concern had a balance of $1,318.54. The western work was an inviting field — ripe and ready for the harvest. The work in these parts was known as "Western Missions," and was begun in 1840. By 1842 there were eight circuits and stations with about eight or nine hundred members.

CHAPTER IV

An Eventful Period

Behold, I make all things new. — REVELATION 21:5

There is a tide in the affairs of men,
Which, taken at the flood, leads on to fortune;
Omitted, all the voyage of their life
Is bound in shallows and miseries.
On such a full sea are we now afloat,
And we must take the current when it serves,
Or lose our ventures.—SHAKESPEARE, *Julius Caesar* IV, 3

The year 1848 ushered in one of the most eventful periods in the political and ecclesiastical history of the United States. The stage was about to be set for the great drama of free labor versus slave labor. From that time onward to the election of Abraham Lincoln to the Presidency, either a Southerner or a "doughface" occupied the White House, and the slave interests became more strongly intrenched. In sections where the institution could not be maintained to economic profit, there was a rising tide of reaction and opposition. In the meantime the abolitionists became more vocal and assertive. The schism in the Methodist Church foreshadowed what was destined to be the fate of the nation — four long years of bloody domestic strife.

Bishop Payne says: "With the year 1844 a new period in the history of the African M. E. Church opens." In the previous chapter we have seen how the early pioneers, building upon the foundation laid by Allen, and his associates, spread the Church in the West beyond the mountains. A new era of prosperity now opens. The General Conference of 1844 met at Pittsburgh on May 6. Bishops Morris Brown and Edward Waters were present. There were sixty-eight members in this body. The Book of Discipline was revised. The phrases "Junior" and "Senior" Bishop were altered to "Joint Bishops." The basis of election of delegates to the General Conference was changed to read: "One delegate to every four hundred lay members returned at the previous Annual Conference." This made for a representative General Conference based upon the membership of the Church. Now the representation is based upon the number of ministerial members in an Annual Conference: "Two ministerial delegates for every Annual Conference actually existing, but for each Annual Conference of more than eighty ministerial members, one ministerial delegate for every *forty ministerial members* or final fraction exceeding twenty." In 1848: "One ministerial, and one lay delegate for each forty (40) ministerial members of an Annual Conference or fraction over sixteen. No Conference shall have less than three ministerial and three lay delegates." The effort to secure lay membership in the General Conference began at this time. There was so much antipathy to it that only local preachers were permitted to represent the laity. It could not be foreseen that eighty-four years afterwards the Chicago General Conference of 1928 would grant *equal* lay representation, nor that the Cleveland General Conference of 1932 would give the laymen equal representation on the Episcopal Committee. Now there is equal lay representation in the Annual Conferences.[1]

Two men were present and took part in the deliberations whose names have emblazoned the pages of history of the denominations: Paul Quinn and Daniel Alexander Payne. The former was born about the year 1788 in India. He came to the United States via England, and became a member of the African M. E. Church. He was present at the time of its organization, being about eighteen years old. He was made of stern stuff and possessed a rugged physique, which fitted him for the rigors and hardships of frontier life. He was an ideal missionary, and the first Circuit Rider in the Church. The early western advance of the Church is synonomous with the endeavors of this flaming herald of the Cross. Reverend J. W. Early and others had entered the field and were Quinn's contemporaries. But Quinn's labors were more fruitful and impressive than theirs. When he came to the General Conference, the Easterners were not in favor of him but when he read his report, sentiment was changed. The Easterners were compelled to cast aside whatever prejudices they may have had,

---

1. *A. M. E. Discipline,* 1932, 206 f.; *Discipline,* 1948, Sec. 108, p. 154; Daniel A. Payne, *History of the A. M. E. Church,* 168.

and to elect Quinn solely upon the basis of merit and achievement. He stands out in a class by himself. The hounds of slavery were ever on his heels; some white people were domineering and intolerant, while his own people were timid; the Fugitive Slave Law had practically set up a system of espionage over the movement of Negroes in the North and deterred them from going into slave territory. But in spite of these handicaps, Quinn sallied forth like a plumed knight of God, and planted the Church in such slave centers as Louisville and St. Louis.[2]

Payne was born in Charleston. He was a precocious child, and soon gave evidence of a great penchant for learning. He read and mastered whatever books he could obtain. After his day's work was done he would study until midnight, and, rising early the next morning, he would be at his books from four to six. At fifteen he gave his life to God, became a schoolteacher, and followed the bent of his soul. His three pupils gave him fifty cents each. Three slaves whom he taught at night gave him one dollar each. Education was his master-passion throughout his life. It distinguished him in the Episcopacy. The success of Payne's educational venture aroused curiosity and hostility on the part of the whites in Charleston. The State Legislature enacted a law in 1833 which made it a punishable crime to teach Negroes. Thus Payne's educational career as a teacher was cut short. He was forced to close his little school. When he arrived in the East, he matriculated in a Luthern theological seminary at Gettysburg. Later he joined the African M. E. Church and soon became one of the leaders. He soon saw the need for training and worked with unflagging zeal for the uplift of his people, and for the ministry. At the General Conference in 1844 Payne introduced his resolution calling for Annual Conference Studies, and saw it voted down unanimously. He also saw it passed the next day unanimously, upon a motion offered by the Reverend A. D. Lewis, a brother of lofty stature, venerable in appearance, of dignified mien, and delectable countenance. It was he who called for reconsideration. It has been over a hundred years since this epochal event transpired. Bishop Morris Brown spoke that day until the faces of the delegates were bathed in tears. They cried, they wept. Since then the Church has been committed to ministerial educa-

---

2. Payne, *op. cit.*, 171; C. S. Smith, *History of the A. M. E. Church*, 16 f.

tion. The record justifies the determination, courage, and vision of Payne, the co-operation of Lewis, and the co-operative support of Morris Brown.[3]

The office of Book Steward was created and filled by Reverend George Hogarth. The Reverend M. M. Clark, an honor graduate from Jefferson College, Cannonsburg, in 1853, was elected Traveling Agent. The Parent Home and Foreign Missionary Society was organized. It was the general consensus of opinion that this General Conference represented the largest concentration of talent and ability ever assembled in an ecclesiastical capacity since the memorable Convention of 1816. The delegates left for their homes with high hopes of abundant success during the next Quadrennium.[4]

By 1848 the membership of the entire Church was 17,000. The Book Concern was in a fair condition. The level of intelligence among the people was low, and here and there voices were raised on behalf of education. Payne was most persistent. That early zeal for mental development which fired his soul in the Charleston days flamed and burned with consuming passion. He completed a series of essays on the "Education of the Ministry." This year witnessed the ordination of Alexander Wayman as a Deacon in the Philadelphia Conference. He was from the Eastern Shore, Maryland, a state that has given the Church an array of able men. He was one of the giants in those days, and over a long period of time did the work of an evangelist, and made full proof of his ministry. He was rough and ready, rugged, up-and-coming, yet he was a preacher of no mean ability. His popularity was known and heralded far and wide. He has left the Church a most important work, a sort of diary: *Wayman's Recollections* and *Wayman on the Discipline*.[5]

T. M. D. Ward was the incarnation of the Divine Spirit in a unique way. He was the living embodiment of the idea that the All Highest is ever drawing nigh unto His people, inspiring men and raising up leaders. Ward has been regarded as the greatest preacher the Church ever produced. Like most men of his day, he was not a product of the schools. The older men who saw and

3.   James A. Buckley, *History of Methodism,* II, 295 f.
4.   B. W. Arnett, *Budget, 1900,* 221.
5.   A. W. Wayman, *My Recollections.*

heard him, say that he had "an eagle eye" which pierced the hearts of his listeners. His voice was irresistible, his look penetrating. He was a natural orator. In his class there was no equal. His sermons were very brief. Bishop H. B. Parks says that Ward's sermon at the General Conference of 1868 elected him to the Bishopric. The entire assembly was lifted to its feet.[6]

For the first time a written Episcopal Address was delivered by Paul Quinn before the Eighth General Conference which met at Philadelphia on Monday, May 1, 1848.[7] Heretofore the Episcopal Address had been referred to secretaries. Presiding Elders were recommended, but the proposition was lost by a vote of 40 to 33. The *Christian Recorder* was founded with the Reverend Augustus R. Green as Editor. The name was the *Christian Herald*. The Book Concern was removed from Pittsburgh to Philadelphia. Daniel A. Payne was appointed to write the history of the Church. He spent forty years in traveling, collecting data, and preparing the monumental volume. The Society of Methodists in New Orleans petitioned the Indiana Conference to consider the propriety of establishing the African M. E. Church in that city. The prayer was granted, and brother Charles Doughty, who brought it, himself a native Louisianian and a Licentiate in the Methodist Church, was ordained a Deacon and sent back to take charge of the "Louisiana Mission." This was the beginning of St. James,[8] the beautiful church on North Roman Street. It was the first instance of expansion of the Church into the deep South since the formation of society at Mobile, Alabama.[9]

The Ninth General Conference was convened at New York in 1852. The only member of the Episcopate was Paul Quinn. It was a remarkable Conference. One hundred and thirty-nine were enrolled as delegates, though not all were present. Bishop Quinn privately urged Payne to deliver one of the sermons. After much persuasion he reluctantly agreed.[10] The Episcopal Address was read by the Reverend Alexander W. Wayman. The name of the

---

6. H. B. Parks related this to the author in the presence of Bishop Heard in 1938 in the parsonage at Peoria, Illinois, when the Annual Conference was meeting in Ward Chapel A. M. E. Church.
7. Payne, *op. cit.*, 217.
8. Smith, *op. cit.*, 20.
9. W. H. Mixon, *History of the A. M. E. Church in Alabama*, 29.
10. Payne, *op. cit.*, 268-71.

Christian Herald was changed to that of the *Christian Recorder*, and the first issue was sent forth on July 1st, 1852. This periodical has the distinction of being the oldest published by Negroes the world over. The name is still the same.[11] The proposal to grant license to women to preach was rejected. When the time for election of Bishops had arrived, the delegates chose Daniel A. Payne and Willis Nazrey. An unusual thing happened. Even though Nazrey was elected first, Payne was set apart first. The delegates felt that Payne should, in any eventuality, be the senior Bishop. Then the election and priority of Payne would set at rest the current comment that the African M. E. Church abetted ignorance and abhorred education. Payne turned out to be in the Church of his choice what Paul was to the early Church. He was the undisputed leader, stood in front of the Church and the sacramental Host for more than a half-century. After a long and useful life he passed into the great beyond at his home, Evergreen Cottage, on the campus of his beloved Wilberforce, in the year 1893. At the time he was Bishop of Florida.

Incidentally, two things must take place to make an Elder a Bishop. He must be elected and "consecrated." Even though he may be elected, he must be set apart by his brethren. Thus the setting apart of Payne first constituted his seniority over Nazrey. In this connection, Daniel Coker was elected a Bishop in 1816, but he was not "set apart." It is true that he resigned, but had he not done so, in the absence of Consecration, he would not have been regarded as a Bishop. Priority comes in "the laying on of hands."[12] Both Handy and Smith take the position that election constitutes priority. Handy says: "Bishop Nazrey having received the largest number of votes, and being elected first, was the Senior, and Bishop Payne, while he was ordained first, yet was the Junior, and this has been the rule governing our General Conference ever since." Bishop Charles Spencer Smith follows Handy: "The first and paramount requisite is election; Consecration is secondary." The General Conference does whatsoever it chooses. Regardless of the order of election, if it sees fit to complete the work of constituting a Bishop by taking the one second in the

---

11. *Ibid.*, 278.
12. Wayman, *op. cit.*, 49 f.

election and setting him apart first, the final act of the General Conference is supreme.

The Bishops divided the work into Districts, and assigned themselves as follows:

First District: Daniel Alexander Payne. The Philadelphia and New England Conferences.

Second District: Willis Nazrey. The Baltimore and New York Conferences.

Third District: William Paul Quinn. The Ohio, Indiana, and Canada Conferences.

At the close of this year the First Council of Bishops was held.[13] The Churches throughout the Connection showed a prosperous condition; however, the *Christian Recorder* was suspended for want of means. The Editor, Reverend M. M. Clark, who was also General Book Steward, resigned his twofold office. He had come into double service because of the resignation of the Reverend William Catto, who joined the old Presbyterian Church. Reverend Clark served for two years, and said he was going to leave the East to go west, "to secure a cage in which to place a bird to sing and cheer him in his declining years."[14] The Canadian Churches were separated from the Connection upon their own request. Bishop Quinn was enthusiastic and thought that in time his episcopal colleagues would be forced to follow. The Fugitive Slave Law might have influenced his thinking. Richard Allen had remarked in his day that "slavery is a bitter pill." The Canadian Church was another reaction against the custom of buying and selling human flesh.

In 1855 the Missouri Conference was formed. Slowly the Church was making its way westward. It had reached the "Father of Waters." Missouri and Kentucky were slave territory. It required a high degree of courage to plant the Church in this area at such a time when war clouds were gathering on the nation's horizon. Preparation was being made for a death struggle to preserve the Union in the face of those who would destroy it to

---

13. Smith, *op. cit.,* 24.
14. *Ibid.,* 25.

preserve their "peculiar institution." The first session of this Conference was held September 13, 1855, at Louisville in Quinn Chapel. Bishops Quinn and Payne were present. The newly formed Conference had 1,698 lay members within its confines. Contingent money collected amounted to $67.43.

The burning question before the Cincinnati General Conference of 1856, one year later, was slavery. It was the all-absorbing topic of discussion everywhere. Thousands of immigrants had entered the country from Europe, where they had striven for the ideal of freedom and democracy. At first they realized the significance of the slavery question; many of their number, however, were pro-Southern. But after the issues were sharply drawn, and made clear, they cast their lot on the side of free labor. Large numbers of them settled in the Northwest, and when the Republican Party was born at Ripon, Wisconsin, February 18, 1864, and in July of the same year at Jackson, Michigan, these liberty-loving newcomers identified themselves with the new party.

The great triumvirate of Calhoun, Clay, and Webster had recently passed from the political scene. A new group of leaders appeared, who had been nurtured in the era of sectional controversy. They would stop at nothing, not even the dismemberment of the Union itself, to realize their dreams and attain their goals. The time for compromise had passed. From the free states such men had come as Seward from New York, Salmon P. Chase from Ohio who figured in the founding of Wilberforce, Thaddeus Stevens from Pennsylvania, and Charles Sumner from Massachusetts. From the slave states such men had come onto the political scene as Alexander H. Stephens and Robert Toombs of Georgia, Howell Cobb and Governor Brown. The acknowledged leader of this group was Jefferson Davis of Mississippi. By them the Union was evaluated in terms of slavery. The West was ably represented by Stephen A. Douglas, of "popular sovereignty" fame. He did not care "whether slavery was voted up or down in the territories." The Kansas and Nebraska Act was one of the most important pieces of legislation ever enacted by the United States Congress. By its enactment the Missouri Compromise was repealed, and the people of the newly created territories were left to regulate their domestic institutions as they chose "subject to the Constitution of the United States." The contest was bitter, and the law produced momentous consequences. While the bill was yet before Congress, Chase predicted, "It will light up a fire in the country which may, perhaps, consume those who kindle it." A few years more proved his prophecy true. In 1856 the Democrats met in their National Convention in Cincinnati, Ohio, and nominated James Buchanan as their standard-bearer. He was a Northern man with Southern principles. The Republicans met at Philadelphia on June 17, the anniversary of the battle of Bunker Hill. They named John C. Fremont of California for the Presidency, and passed up Abraham Lincoln for the Vice-Presidency, naming W. L. Dayton of New Jersey. In the election, Buchanan won. The contest was virtually on between "opposing and enduring forces," with the Negro as the bone of contention.

Bishop William Paul Quinn opened the General Conference by giving out the hymn: "Come let us use the grace divine," and offered prayer. An able Episcopal Address was read. The office of Editor of the *Christian Recorder* was combined with that of General Book Steward. The paper had had rough sailing; only nineteen numbers were published in the city of Philadelphia, yet there were 2,207 Church members, and in the District 5,736. While slavery agitated the nation, it was of chief concern to the members of the African M. E. Church. The slave population was composed of their fellow-sufferers in trials and tribulations. Larger space will be devoted to the manner in which the General Conference met the issue subsequently.

DIVORCE

The question of divorce was brought up and discussed. From 1848 to 1852 the law read: "If any minister, preacher, exhorter, or member of our society who has been married, and shall separate and marry again while the former companion is living, he or she shall be expelled, and shall never be admitted during the lifetime of the parties. And any minister who shall marry such knowingly, shall forfeit his standing in the Connection." Four years previously an amendment had been proposed to allow any one of our members to marry after divorce, if he or she had obtained a divorce legally and upon the grounds of infidelity. This alter-

ing amendment was omitted from the Discipline of 1852. Therefore in 1856, Dr. J. G. Bias made a motion that this section of the
Discipline be changed, and the rule of 1852 inserted. A long debate ensued. The result was an indefinite postponement. Such a
question was dealt with by Richard Allen. He decided that it was
right for the Reverend Dutton, whose wife had been torn from
him by the slave power, to serve another woman.

The present law reads:

(1) If any minister, preacher, exhorter, or lay member, who has been legally married, shall leave his wife or
husband, save for the cause of adultery, and marry again
(which we believe to be a crime expressly forbidden by
the word of God), while the former wife, or husband is
living, he or she shall be expelled and shall not be admitted to any of our churches during the natural life of the
forsaken party.

(2) Any lay member, male or female who shall legally separate from his wife, or her husband and marry
again while the former wife or husband is living, he or
she shall be required to file with the Quarterly Conference to which he or she is amenable, a transcript of the
records in the case of the court which granted said bill
of separation, showing that it was granted on scriptural
grounds, and upon failure to do so, he or she shall be expelled.

(3) Any minister who shall legally separate from his
wife and marry again while the former wife is living,
shall be required to file with the Annual Conference, of
which he is a member, a transcript of the records in the
case of the court which granted said bill of separation,
showing that it was granted on scriptural grounds. And
any minister refusing to do so when requested by said
Conference shall be expelled.[15]

It is apparent from the foregoing that the law of 1848-52 had

---

15. John M. Brown, (ed.), *Repository of Religion and Literature*, III, 1-4;
Wayman, *op. cit.*, 51.

STEPHEN HILL

Wealthy lumber merchant; pioneer in the Church. Founded Old
Folks Home and Zion in Philadelphia

DANIEL ALEXANDER PAYNE

Apostle of Education; Church historian, editor, author, musical
organizer. Founded Wilberforce University

HENRY MCNEAL TURNER

Ex-slave; first colored Chaplain to U. S. Army; orator, Georgia
Legislator; Bishop in 1880

T. M. D. WARD

"The old man eloquent." A powerful preacher-orator. Trail-
blazer of the Church to the Pacific

been liberalized, and divorce recognizable upon the grounds of marital infidelity, based upon the teaching of Jesus. This the evident meaning of paragraphs 1 and 2 quoted above. Under this law divorce is permissible in the Church. The lay member will be "required" to file a transcript of the records of the court granting the separation with the Quarterly Conference to which he or she is amenable, showing that it was granted upon scriptural grounds. Expulsion results if or when the person involved fails to comply with the request as stated. In the case of a minister, that is, an Elder or Deacon, he shall follow a similar procedure to that of the lay member, except that he files his transcript with his Annual Conference, if or when requested to do so. Should his Annual Conference request a transcript, and he should fail to file it, "he shall be expelled."[16]

A proposal for Presiding Elders was again rejected; the time limit of circuit preachers was fixed at two years, city pastors four years. An article was inserted in the law to preserve the General Superintendency. The salary of a Bishop was fixed at two-hundred dollars per year, with board for himself, wife and children under twelve years of age, also house rent, fuel and traveling expenses. A traveling preacher's allowance was to be the same as a Bishop's. Several important resolutions were adopted, but not all were executed. Bishop Payne was designated to have an Episcopal Seal ordered. "Its face is embellished with an open Bible, from which Divine light is radiating; the heavenly cross lying upon the Book; the eternal Spirit, in the form of a dove, hovering over it; the title of the denomination below the Bible. Upon the border of the seal is the motto: 'God our Father, Christ our Redeemer, Man our Brother.'" A resolution was also passed to allow the Bishop twenty-five cents on every dollar accruing from the sale of his *History of the A. M. E. Church.*[17] It has already been stated that the question of divorce was discussed by the members of the General Conference of 1856, and certain definite action taken. An attempt to revise that section of the Discipline which pertains to divorce was made in 1860. The test clause was: "Except where parties have been separated by the law for the

---

16. Payne, *op. cit.,* 335 ff.
17. *Ibid.,* 346.

cause of fornication." The report from the Committee on Revision was adopted as a substitute.[18]

An attempt was made to amend the Divorce Canon in the General Conference of 1864, but the Journal is not clear on what was attempted. It did pass a motion made by John M. Brown that the law remain as "it was prior to the General Conference."[19] The present law dates from 1908.

Bishops were held to strict accountability for the sacred performance of their duties, supervision and administration. The General Conference selected the next place of meeting. Such a task is now left with the General Conference Commission. The time is fixed by law, once in every four years, opening on the first Wednesday in May.[20]

While the country was becoming increasingly agitated over sectionalism and cotton capitalism, which endangered the preservation of the Union; and while slavery inconvenienced and hampered those who sought to extend the Church and its saving influence among the people, there were certain forces at work that made compromise and pacification impossible. The Church saw the issue as a moral one, of right against wrong. So it stood on the side of what it conceived to be right.

---

18. *Ibid.,* 359.
19. *Ibid.,* 348; *General Conference Minutes,* 1864; Smith, *op. cit.,* 201.
20. *Ibid.*

CHAPTER V

The Church and Slavery

Remember them that are in bonds as bound with them.
— HEBREWS 13:3

Slavery is the execrable sum of all villainies. — JOHN WESLEY

Slavery is the assumption that it is right for one man to hold property in another. — DANIEL ALEXANDER PAYNE

The historic attitude of the Methodist Church was antislavery. The founder, John Wesley, was outspoken in his condemnation of what he regarded as "the execrable sum of all villainies." He said: "I strike at the root of this complicated villainy. I absolutely deny all slave-holding to be consistent with any degree of natural justice. Much less is it possible that any child of man should ever be born a slave. Liberty is the right of every human creature as soon as he breathes the vital air, and no human law can deprive him of that right." Four days before his death, February 24, 1791, Wesley wrote to William Wilberforce:

> MY DEAR SIR:
> Unless the Divine Power has raised you up to be an Athanasius, *contra mundum*, I see not how you can get through your glorious enterprise in opposing that execrable villainy which is the scandal of religion, of England, and of human nature. Unless God has raised you up for this very thing, you will be worn out by the opposition of men and devils; but if God be for you, who can be against you?[1]

Wesley's antislavery force was as "the little stone at first cut out of the mountain without hands, but it became an overwhelm-

---

1. James M. Buckley, *History of Methodism*, I, 227.

ing power against oppression, and lifted high up in the scale of
being redeemed millions of the sons of Africa." His uttered and
written word against slavery demonstrates the transforming power
of an ideal; for within less than one hundred years after he had
expressed himself, all the slaves of every island controlled by
European nations, and the millions in the United States were
declared "henceforth and forever free."

No action was taken with reference to slavery at the first
Methodist Conference which met at Philadelphia in 1793. Freeborn Garretson, under whose preaching Richard Allen felt his
dungeon shake and his chains fall off, was impressed with the
iniquity of the system on the Lord's Day while reading the Bible.
The thought haunted him: "It is not right for you to keep your
fellow-creatures in bondage. You must let the oppressed go free."
After this feeling came over him, an unutterable sweetness filled
his breast. "Had I the tongue of an angel I could not fully
describe what I felt." Henceforth he believed it "to be a crying
sin." Francis Asbury was a strong antagonist to slavery. He once
said: "O Lord, banish the infernal spirit of slavery from thy dear
Zion!" "I pity the poor slaves!" He was one of a group that
waited upon George Washington and got his views on slavery.
Dr. Thomas Coke, who was set apart as Superintendent for the
American work by Wesley in 1784, was strong in his opposition
to slavery. In Virginia he became openly hostile to the institution and risked bodily danger. As a result of his preaching against
the evil, many slaves received their freedom. The learned Bishop
was a personal friend of Richard Allen, and preached often in
Bethel. On several occasions he, along with Dr. Benjamin Rush,
went home with Allen, and dined at his table.[2]

The early Annual Conference of Methodism went on record
against slavery, especially while the Church was under the influence of Wesley. High ground was taken in opposing the system. Conferences were had with the President of the nation, with
governors of states, and their pleas were heard in legislative halls.
John Marshall of Virginia, afterward Chief Justice of the United
States Supreme Court, urged in a discussion that if the government countenanced slavery it would lose the support of the Methodists. This opinion was expressed at the Convention where the

---

2. *Autobiography of Benjamin Rush*, 234, 250.

Constitution of the United States was formed, but was not allowed in the highest law of our land.[3]

In 1743 Wesley prepared The General Rules for the English Societies, and specifically stated that "the buying or selling the bodies and souls of men, women, or children, with an intention to enslave them" was forbidden. In addition, steps were taken to extirpate the evil.[4] Special rules were adopted requiring slave-holding members to grant a deed of manumission to their slaves within twelve months. All infants born after the Rules went into effect were to be given their immediate freedom. Non-complying members were to be allowed to withdraw within twelve months. The Sacrament of the Lord's Supper was denied to all such thenceforward, and no slaveholders were to be admitted thereafter to the Communion Table or to membership in the Church. And any member who bought, sold, or gave slaves away, except on purpose to free them, was immediately to be expelled.

A Mr. Samuel Davis, of New York City, who lived in the slave states from before the organization of the Methodist Church in America until 1826, wrote the following letter to Dr. Fisk, and it was published in the *Zion's Watchman*, April 8, 1838:

> I know it was required of all those who joined our Church, in our District, in those early days of Methodism, that they should execute an instrument of emancipation of all the slaves in their possession, which they had inherited, according to their respective ages and circumstances; and if any members had bought, or should buy, for their own use, any slave, a committee was appointed to determine how long the slave should serve; and this committee was regulated in its estimates by the age, health and cost of the slaves, after which none of those thus emancipated were considered by us as slaves. So universally were these rules attended to, that I never knew but one instance of any member's neglecting them, and that was my next neighbor, at whose house our Presiding Elder called on business with a preacher who was then stationed there in 1792. When the Elder was about to

---

3. Carl Van Doren, *The Great Rehearsal*, 118 f.
4. L. C. Matlack, *Anti-Slavery Struggle*, 58 f.

retire, the gentleman of the house invited him to stay to dinner. The reply was, "I never eat a meal in a Methodist slave-holder's house," and he immediately left him. I have heard Bishop Asbury and many of the early preachers preach pointedly against slavery. At our Quarterly Meetings, where hundreds were present with their slaves, I have repeatedly heard our preachers condemn the practice as a vile sin against God, morally, socially, and politically wrong, no one molesting nor interrupting the man of God. And I have no doubt, had all our ministers done their duty, there would not have been a slave left in this country twenty years ago. For I know that about that time, and a few years previous, there were hundreds of slaves set free by the members of the Methodist Episcopal Church.[5]

A great teacher of Church History once said to his class in the course of a lecture: "The moral insight always outruns the economic." The attitude of the Church toward slavery is a case in point. With lofty and transcendent idealism the Church opposed the institution, but in those sections in which tobacco capitalism and cotton culture were of profit, there was a different point of view. Human values were sacrificed upon the altar of agricultural profit-taking. The passionate aim was economic gain. Everything else was subordinate. With the invention of the cotton gin in 1793, and accompanying labor-saving devices, the Church in certain sections of the country lost its mind. When cotton became king, the slave-holding states lost their heads. During the decade between 1850 and 1860, they regarded slavery as a positive good, and they lost their souls. In this moral lapse the Church in the Cotton Kingdom followed the dollar and led the way.

The Ninth Annual Conference was held at Baltimore, April 24, 1780. Certain questions were asked and answers given.

Question 16: Ought not this Conference to require those traveling preachers who hold slaves to give promise to set them free?
Answer: Yes.

---

5. Buckley, *loc. cit.*

Question 17: Does the Conference acknowledge that slavery is contrary to the laws of God, and nature, and hurtful to society, contrary to the dictates of conscience and pure religion, and doing that which we would not that others should do to us and ours? Do we pass our disapprobation on all our friends who keep slaves, and advise their freedom?

Answer: Yes.

"At the Virginia Conference of 1785 several petitions were presented by some of the principal members, urging the suspension of the rules on slavery." Dr. Thomas Coke stood fast for the rules. The Baltimore Conference "recommended to all our brethren to suspend the execution of the minute on slavery till the deliberations of a future Conference; and that an equal space of time be allowed all our members for consideration, when the minute shall be put in force." Lee says in his *History of the Methodists* that "these rules were offensive to most of our Southern friends, and were much opposed by many of our private members, local preachers, and some of the traveling preachers, and they were never afterward carried into full force." In 1800 the Church addressed a special letter to "all their brethren and friends in the United States," in which attention was called to the evil of slavery. This was one of the strongest statements ever offered by an ecclesiastical body against the institution.

This antislavery platform was vigorously opposed by the extreme South, and for twenty-four years from 1800 on there was an attitude of tolerance to slavery in the Methodist Church. One of the leaders in the South was Bishop William Capers of South Carolina, whose dust lies entombed in Columbia, the state capital. His view of slavery was that of a successful planter in his day, and he sought to salve his conscience by giving a form of religious instruction to the slaves of his state on the various plantations. That is, do not change the situation. It is heaven's decree and must be so recognized. The Negro is a servant of servants to his brothers in white, as borne out by scriptural prophecy. The thing to do is to give it the sanction of the Church, and baptize it with the spirit of the Christ. The Georgia Conference of 1837 said, by a unanimous vote:

Whereas, There is a clause in the Discipline of our Church which states that we are as much as ever convinced of the great evil of slavery; and,

Whereas, The said clause has been perverted by some, and used in such a manner as to produce the impression that the Methodist Episcopal Church believed slavery to be a moral evil;

therefore,

Resolved (1) That it is the sense of The Georgia Annual Conference, that slavery, as it exists in the United States, is not a moral evil;

Resolved (2) That we view slavery as a civil and domestic institution, and one with which, as Ministers of Christ, we have nothing to do, further than to ameliorate the condition of the slave, by endeavoring to impart to him and his master the benign influence of Christ, and aiding both on their way to heaven.

This is typical and representative of the Church in the South. Philosophy is always an afterthought. An attempt at justification inevitably follows the act. Religion was thus interpreted in a way to favor and rationalize the status quo. The Negro was no more than a mule, a beast of burden, a thing to be exploited, bought, used and sold. Man made in the image and likeness of God was dehumanized. One of the darkest pages in the history of the American Church is that which reveals religion and the Bible being used to buttress the system of slavery.

In 1838 the South Carolina Conference took the position that "Slavery in these United States is not one proper (subject) for the action of the Church, but it is exclusively appropriate to the civil authorities; therefore, Resolved, That this Conference will not intermeddle with it further than to express our regret that it has ever been introduced, in any form, into any one of the judicatories of the Church." The motion to adopt was made by Dr. Capers, who explained that "if slavery were a moral evil that is sinful, the Church would be bound to take cognizance of it; but our affirmation is, that it is not sinful." The adoption was unanimous.

The General Conference of 1840 was of the opinion that no

new legislation upon the subject of slavery would achieve the desired results: "Preserve the peace and unity of the whole body, promote the greatest happiness of the slave population and advance generally in the slave-holding community of our country the humane and hallowing influence of our holy religion." Even though the leaders saw the necessity of expressing an opinion in view of conflicting interpretations or attitudes toward the rule regarding slavery, none was made. Abolitionism was opposed, slavery agitation condemned, and it was decided not to change regulations touching slavery among its own members. Yet the abolition movement gained momentum, and had the power of molding public opinion. It was a small but influential group. In the South it was hated most cordially, and religiously despised. Some of the prominent abolition writers were: La Roy Sunderland, Orange Scott, George Storrs, Phineas Crandall, Joseph Merrill, Timothy Merritt, Frederick P. Tracy, Jotham Horton, Gershom F. Cox, James Porter, Luther Lee, Jonathan D. Bridge, Charles Adams, Cyrus Prindle, Daniel Wise, and Robert Boyd. Among the early conservatives were: Dr. Fisk, Professor Whedon, Dr. Nathan Bangs, Durbin, Luckey, Amos Binney, Bishop Hedding, Dr. Bond, and Bishop Emory. In 1859 *Uncle Tom's Cabin* by Harriet Beecher Stowe appeared and fell upon the thinking of the nation with tremendous incidence. The hero was Josiah Henson, an African Methodist preacher, who had escaped to Canada. *The Impending Crisis* by Hinton Rowan Helper, a poor North Carolina white, was so upsetting that it was *verboten* in the South. By 1843 the antislavery agitation bore fruit in the formation of the Wesleyan Methodist Episcopal Church of America, a withdrawal of about six thousand from the Methodist Episcopal body. The organizing convention was held at Utica, New York, May 31, 1843.

Eighteen forty-four was the year of the great schism in the Methodist Church. The story has been told in full by others. In such an account as this, it is only necessary to say that by 1844 a crisis had come within the Methodist Church. Events occurred which thrust the slavery question onto the center of the stage. The General Conference of that year met at New York City. The abolitionists and the conservatives had girded themselves for determinative action. The South contended that a slave-holding preacher, who had been suspended by the Baltimore Annual Conference, should be restored, and that a slave-holding Bishop should be allowed to remain undisturbed in office. Could the Church be true to the genius of Methodism, and countenance within its ranks a slave-holding Bishop? Had she a precedent or grounds for suspension or expulsion? The famous Bishop Andrews case engaged the time and thought of the General Conference. He was a Bishop who had inherited some slaves, and the Southern members of the General Conference were determined to support him.

A heated discussion ensued, which finally resulted in a division of the Church practically along the Mason-Dixon Line. This momentous General Conference adjourned sine die, at midnight, June 10, 1844, or June 11, at 12:15 A.M. A century has passed since the bitter struggle which bade fair to divide the nation. It was presaged by a schism in the Church.

The General Conference of 1856, on the eve of the Rebellion, was a forum for the heated discussion of the slavery issue. Many men of distinction participated in it, among them Miner Raymond of the New England Conference, Chairman of the Committee on Slavery; Collins, Chairman of the minority which presented a report; Hiram Mattison, George R. Crooks, Edward Thompson, Abel Stevens, Samuel Y. Morris, George Peck, John Dempster, Israel Chamberlayne, and John McClintock.

"The indirect refusal to take up the report of slavery by laying on the table the preliminary motion to suspend the order of the day indicated that any further action on the subject was not practicable during that session of the General Conference. A large majority, one hundred and twenty-two, had recorded their names in favor of prohibiting all slave-holding by a change in the General Rules with the concurring vote of the Annual Conferences. Of this number ninety-one were radical abolitionists and in favor of partial prohibition by direct and immediate legislation. Comparing the different votes taken by the yeas and nays, three classes of votes are recorded, — the conservatives, the constitutional abolitionists, and the radical abolitionists. The last class, numbering in all thirty-one, to prevent prohibition of slave-holding by direct legislation, united with the conservatives and threw the balance of power in favor of postponing further action, as before noted. Final antislavery action was thus deferred rather than defeated."[6]

The controversy continued after the adjournment and much space was occupied in Church papers. Abel Stevens, the later Church Historian, strenuously maintained that the slaveholder had a constitutional right to membership in the Church. His position was attacked by Professor W. L. Harris in a series of brilliant articles, which later appeared in a small work entitled, *Powers of the General Conference*. In substance he held that the General Conference has power to make rules which do not revoke or change a General Rule; that a Statutory Rule excluding slaveholders would not revoke or change the General Rule; that if it had been the intention to guard by constitutional provision the institution of slavery, it would have been done when, in 1808, the Church met to frame the Constitution; it was not done; hence the General Conference had power to refuse to tolerate slavery any longer. Others argued that no change was necessary to give authority to exclude slaveholders. Editor Daniel Wise of the *Sunday School Advocate* wrote pointed paragraphs against slavery and in favor of freedom. He was assailed before Annual Conferences and a boycott of his paper threatened. But he was adamant and replied: "The *Advocate* is expected to teach our children the doctrines and ethics of our Church; that slave-holding is a violation of Christian and Methodist ethics; and consequently it is my duty to teach the children to think of it as a sin; so long as I am Editor of the paper I shall firmly but judiciously so instruct them. If the General Conference shall condemn my course, it can of course, replace me with another Editor."

The battle of words, the logomachy, continued. Others entered the lists. Stevens thundered forth through the columns of the *Advocate* on "What the Next General Conference Should Do on the Question of Slavery." He was answered by D. D. Whedon in the *New York Tribune*, made famous by the impressive and colorful Horace Greeley, with his linen duster, one breeches leg in the top of a boot, and the other dragging the ground, later to pen his immortal "Prayer of Twenty Millions" to President Lincoln on the question of slavery.

---

6. *Ibid.* 59 f.

We have noted the formation of the Wesleyan Church in 1843, the split in the Methodist Church ranks which resulted in the Methodist Church South in 1844-45, and it may not be amiss to state briefly the cases of the other prominent American Churches. The Protestant Episcopalians "remained a mute and careless spectator of this great conflict." The Baptist Church being "a movement" and not an organization with a central body holding general jurisdiction, could not speak as a unit. In its convention each individual church is sovereign and independent. Several did, however, give antislavery testimonies. In the denomination as a whole there was no great antislavery struggle; but a separate antislavery Mission Board was maintained for several years. A crisis came in the Board in 1845, which resulted in a schism. The Free-Will Baptists denied fellowship to slaveholders as early as 1839, but their scene of operation was not in the South, hence there was no occasion for an antislavery struggle.

As early as 1774 the Presbyterian Church, in the Synod of New York and Pennsylvania, took up the subject of Negro slavery, but deferred action until the next meeting. Thirteen years later they went on record "in warmest terms, to every member of the body, and to all the churches and families under their care, to do everything in their power, consistent with the civil rights of society, to promote the abolition of slavery." In 1793 this was reaffirmed. The same year the General Assembly notified "all the former churches under their care that they view with the deepest concern any vestiges of slavery which may exist in our country." In 1815 The General Assembly reaffirmed their former position and added that "they consider the buying and selling of slaves by way of traffic inconsistent with the spirit of the Gospel." Three years later the system of slavery was condemned, as "inconsistent with the Law of God . . . irreconcilable with the spirit and principles of the Gospel of Christ," and a "blot on our holy religion." They urged speedy efforts "to obtain the complete abolition of slavery throughout Christendom and the world."

In 1836 the subject of slavery was indefinitely postponed by a vote of 154 to 87. This vote is indicative of a change of front, and is reflective of the growing importance of the slave system with the planters and certain individuals. This action was taken just before the appearance of the two Assemblies — the Old School and the New School. The latter referred the matter of slavery to the lower judicatories. By 1840 they did "not think it for the edification of the Church to take any action on the subject," but in 1846 the system was condemned as "intrinsically unrighteous and oppressive." They did not, however, exclude owners of slaves from Christian fellowship. Strong statements condemnatory of slavery were issued in reaffirmation of former attitudes, and by 1856 the Assembly took the position that it could only reprove and warn, and recommend reform. This it did in the case of the Lexington Presbytery, South, which had taken a proslavery position.

The Old School went proslavery by a vote of 168 to 13, and by 1850 it was decided not to discuss the issue, and the whole subject was laid on the table until the Rebellion. During the war the Old School held to its former position. However, in 1862 the "Deliverance" of the Assembly was adopted 190 to 20. It stated that "the system that makes or proposes to make, the relation of master and slave hereditary, perpetual, and absolute, must be wrong, as it is a negation of the principles and precepts of the Gospel, and of every idea of civil liberty and of inalienable rights." Just prior to the Rebellion the New School Assembly went on record by refusing "to instruct their Church Extension Society not to aid any Church that has in its communion one or more slaveholders." The Philadelphia Assembly of 1863 adopted a report on the state of the country, prepared by the Reverend Dr. Barnes, which condemned slavery as a violation of human rights. The report indorsed President Lincoln's Proclamation of Emancipation. The Presbyterians went still farther in 1865 by unanimously adopting a memorial demanding the right of enfranchisement for the Negroes.

The Congregational Church operated chiefly in free territory, had no connectional bond and were not implicated in the slavery agitation. The Episcopal Church did not recognize the withdrawal of their Southern brethren, and thus avoided a schism. The slavery question was the concern chiefly of the great evangelical Churches, namely, the Methodists, Baptists, and the Presbyterians. As one looks backward upon the great issues that created acute tensions in the denominations, and caused brethren of the same Communion to walk no longer together in faith and fellowship of the Spirit, one can and must sympathize with those who were grappling with a vital question in the light of their experience, knowledge, and enfolding environmental circumstances. But our main concern is with the Methodist Church, and its attitude toward the institution of Negro slavery; out of it came Richard Allen, the Apostle of Freedom, founder and organizer of the African M. E. Church.

CHAPTER VI

Meeting a Vital Issue

I know there is a God, and that He hates injustice and slavery. I see the storm coming, and I know that His hand is in it. If He has a place and work for me, — and I think He has — I believe I am ready.

I am nothing, but truth is everything. I know I am right because I know that liberty is right, for Christ teaches it, and Christ is God. —ABRAHAM LINCOLN

The historic position of the African M. E. Church would naturally be antislavery. Was not the Church begun because of certain discriminatory attitudes to peoples of African descent as a direct result of the traffic in men in America? Was not the entire African Church movement a reaction and a protest against such? From the outset it placed its stamp of disapproval upon slavery and couched its opinion in the first Book of Discipline published in 1817. Article 3 of the General Rules for the United Societies embodied the Wesleyan ideal:

The buying and selling of men, women and children, with an intention to enslave them is prohibited by any member or members of the Church.[1]

The Fathers who founded the Church knew that the birth and rise of Bethel was occasioned by slavery, and they took a definite position against it.

Difficulty arose in Philadelphia, Baltimore, and Charleston concerning the white and colored members sitting in the same pews and kneeling at the same altars. The Negroes had to sit in certain designated places, in the gallery, the rear, or around the walls on the fringe of the white worshipers. In some instances they were

1. *A. M. E. Discipline, 1948,* 81, Sec. 1, Art. 3.

compelled to wait for the Communion of the Lord's Supper until
after their white brethren had finished.[2] After the organization of
the Church in 1816, its spread in the South was arrested by the
slave power. Morris Brown and his associates were forced to leave
Charleston for Baltimore and Philadelphia.

While the American democratic churches were wrestling with
the question of slavery which finally split them asunder, the African M. E. Church presented a solid front against the iniquitous
system. It represented the enslaved group. Often has it been asked
why the Church in its Conferences did not take a more militant
attitude. It has even been asked why the slaves did not join in a
revolution, a group war against cotton and tobacco capitalism.
In the first place the Fathers did come to vital grips with the issue
in an understandable way. They were wise and judicious. They
realized that they were Christians, carrying forward the spirit of
forbearance and forgiveness. They believed in the ultimate triumph of justice on the earth. On the other hand, they did not
desire to do anything that would work hardship upon their
brothers in chains, and fellow-sufferers in tribulation. Here and
there a voice was heard crying in the wilderness against slavery.
From time to time the General Conference and Annual Conference took an uncompromising attitude upon the slavery question. The 1844 General Conference was silent in reference to the
institution. But the Canadian Conference of 1845 passed a resolution prohibiting the use of their pulpits to slaveholders. Canada
was a haven of freedom for runaway slaves from the southern
plantations. It was the terminus of the Underground Railway. On
the other hand, many Negroes there were born free, and hostile
to slavery. The New York Conference about the same time
adopted a resolution that called for three days' fasting and humiliation "in order that the God of the oppressed might terminate their
degradation and oppression."[3]

The New England Conference which met at New Bedford in
1852 passed the following resolution, signed by D. Dorrell, W. J.
Fuller, and T. M. D. Ward:

Resolved: That while we inhale the soft and sweet air of
liberty, we as Christians cannot forget the forlorn and

2. J. A. Handy, *Scraps of A. M. E. Church History*, 13.
3. C. S. Smith, *History of the A. M. E. Church*, 13.

mournful condition of those our own brethren who are
held in chains and obeying the scriptural command to
remember those that are in bonds, as being bound with
them, we will ever invoke the power and protection of
that God who executed righteousness for all them that
are oppressed. . . .[4]

In 1856 it decried slavery as "a gross outrage against humanity,
a positive violation of every one of the Ten Commandments,
destructive of all political, moral and religious rites, which is in
itself theft, murder, robbery, licentiousness, concubinage, and
everything else that is sinful and devilish between heaven and
earth."[5] This General Conference attitude was taken just three
years before John Brown raided Harper's Ferry, and four years
before the election of Lincoln which was a signal for war. It will
be treated more fully in the following chapter.

The march of events gave evidence of a crisis that was impending in the affairs of the nation. It will be remembered that three
great American bodies of Christians had already parted company
at least twelve years prior to this time, showing the way to the
nation in 1861. In the General Conference of 1856 which met at
Cincinnati, slavery agitation was at fever heat. The Missouri Compromise of 1820 had virtually been repealed by the Kansas and
Nebraska Bill of 1854. There was the Fugitive Slave Law of 1850
that legalized slaves as so much property. In 1857 the United
States Supreme Court's decision handed down by Chief Justice
Roger B. Taney in the case of Dred Scott, legalized the deperson-
alization and dehumanizing of the Negro. Legislatures in northern
states passed resolutions condemning the decision and the Republican platform of 1860 characterized the dogma that the Constitution carried slavery into the territories as "a dangerous political
heresy at variance with the explicit provisions of that instrument
itself . . . with legislative and judicial precedent . . . revolutionary
in tendency and subversive of the peace and harmony of the
country." Lincoln said: "We know the Court that made it has
often overruled its own decisions and we shall do what we can to
have it overrule this."

Men of high and low estate saw the coming storm that would

---

4. *Minutes of the New England Conference, 1852,* 14.
5. Handy, *loc., cit.*

soon break in mad fury over the nation. Henry Clay and others tried in vain to stay its coming with compromises. But there is no compromise between right and wrong. The conflict between two contrary and opposite conceptions of religion as well as of economics and labor had to be settled. It had to be settled right. The cold war went on in the nation. In the Churches the war of words continued.

The Churches in the South stood generally for the political philosophy of states' rights, which meant the right to deal with the "peculiar institution" and slave economy as it saw fit. Religion was so interpreted. The men in the South who were determined to perpetuate and extend the slave power were in the main leaders in the Church. The North was equally determined to prevent the extension of the slave power and maintain free labor. There were many in this section of the country whose sympathies were with the slavocracy. A very able and scholarly discussion of this phase of our story may be found in DuBois' *Black Reconstruction*. Such a lengthy treatise would be out of place here.

The Negroes, about whom the unity of religion and the preservation of the Union centered, by their own reproduction had increased to 3,638,808 in 1850, and before the War of the Rebellion they had reached the figure of 4,441,830. They constituted 10 per cent of the whole population of the nation in 1700, 22 per cent in 1750, 18.9 per cent in 1800, and 11.6 per cent in 1900. The people who owned slaves were respectable Church members and "Christians." They were leaders in their several communities. The slaves represented so much invested property. One planter regarded the newborn baby of a slave mother as worth $300. At the beginning of the nineteenth century, a slave brought an average price of $200, while in 1860 the price ranged from $1,400 to $2,000. In 1791, the production of cotton was 9,000 bales. The cotton gin was invented in 1793, and within nine years the annual production was increased to 79,000 bales. There ensued an economic revolution, and by 1822 the cotton crop had reached the astronomical figure of 1,500,000 bales. In 1850 cotton sold for $102,000,000; sugar for $14,800,000; rice for $2,600,000 — a total of $119,400,000. These figures are more eloquent than words, and gauge correctly the sentiment back of the actions of southern churchmen and planters.

The rapid increase of wealth makes one hunger the more for

greater wealth, and a wider area for one's operations. There was feverish activity in the acquisition of new lands. In the tobacco country of Maryland and Virginia the law of diminishing returns began to operate inexorably. These states turned to breeding slaves for the Deep South. John Randolph was so hard pressed that he talked of leaving Virginia. A southerner wrote to Frederick Law Olmsted:

> In the states of Maryland, Virginia, North Carolina, Kentucky, Tennessee, and Missouri, as much attention was paid to the breeding and growth of Negroes as to that of horses and mules. Further South, we raise them both for use and for market. Planters command their girls and women (married and unmarried) to have children; I have known a good many Negro girls to be sold off because they did not have children. A breeding woman is worth from one-sixth to one-fourth more than one that does not breed.[6]

From 1840 to 1850 Virginia bred and exported to the cotton kingdom no less than 100,000, which at $500 a head would have yielded $50,000,000.

The wealth-hunger possessed the lower South during the two decades prior to the Rebellion. When the leaders in Church and State arrived at the position where they considered slavery a "positive good," they vied with each other in trying to justify the institution at the expense of the slaves. Men of the cotton country who were not members of the Church might live freely, partake of the joys of the world, and might even deny the fundamentals of the Christian faith without the feeling that everlasting penance must be done in the world to come. Nor were there great religious or social scruples, if aristocratic blood ran in Negro veins, or if fine young gentlemen kept half-breed mistresses.[7] In New Orleans a group of distinguished men was dining at a fashionable hotel, and one of the number pointed out a handsome young waiter, and said that he was the son of President Andrew Jackson.[8]

Religion was merely a means to an end, which was twofold:

---

6. W. E. B. Du Bois, *Black Reconstruction,* 13.
7. W. E. Dodd, *The Cotton Kingdom,* 13.
8. James Ford Rhodes, *History of the United States,* I., 134 f.

to justify the existing institution, and to serve as an opiate for the slaves. They were told that their lot had been ordained of God; their sole duty was to obey their masters in the Lord as good servants. By and by they would lay down their heavy load, cross over Jordan in a calm time, and rest forevermore in an apocalyptic heaven with a superabundance of milk and honey. A religious philosophy was evolved that would guarantee and maintain the status quo at all costs. The idea of religion in terms of brotherhood was foreign, and social justice was unthinkable. The slave was not a man or a person. He was a brute, a beast, a thing. In the meantime, the weight of the exploitative economic order rested upon the broad, bent, black backs of the enslaved Africans. In the North where the institution was not profitable economically, there was a rising tide of opposition. Various Church groups, the abolitionists, free press, orators, and labor organizations took up the gauge of battle. It was forbidden in the prairie states of the Northwest; civil war broke out in Kansas. Leading clergymen in the North like Henry Ward Beecher, Phillips Brooks, and Theodore Parker inveighed against slavery. Scores of men whose names are unknown, North and South, joined issues. The leaders in the South, Chancellor Harper, President Thornwell, the Reverend McMaster espoused a type of religion that countenanced slavery. Thomas R. Dew attempted to show that slavery was the principal cause of civilization. Hammond based his justification of slavery upon the holy Scriptures. Parson Brownlow of Knoxville espoused the cause of freedom.

With the leading religious denominations that operated in the South, torn asunder by the slave question; with the passion for wealth increasing; with the Southern clergy actually attempting to prove slavery to be ordained of God; with cotton culture reaching the astounding figure of 5,000,000 bales in 1860; with 5,236,000 spindles in the North, and 290,000 in the South, a new level never before reached, the South was ready to go to war to perpetuate the system in 1861. The election of Abraham Lincoln was meaningful.

During the four years of strife, the Southern Church stood steadfastly by the Confederacy, encouraged loyalty to the Stars and Bars, and prayed for victory on the field of battle. On the other hand the Northern Church encouraged fidelity and loyalty to the Union and prayed for ultimate victory for the armies of Grant, Sherman, and Sheridan. Finally it urged the emancipation of the slaves. In 1864 a committee from the Methodist Church Conference, held in Philadelphia, visited President Lincoln in Washington. He said to them: "God bless all the Churches, and blessed be God! Who, in this our great trial giveth us the Churches."[9] Another caller at the White House to urge emancipation was Daniel Alexander Payne, Bishop in the African M. E. Church. Neither he nor Carl Schurz succeeded in causing Mr. Lincoln to commit himself but he did reply with a slightly bent head:

> Well, I must believe that God has led me thus far, for I am conscious that I never would have accomplished what has been done, if He had not been with me to counsel and to shield.[10]

Again we turn to the attempt of the African M. E. Church in its effort to meet the slavery issue. The General Conference of 1856 which met at Cincinnati was the most important gathering in the history of the denomination for discussion and debate of the slavery question. Looking backward upon that era from the vantage-ground of time, the lengthening perspective enables one to see the intelligence, sincerity, and spirit of Christianity with which the men of that day came to grips with a problem that within four or five years would see the country bathed in the blood of brothers. It might have been averted, perhaps, had the Christian pulpit all over the land raised a united voice against slavery. But alas, it was divided. The house was divided against itself. It has already been shown how the Church in the South, and some men in the North interpreted their religion in terms of slave-holding. Many of these Christians sealed their faith, political and religious, with their lifeblood. One southern Bishop, an owner of slaves, became a general in the army of the South.

Considerable discussion ensued upon the adoption of a report on slavery. It was feared that the majority report was too radical as it condemned "slave-holding, as practiced in this country, as

9. Osborn H. Oldroyd, *Words of Lincoln,* 134 f.
10. John Wesley Cromwell, *The Negro in American History,* 121.

a sin of the first magnitude, and should not for one moment be allowed in the holy Communion of the Church of God."

> (1) That the sin of slave-holding, as practiced in the American Churches, is a sin of the first degree, and the greatest known in the category of crimes — the highest violation of God's Law, a shameful abuse of God's creatures, shocking the enlightened humanity, and should unchurch, and does unchristianize every man and woman who is a slaveholder.
>
> (2) That the A. M. E. Church, composed, as it is, of colored persons identified with the slaves in chains, who never can be dissevered from them in their sufferings, do deeply sympathize with them in their tears and blood, and they shall have our constant prayers, good wishes and help as it may be in our power to render them.

A motion was made to adopt, when a minority report was offered: "In our Book of Discipline, under page 124, in the Rules, we find the buying and selling of men, women and children, with an intent to enslave them, expressly forbidden. Also under page 136, we find in positive terms the following: 'We will not receive any person into our society as a member who is a slaveholder. Any person now a member having slaves, who shall refuse to emancipate them after due notice has been given by the preacher in charge, shall be expelled.' We are of the opinion that in the above sentiments as a Church are fully expressed. And while we deeply deplore that American slavery exists, we can do no more than pray that God, in His providence, may hasten the day when equity and justice shall be equally distributed to all mankind, and insist that our laws on that subject be rigidly enforced. We further recommend the passage of the following resolutions:

> (1) That we deprecate the spirit in any professing Christian denomination that would attempt to excuse its members from the sin of slave-holding by offering as an apology the example of the Apostolic Church.
>
> (2) That there is not the most distant likeness be-

tween them; for while the Apostolic Church in the then
existing government was held in a similar position to
the A. M. E. Church now in government, both Apostles
and followers were deprived from any protection from
the existing laws, much less to vote in making or abolish-
ing them, as we are now.

(3) That while we have no voice in the affairs of
this nation, we recommend that both our preachers and
people, like Israel of old, set apart special days of fasting
and prayer to Almighty God that He, in His divine providence, may hasten the day when all oppression shall
come to an end, and when the whole earth shall be filled
with His glory.

(4) That while we as a denomination have no power,
so far as political rights are concerned, but are groaning
under the yoke and burdens of oppressive laws, we do
earnestly recommend the enforcement of our law, as it
is, on slavery.[11]

In the long discussion that followed, there was fear that the
minority report was not sufficiently radical. It was developed
in the debate that there were slave-holding members in the
Church. An anomalous situation was revealed in that Louisiana
had incorporated the A. M. E. Church with an antislavery Discipline. The minority report was finally adopted.

In 1860 when the General Conference was convened, the
question of slavery was again considered. A resolution was agreed
to which excluded slave-holding members from the Church; that
is, providing they refused to set them free immediately. Such
slave-holding members who refused to emancipate their slaves
would be expelled from Church membership. Sympathy was expressed for that part of the Church in chains, and deprecation for
any professing Christian denomination that would attempt to ex-
cuse its members from the sin of slave-holding.

The Church elected to pursue the path of trying to christian-
ize public opinion, and to use what spiritual means were at hand,
rather than incite a revolt, or do anything that would in their
opinion jeopardize their brethren in the house of bondage. That

11. D. A. Payne, *History of the A. M. E. Church*, 23, 213, 323, 326.

was the official position of the African M. E. Church, but the story of attitudes of individual ministers and members will never be chronicled. The system of American slavery operated in such a way as to break up tribal groups, and families. This made for a weakening of the least semblance of unified, co-ordinated effort. Yet there are several instances of slave uprisings to cast off the yoke of oppression. On the other hand, the police system always had to keep a watchful eye upon the slaves. This accounts in part for the failure of the Negroes to engage in a large-scale attempt to overthrow the plantation system in the South. Again, the slave-owners were quick to see the danger of mental improvement. Most of the "education" came as a result of contact with the "big house," or it was acquired clandestinely. The writer has heard Bishop Henry McNeal Turner tell of how he learned to read. When his master was not looking, he would steal a glimpse of a word in a dictionary, the Bible, or Webster's Blue Back Speller, and watch to see if prying eyes saw him. Sometimes a kind master, his wife, or children would help him.

Shields Green said, when about to join in the Harper's Ferry raid: "I think I'll go down wid de ole man." Nat Turner raised the flag of revolt in South Hampton, Va. Denmark Vasey's plot in Charleston was revealed by one of his own men. It is clear what might have been the result had there been a general uprising.[12]

War clouds were lowering. All attempts at compromise had failed. Both sides girded themselves for the conflict. An antislavery man from Illinois was in the White House. There were grave threats of secession by the cotton states. Garrison was busy with *The Liberator*, and Horace Greeley with the *New York Tribune*. Robert Barnwell Rhett and W. Y. Yancey were spilling vitriolic ink in the *Charleston Mercury*, and the *Mobile Register*. An army of blue invaded the South, and for four years heard the "Rebel yell" from the throats of gray-uniformed soldiers who followed the leadership of Robert E. Lee. Upon the shoulders of Jefferson Davis had fallen the mantle of Calhoun. The South sold her soul for silver fleece, which turned out to be more costly than

---

12. *General Conference Journal*, May 1860; J. A. Rogers, *World's Great Men of Color*, II, 531-36.

the price of freedom. Both sides implored the same Providence; Churches on either side of the Potomac and the Ohio prayed to the same God. The African M. E. Church waited, hoped, trusted that the God of all the universe would do right. It believed that justice eternal is interwoven with the very fibre and texture of the universe, and that in the long run right would prevail. "As it was said three thousand years ago, so still must it be said, 'The judgments of the Lord are true and righteous altogether.' "

CHAPTER VII

The Missionary Enterprise

They went out and preached everywhere. — MARK 16:20

Go west, and build up the Church. — MORRIS BROWN

The Christian Church is a missionary enterprise, and when it loses its impulse to propagate itself by carrying the Gospel of the Lord, its unique distinction will be gone. The Divine command is to "go." Realizing this fact, very shortly after the beginning of the African M. E. Church, the early Fathers were fired with a holy zeal to extend its borders and range of influence. The movement out of Philadelphia is like another chapter to be added to the Acts of the Apostles. The men who carried the banner of African Methodism to the most far-distant frontier regions were heralds of a burning passion, who set no value upon their own lives in order that they might execute the great commission of their Lord. Their overmastering purpose was to plant the Church to the glory of God.

The Church had been organized in 1816. In 1820 Daniel Coker, the flaming evangel of Baltimore, set sail for Liberia on the west coast of Africa. While on the high seas, he organized a branch of the Church among those who were on board the ship. Like the great Apostle unto the Gentiles he made use of every opportunity to proclaim the story of the Cross. Coker subsequently went to Sierra Leone, a British colony adjacent to Liberia. This heroic spirit was in the first company of emigrants who left this country for the fatherland under the auspices of The American Colonization Society. When death had claimed the leader, Coker was in charge of the little band, and standing alone with a dark future, but strong faith in God he writes:

We have met with trials; we are but a handful; our provisions are running low; we are in a strange land; we have

not heard from America and know not whether more
provisions or people will be sent out, yet, thank the
Lord, *my confidence is strong in the veracity of His
promises*. Tell my brethren to come — fear not — this
land is good; it only wants men to possess it. I have
opened a little Sunday School for native children. Oh, it
would do your heart good to see the little naked sons of
Africa around me. *Tell the colored people to come up to
the help of the Lord*. Let nothing discourage the Society,
or the colored people.[1]

This work was done in Sierra Leone. Nothing is known of his
work in Liberia. This is another view of the indefatigable worker
who planted the Church in Maryland, founded Bethel on Druid
Hill, Baltimore, and was so highly esteemed that his brethren
elected him to the Episcopacy in 1816. The figure of Coker looms
larger with the flight of time. He was a pioneer missionary. Bishop
Jabez Pitt Campbell is of the opinion that the grand honor should
go to John Boggs, who, however did not go to the field until
1824. Truly Coker went on other business, and his missionary
work was incidental. He felt the "woe is me." Boggs was sent out
by the Church.[2]

By the meeting of the General Conference of 1824 the missionaries had made their way across the mountains into the valley
of the Monongahela. The mighty leaders were none other than
the same Boggs, William Paul Quinn, and John Charleston.[3]
Quinn's labors carried him through Pennsylvania, Ohio, Indiana,
Illinois, Kentucky, Tennessee, and Missouri. He is to African
Methodism what Peter Cartwright was to Methodism in the frontier period of the Church. John Boggs left his footprints in Ohio,
and nearly five hundred miles beyond the western spur of the
Alleghenies. In 1823, only seven years after the Philadelphia Convention, the advancing missionaries had founded the Church at
Steubenville, Ohio. By February, 1824, Moses Freeman had established what is now Allen Temple in Cincinnati. A magnificent
edifice now stands at the corner of Sixth Street and Broadway,

---

1. J. M. Brown, (ed.), *Repository of Religion and Literature*, III, 99.
2. C. S. Smith, *History of the A. M. E. Church,* 124; L. L. Berry, *A Century of Missions,* 41 f.
3. B. W. Arnett, *Colored Sunday Schools,* 4 f., 12.

a monument to early architecture. The Pastor is the Reverend
Wallace M. Wright. Under his leadership the debt was paid, and
the mortgage burned, September 14, 1945, by Bishop Reverdy
Cassius Ransom. The feat of raising the money was accomplished
without a social or an entertainment.

The first mission field outside the continental limits of the
United States was Haiti. Scipio Beans of the Baltimore Conference unfurled the banner of the Cross in the island after the immortal Toussaint L'Ouverture had led his people to freedom from
Napoleon Bonaparte and the French. The Reverend Beans toiled
in this field heroically until the Lord took his restless spirit home.
From failing hands there is always another to catch the torch and
carry on. In this instance Richard Robinson, Charles W. Mossell,
S. G. Dorce, John Hurst, and others projected and developed the
work so nobly begun by Beans. Robinson did not long remain
in Haiti, though he was ordained for the work. Upon his return
to the country he founded Campbell Chapel in Frankford, a part
of Philadelphia. His grave is to be seen today in front of the
Church. His wife is buried beside him. Boggs died in Philadelphia
in 1848. John Hurst came to America and became Financial Secretary. In 1912 at Kansas City he was elected one of the Bishops.
His constructive work in Florida and South Carolina is monumental. In spite of the zeal and sacrifices of Boggs, Beans, and
their company, the Church was not awakened to the religious
imperative and responsibilities of the missionary enterprise in the
islands as in Africa.[4] The redeeming feature is the vision and interest manifested by the Fathers.

Africa was set apart as a mission field by the General Conference of 1856.[5] This was an epochal event. The Reverend J. R. V.
Morgan was appointed missionary. He was born in Kent County,
Maryland but reared in Philadelphia. In early life he was apt, but
wild. He served in the Union Army during the Rebellion. He
served in the New Jersey Conference, New England, California,
and Colorado. When dying, he was heard to exclaim: "This is
the last of John R. V. Morgan."

The Reverend David Smith was one of the early pioneers in
Maryland and Pennsylvania. He was a tireless worker for the Lord

---

4.   James A. Handy, *Scraps of A. M. E. Church History*, 332 ff.
5.   B. W. Arnett, *Budget, 1888*, 17.

in preaching, laying out circuits, and doing the task of a missionary. Smith was ordained in 1817 by Allen at the first session of the Baltimore Conference, and appointed to the Harrisburg Circuit, which he traveled on foot. The points were Harrisburg, Carlisle, Chambersburg, Shippensbury, and Fredericktown. In 1846 he was Supply Pastor of Allen Temple, Cincinnati. He spent the sunset years of his life at Xenia in Greene County, where he wrote a very valuable autobiography.

The western extension of the Church was largely the work of William Paul Quinn. He was one of the first four men who joined the African M. E. Church, and was present at the time of its organization.[6] Quinn was from Calcutta, India, of Negro and Hindu parentage. His father was a wealthy mahogany dealer. Quinn's religious life was induced by a woman missionary, a Quaker who came from England to India. He developed a hatred for war and drunkenness. His father banished and disowned him for having advocated his religious views; so he came to America via Gibraltar, and Sheffield, England. William Paul Quinn was tall and stood erect, with slightly stooped shoulders. His well-formed head was covered with a shock of black, curly hair, that well adorned a bronze complexion. He wore upon his face a very gentle expression, full eyebrows, arched over keen piercing eyes, aquiline nose, firm mouth, and shapely chin. His physique was rugged and strong. It seemed that he was prepared by the Almighty for the Herculean task of frontier preaching, at a time when life was hard. The exact date of his birth is doubtful. Some claim 1788, some 1799. His tombstone in the cemetery at Richmond, Indiana, where his dust is interred, bears the simple inscription: "PAUL QUINN, 1800."

He was the first preacher to mount a horse and ride a circuit. In 1836 he was commissioned by Morris Brown to go west and "build up the Church." Apparently all the preparation he needed was to have a good night's sleep, saddle his horse and start. Often he was compelled to engage in physical combat with rowdies and Kluxers before concluding his sermon. In both he would come out victorious, and the enemies of the Church would be subdued. This rigorous missionary work marked him for life. In 1840 he was selected by the General Conference to be a missionary to the ter-

---

6.   Daniel A. Payne, *History of the A. M. E. Church,* 375.

ritory west of Ohio; the only time such an assignment has ever been made.[7]

Quinn attended the General Conference of 1844. The delegates from the East did not like him, and did not wish to see him elevated to the Episcopacy. But when he read his report they had the good sense to elect him upon the basis of merit and promise of an outstanding contribution in the high office. He served as Bishop from 1844 to 1873, and as Senior Bishop from 1848, or twenty-five years. The report which turned the tide of sentiment in his favor included 47 churches established and organized, with 2,000 members; 7 traveling Elders; 20 traveling preachers, 27 local preachers, 50 Sunday schools, 200 teachers, 2,000 scholars, 40 temperance societies, and 17 Camp Meetings.

It has been observed that when the physical and legal difficulties that Elder Quinn had to encounter are considered — that the hounds of slavery were scenting his footsteps at every turn he took; that many of the white people were timid; that the Fugitive Slave Law practically established a system of espionage over the movements of the colored people in the North that deterred them from going into slave territory — that despite these untoward circumstances and galling restrictions, he should have possessed the moral and physical courage to defy the slave power by planting the banner of the African Methodist Episcopal Church in two great slave centers, Louisville and St. Louis, makes one, even at this distant time, feel like reviving the plaudits that greeted him when he submitted his report to the General Conference of 1844. At Alton, Ill., the mighty warrior for God preached the Gospel to the slaves across the Mississippi River over on the Missouri side. Priscilla Baltimore frequently ferried him across the river in the early hours of the night. He was accompanied by Ezekiel Pines, a devout man, who was a regular attendant at five o'clock Sunday morning prayer meetings when St. Paul Chapel, St. Louis was founded. The great church now stands at the corner of Leffingwell and Lawton Streets.

Priscilla Baltimore was born in Bourbon County, Kentucky, May 13, 1801. She was owned in slavery by her father, and was converted under the preaching of Bishop Eugene R. Hendrick of

---

7. Handy, *op. cit.*, 165.

the M. E. Church. A missionary purchased her freedom for $1,100, and in turn gave her the opportunity of purchasing her own freedom, which she accomplished in seven years. She was a missionary indeed. So great was her influence that slave masters permitted her to gather their slaves for religious services. Once she was allowed to carry three hundred of them from Missouri into Illinois that they might hear the Gospel. This good woman ministered unto Quinn of her means, and cheered his heart in his difficult and heroic task of planting the Church in Missouri. She fell asleep in 1882 at a ripe old age. Dr. T. W. Henderson preached the funeral from the text: "But a woman that feareth the Lord, she shall be praised. Give her the fruit of her hands, and let her own words praise her in the gates" (Proverbs 31:30-31).[8]

William Paul Quinn had the daring and faith of Paul, the intrepidity of Francis Asbury, the blood and iron of Bismarck, and the zeal of Peter Cartwright. He was matchless in heroism, superb in courage, and relentless in his attacks on the foes of his people. He was a militant soldier of the Cross. He was a giant in his day. His life and labors are both a lesson and a rebuke to the timid and faint-hearted of this day; to those in the North who shrink from accepting a place in our ministry in the South because there are Jim Crow cars and other restrictions and inconveniences to which people of color in that section are subjected. What are Jim Crow cars, restrictions, and inconveniences to the restrictions imposed by slavery? At times this man of God could find no means of conveyance other than an ox cart, and there were others when he had no place to lay his head. Only a superman could have borne the brunt of the battle as he did and so gloriously. There is dire need today for men of his spirit and type.

When Bishop Quinn fell asleep, and the General Conference of 1876 held appropriate memorial services for him, Bishop Jabez Pitt Campbell said:

William Paul Quinn, the missionary! That is just what he was — a missionary. And so were all the first preachers. William Paul Quinn was the first to mount a horse, the first to lay out a circuit in the bounds of the Philadel-

---

8. Elaine Welch, *William Paul Quinn*, 11.

phia Conference, labored in the Baltimore Conference,
and traveled on out west to push on the victory of the
Cross. He traveled all of the circuits east of the Allegheny Mountains, and was exposed to all of the hardships
which some of you well know; yet he would not give up
the cause. In 1832 he went into the Mississippi Valley.
His course was onward, and westward at that time. He
was made of such material that he feared neither man nor
devils. If he wanted to hold outdoor meetings, he would
hold them and conquer mobs and still go on. He was just
such a man. God made him so that he could preach in the
pulpit, go down and whip the devil, and then go preach
again. He could do more than all the sheriffs and con-
stables put together. He was able to do it. And still I
never saw him angry with a wicked man.

He lived in his day and served his generation well. He
carried the battle to the gates, as Hannibal carried it to
the gates of Rome. Just before he died, the battle-
scarred veteran of the Cross said to one of his brethren
who was near by: "I see before me a great light making
visible the other side."[9]

Bishop Quinn was a Master Mason. The Quakers were somewhat against secret societies, and the craft had difficulty in rent-
ing a lodge hall in Richmond, Ind. Quinn permitted them to meet
in one of his houses. He is now the patron saint of the Paul Quinn
Lodge. His masonic membership was in New York. It might be
said of him as of another: "From the mystic tie, he has passed
away. Over the curve of the ever-living arch hang the insignia
of his office. The gavel and the plumb never shall he use. Grant,
that when the Royal Master, with the stamp of fate, shall bid us
present our work for inspection, we also, like him who has gone
before, may be able to render good work, such as He shall ap-
prove who once proclaimed: 'Let there be light! and there was
light.' "

To every great man, there are scores and hundreds of unnamed
ones who make his work possible. In writing this narrative it is
impossible to chronicle the deeds and exploits of all that grand

9.   Arnett, *op. cit.*, 179 f.

army of God-intoxicated veterans of the Cross. Were it our desire, it would be impossible as well as impracticable, because the records are not extant. There are multitudes who wrought well, and, unnoticed, slipped away quietly into the enfolding abyss of eternity. The few whose names have been mentioned, and their comrades carried the word into New England, Canada, down the Mississippi to the Gulf and New Orleans, where John Mifflin Brown was five times imprisoned for bravely preaching to the enslaved brethren. Strange to say that his incarceration was due to hostility on the part of the very people he was trying to help. Slaves would slip into the services to participate in the worship. Exception was taken to this by some of the free people of color, and it led to Brown's imprisonment. But his firm stand won out in the end to the glory of God and the benefit of the Church. St. James on North Roman Street, New Orleans, is a monument to his memory.

The early Fathers of the Church saw new fields of missionary endeavor other than the continent of Africa and Haiti. They looked with longing eyes toward Central America, South America, Cuba, and the West Indies. At the General Conference of 1856, a Brother Smith made a report of his labors at Greytown, Central America. This society was made up "partly of English persons, and partly of colored persons." It did "not comprehend the distinction of color," and would not have understood the Discipline, according to Brother Smith. Brother G. W. Lawrence seems to have been the real founder of the point. He gave Bishop Payne letters to prove his contention. He prosecuted his labors as a British subject.[10]

Organizational machinery for missionary activities was set up by an act of the General Conference of 1844,[11] but under the Baltimore Annual Conference. A Constitution for the Parent Home and Foreign Missionary Society was adopted by the General Conference of 1864. The Reverend Dr. John M. Brown was elected as Secretary, and a General Board was provided. The following persons have served as secretaries: John M. Brown, 1864-68; James A. Handy, 1868-72; George W. Brodie, 1872-76; Richard Harvey

---

10. Welch *op. cit.*, 11.
11. Charles S. Hunter, *History of St. Paul A. M. E. Church, St. Louis, Missouri;* 9 f.; Arnett, *Colored Sunday Schools,* 8; Payne, *op. cit.,* 384 f.

Cain, 1876-80; J. M. Townsend, 1880-88; W. B. Derrick, 1888-96; Henry Blanton Parks, 1898-1908; William Wesley Beckett, 1908-12; J. W. Rankin, 1912-24; Edmund Howard Coit, 1924-32; L. L. Berry, 1932- . Dr. Coit purchased the building where the Department is now housed at 112 West 120th Street, New York City. The indebtedness was paid by Dr. Berry, who was elected by the Board upon the death of his predecessor. He was a member of the Board from the Virginia Conference, and Pastor of historic St. John, Norfolk, where he had the largest Sunday School in the Connection.

Immediately after the funeral of Dr. Coit, the Board filled the vacancy by selecting Dr. Berry. Subsequently the Bishops met at Wilberforce in council during the month of June, and attempted to set aside the work of the Board upon the grounds that it was not properly called, holding that a quorum was not present. They chose Dr. Carl F. Flipper, son of Bishop J. S. Flipper. He was Pastor of Ebenezer at Kansas City, Missouri. Thus the Church had two Secretaries of Missions — each attempting to function, each clothed with authority. Dr. Berry worked out of New York, and Dr. Flipper from Kansas City. A delicate situation was adjusted when a regular session of the Board, meeting the next year at New York, by unanimous vote settled upon Dr. Berry. Senior Bishop H. B. Parks was present. This elaboration is made because it was the first time in the history of the Church that such ever occurred. The wisdom of the Board has been fully justified. Dr. Berry has made an excellent Secretary. He is an author of books on Missions, has traveled in West and South Africa, South America, Canada, and the islands of the West Indies. He has visited all of our Mission work. He is a thirty-third degree Mason, a loyal son of the Church, and was a prominent aspirant for the Episcopacy at Kansas City, Kansas, in 1948.

The Department of Missions has supervision of the missionary activity of the Church, home and foreign. The Fourteenth Episcopal District embraces Liberia, Sierra Leone, Nigeria, and the Gold Coast Conferences. It is supervised by Bishop Carey A. Gibbs. The Fifteenth and Seventeenth Districts embrace South Africa: Cape Colony, Orange Free State, Natal, Swaziland, and Southwest Conferences; the Transvaal, Zambezi, Central Africa, and Belgian Congo. The Presiding Bishop is I. H. Bonner. The

Sixteenth District is presided over by Bishop W. R. Wilkes, and embraces the Windward Islands, Cuba, Bahama, Jamaica, Guiana, Haiti, Santo Domingo, and South American Conferences. The two Districts in South Africa were made by the Philadelphia General Conference of 1944. Up to that time one District embraced the entire territory of South Africa. It also made South America and the Islands an Episcopal District.

The mission work is supported by monies paid into the Department of Missions, which receives 5 per cent of the Dollar Money directly from the Annual Conferences. One-half to be used for foreign work, and one-half for home work. The Department receives one-half of the Easter Day collection. The other half is used for sustaining mission preachers. Annual dues of pastors, local members of the Conference, and annual dues of the laity in each charge go to increase the fund.

For a long time there were two Missionary Societies for the women of the Connection: the Women's Mite Missionary Society, and Women's Home and Foreign Missionary Society. The former assisted with the work in West Africa, and the Islands, and the latter with South Africa. The two Presidents were Mrs. Christine Shoecraft Smith, widow of the lamented Bishop C. S. Smith, and Lucy Medorah Hughes of Cameron, Texas. There was much agitation for merging these two societies because their overhead was too great and made for sectionalism. The Mites operated in the North, and the W. H. & F. worked in the South. The General Conference of 1932 which met in Rockland Palace, Cleveland, ordered a merger, but did not set up the machinery. A Commission was named from both groups. They met at Quinn Chapel, Twenty-fourth and Wabash, Chicago, and discussed "ways and means" of merging. There was strong opposition spearheaded by President Smith. Lucy Hughes was conciliatory. The Commission later met in Pearl Street Church, Jackson, Miss. Senior Bishop H. B. Parks presided. He was an ultraconservative, and was in sympathy with Mrs. Smith. He permitted a filibuster to thwart all efforts to consummate the merger. He allowed persons who were not members of the Commission to "state points of order," indefinitely.

When the General Conference of 1936 met in the Casino, 154th Street and Eighth Avenue, New York, the merger was insisted upon. The previous General Conference had voted it. Finally the two societies were brought together under the presidency of Lucy Hughes with Christine Smith as General Secretary. Shortly thereafter, Mrs. Hughes sustained a very painful automobile accident while en route to attend a meeting at New Orleans. She lingered for a year or more, and finally her great spirit passed while she was a patient in her home-town hospital. The writer was constantly at her bedside until the last, being President of Paul Quinn College, Waco, not far distant. The funeral was preached by Bishop W. A. Fountain, a true friend. It was held in the A. M. E. Church.

Upon Mrs. Hughes' death, Mrs. Anne E. Heath of St. Petersburg, Florida, a very polished and accomplished lady, was elevated from the Vice-Presidency by virtue of her office. She and the deceased had been warm personal friends. Mrs. Heath is of a pleasing personality, and an eloquent speaker. The merged society has offices in the Allen Building, Philadelphia. The First Quadrennial meeting of the Society was held in Union Bethel, New Orleans, Dr. H. Thomas Primm, Pastor; S. L. Greene, Bishop. It was in the month of August and the weather was uncomfortably hot. I accompanied the delegation from South Carolina in a special Pullman train. The hundreds of delegates were thrilled to see the "Sherman L. Greene Four Freedoms' Building," erected under the pastoral leadership of Pastor Primm. It is for religious education purposes, and the finest in the Connection. At this meeting Mrs. Smith was retired. Mrs. Heath is ably assisted by Mrs. Norah L. Link of Chester, Pennsylvania, President of the Delaware Conference Branch.

The "mouthpiece" of the women is the *Women's Missionary Recorder*, edited by Mrs. A. B. Williams of Jacksonville, Florida. She succeeded Mrs. Bertie L. DeLyles of Tulsa, Oklahoma. The President of the Young Peoples Department is Mrs. Alma Polk of Pittsburgh, Pennsylvania. The organ of the Department of Missions is the *Voice of Missions*.

Since the Church entered the missionary field in an organized way, thousands of dollars have been collected and expended in this all-important cause, yet there is much that needs to be done by way of medical missions, and a new emphasis upon education that will meet the needs of the recipients. There must be an awakening to the task of world redemption. Africa, with its teeming millions of dark-skinned peoples, calls. The world's open sore is yet to be healed. Because of poverty, the African M. E. Church cannot meet all of the needs, but she can, must and will play her part. God wills it!

CHAPTER VIII

An Adventure in Education

Choose instruction rather than silver, and knowledge rather than rare gold; for wisdom is better than rubies, no treasure is equal to her. — PROVERBS 8:10

Out of the wilderness, and out of the night,
Has the black man crawled to the dawn of light;
Beaten by lashes and bound by chains,
A beast of burden with soul and brains;
He has come through sorrow and pain and woe,
And the cry of his heart is to know, to know.
— WILCOX

The educational efforts of the African M. E. Church moved along two well-defined lines: publication, and encouraging education in the Annual Conferences, which later took the form of founding schools. The Church came into existence during the formative period of the government, and that of several denominations, immediately after the War for Independence. It shared their common interest in education. The American Church pioneered in the field. To be sure, the founding Fathers of the African M. E. Church were not men of formal training. Their background was the African jungles and American slavery. A man of a modicum of training among them was a rarity. Yet they had a fine sense of appreciation for education. Coker had been a teacher in Baltimore, and his school had one hundred and fifty pupils at one time. Richard Allen absorbed his training from his environment, was industrious and wealthy. Stephen Hill was outstanding. Their combined intellectual ability guided the Church in the epoch of its infancy and emphasized the need of training. Allen's autobiography reveals a self-disciplined mind of unusual quality. He was one of the first men in the United States to organize a Mutual Aid Society; was the father of night schools, and an early friend of Sunday schools.[1] Richard Allen was the founder of the Free African Society, a charter member and one of the trustees.

In 1817, a year after the organization of the Church, the first Book of Discipline was published. The first hymnal was brought out and in 1835 an edition of a thousand copies was published. The Reverend Joseph M. Corr, a brilliant young man of twenty-nine years at the time, was the publisher.[2] Within three years he who had taken the Publication Department without any capital, had printed thousands of copies of the Discipline, hymnals, and minutes; and reported over $300 profit. Six years later Joseph Corr and Joseph Cox published an appendix to the Discipline. In 1841 the New York Annual Conference adopted a resolution calling for the publication of a monthly magazine. It was named the *A. M. E. Church Magazine*.[3] George Hogarth was the Editor. For lack of funds it made its appearance quarterly. From this venture evolved the *Christian Herald* in 1848, the Church having purchased the *Mystery* from Major Martin Delaney. The name was changed to the *Christian Recorder* at New York in 1852. This is the oldest journal published by people of color in the world. It was regarded by the slaveholders of the South, and the proslavery group in the North, as a dangerous document, or sheet, and was watched with a critical eye. Its circulation was prevented in the slave-holding states. Neither our ministers or members were permitted to read or handle it. The *Christian Recorder* was taboo until the breaking out of the War of the Rebellion in 1861. Then it rendered valuable aid and assistance to the Union cause, and freedom. It followed the army in blue; went into the hovels of the freedmen, and entered the hospitals. It comforted and inspired those who risked their all to preserve the nation, and to secure the blessings of liberty for themselves and their posterity. The following table shows the names of the managers of the Book Concern, and the editors of the *Christian Recorder*:

---

1. B. W. Arnett, *Budget, 1904,* 92; *Colored Sunday Schools,* 10 f.
2. Daniel A. Payne, *History of the A. M. E. Church,* 110 f.
3. A copy of this rare document is in the possession of the writer. It is about six by eight inches, and contains some interesting articles. The document is owned by Bishop G. W. Baber, who purchased it in Philadelphia for a few cents from a junk dealer.

1818-1826	Richard Allen, as Bishop, and General Book Steward. Jacob Tapsico associated with him.
1826-1835	Joseph M. Corr, first regularly appointed Book Steward.
1835-1848	George Hogarth, New York
1848-1852	Augustus R. Green, also Editor, *Christian Herald*
1852-1854	W. T. Catto. M. M. Clark as Editor, *Christian Recorder*
1854-1860	Jabez P. Campbell, Manager-Editor
1860-1868	Elisha Weaver, Manager-Editor
1868-1869	Joshua Woodlin, Manager; B. T. Tanner, Editor
1869	Joshua Woodlin, Resigned
1869-1871	A. L. Standford, Resigned. Tanner served for him.
1872-1876	W. H. Hunter; B. T. Tanner, Editor
1876-1880	Henry McNeal Turner; B. T. Tanner, Editor
1880-1884	Theopolis Gould; B. T. Tanner, Editor
1884-1888	J. C. Embry; B. F. Lee, Editor
1888-1892	J. C. Embry; B. F. Lee, Editor
1892-1896	J. C. Embrey; H. T. Johnson, Editor
1896-1900	T. W. Henderson; H. T. Johnson, Editor
1900-1904	R. H. W. Leake; H. T. Johnson, Editor
1904-1909	J. H. Collett; H. T. Johnson, Editor
1909-1912	R. R. Wright, Jr., Manager-Editor
1912-1916	J. I. Lowe; R. R. Wright, Jr., Editor
1916-1920	R. R. Wright, Jr., Manager-Editor
1920-1924	D. M. Baxter; R. R. Wright, Jr., Editor
1924-1928	D. M. Baxter; R. R. Wright, Jr., Editor
1928-1932	D. M. Baxter; R. R. Wright, Jr., Editor
1932-1936	D. M. Baxter; R. R. Wright, Jr., Editor
1936	D. M. Baxter; George A. Singleton, Editor
1936-1940	G. E. Curry; George A. Singleton, Editor
1940	W. A. Dorsey; George A. Singleton, Editor
1940-1944	W. K. Hopes; George A. Singleton, Editor
1944-1948	W. K. Hopes; David Norris, Editor
1948-1950	W. D. Johnson; David Norris, Editor

After a few months in office as Manager, Dr. Johnson was relieved, and the management of the Book Concern was given by the Board of Control to Dr. P. C. Williams, as Deputy Manager. He is an experienced printer, and the business is growing. Editor Norris of the *Christian Recorder* passed away during the first week of December, 1950, leaving a very large family. He was funeralized from St. Matthew Church, Fifty-seventh and Summer Streets, Philadelphia. The eulogy was delivered by Bishop D. Ward Nichols. The Board of Control selected Editor Fred A. Hughes of the *Western Christian Recorder* to edit the "mother of the race press" until the General Conference. A part of the salary was to be paid Mrs. Norris by the Financial Department, and the rest to the Editor for running the paper. For the first time in the history of the Church one Editor had charge of two Connectional papers.

The centennial of the *Christian Recorder* was observed during the General Conference of 1948 at Kansas City. Dr. Wright served as Editor of the *Christian Recorder* for twenty-seven years consecutively. From 1909 to 1912 and from 1916 to 1920 he had full control of the publication as Manager-Editor. During that period he paid up the Department's debts. In the quadrennium 1932-36 he was also Acting President of Wilberforce University, and did a good piece of work in each case. He is an able administrator. The General Conference of 1936 elected him to the Episcopacy.

When Dr. Baxter was Manager the country experienced a period of prosperity. Money was plentiful. The old historic site of the Book Concern at 631 Pine Street was sold and a property purchased at 716 South Nineteenth Street. A new, modern, fireproof, six-story building was erected. The architect was Professor L. A. S. Bellinger, of Pittsburgh, a one-time professor in Allen University. The depression after World War I came. The expected revenue from the building never materialized. The Manager failed to be elected to the Bishopric. The Allen Building was lost. Under the direction of Bishop Joshua H. Jones, President of the Board, a three-story building was bought at 1900 South College, or 1230 North Nineteenth Street. In the meantime, shortly after the General Conference of 1936, the Board elected Mr. R.

R. Wright, III as Deputy Business Manager. The College Street building was about to be lost. The Board elected Reverend G. E. Curry of Florida as Business Manager. Shortly after he took over, he succeeded in purchasing the mortgage on the 716 South Nineteenth Street building, and the Book Concern was removed back to its old home. He was very energetic, and convinced the General Conference of 1940 at Detroit that the building was out of debt, and he was elected Bishop. This was over the protest of Bishop R. R. Wright, Jr., who attempted to show that it was still heavily involved. Subsequent history demonstrated the correctness of the Bishop's contention.

During the quadrennium, 1948-52 the Allen Building was listed for sale by the Sheriff of Philadelphia County. It was purchased by Bishop D. Ward Nichols for fifty-odd thousand dollars and held for the Church. His magnanimous act saved embarrassment for the denomination.

During his incumbency as Bishop of the Twelfth Episcopal District charges and specification were brought against Bishop Curry. On March 29, 1946, he was tried at Tulsa, by an Ecclesiastical Court, and suspended. He served out his suspension, but for some reason he was expelled by the Extra Session of the General Conference at Little Rock in November of the same year.

For many years the Book Concern has had a stormy career. In 1948 the General Conference ousted Manager W. K. Hopes, who had done a good piece of work. There was a definite mind-set against him.

Experience has proven that the *Christian Recorder* is more successfully handled when the Editor is also the Manager. This was true during the tenure of Dr. Wright. It was also true under the Editor-Managership of George A. Singleton in 1942-44. Editor Norris had such an arrangement. This is in line with the experience of the *Southern*, and *Western Christian Recorders*, which are published by the Sunday School Union at Nashville.

The *A. M. E. Review* was founded by the General Conference of 1884. Dr. B. T. Tanner had made such a suggestion the previous year. He was interested in a quarterly magazine of a high literary order that would be a vehicle of expression of the best thought of the Church. He served as Editor for four years. Upon his election to the Episcopacy in 1888 at Indianapolis, he was succeeded by Levi Jenkins Coppin. He in turn was followed by the able Dr. H. T. Kealing, a layman, and first President of Paul Quinn College, Waco, Texas. Kealing held on until 1912, when Reverdy Ransom was elected. The editors of the *Review* have been brilliant men. Ransom served until his elevation to the episcopal office at Louisville in 1924. Bishop W. D. Chappelle dominated that assembly, and Caswell W. Crews, a Chicago layman, and one-time professor in Allen University was defeated by Dr. J. G. Robinson, a sturdy, rugged evangelist from Arkansas. He held the post until his retirement at Detroit in 1940. He increased the subscriptions to the largest number in the history of the publication. For sixteen years Dr. Robinson carried on, and the writer was instrumental in having the General Conference give him a pension of $100 per month for the rest of his life.

The *Southern Christian Recorder* was founded by Bishop Turner as a private enterprise in 1886. He saw the wisdom and need of serving the South in a more effective way. The paper was subsequently purchased by Dr. J. C. Embry and recognized as an official organ of the church by the General Conference of 1888. Dr. M. E. Bryant was elected editor. He lived only a short time thereafter. The Council of Bishops meeting at Jacksonville, Fla. in February 1891 chose Dr. C. L. Bradwell to fill out the unexpired term. In 1892 A. M. Green was elected. He was a son of Augustus R. Green, Editor of the *Christian Herald* in 1848, and left the Connection with his father to form the Independent M. E. Church. In 1896 R. M. Cheeks was elected. He died at the General Conference of 1900 in Columbus, Ohio. From 1900 to 1904 the editor was the Reverend G. E. Taylor. He was succeeded by Dr. G. W. Allen of Alabama, a one-time legislator in his state during the Reconstruction days. Editor Allen was re-elected until 1932 at Cleveland, when he retired. His son, Alexander Joseph, was elected a Bishop eight years later at Detroit, Michigan.

Perhaps one of the most energetic, and dynamic editors ever to serve the *Southern Recorder* was Dr. John H. Clayborne of Arkansas. He followed Dr. Allen, and really put the paper before the Church. The result was the largest subscription list of any paper in the denomination. When he took over, he received only a masthead and a list of names. The Church rewarded him by electing him to the Bishopric at Philadelphia in 1944, after a defeat at Detroit four years previously.

The *Western Christian Recorder* has been reactivated, and the Editor is Dr. Fred A. Hughes of St. Louis. The *Allen C. E. League Star* is the young people's paper, and is edited by Dr. S. S. Morris, Sr., Secretary of the League. The New York General Conference of 1936 reorganized the Department of Christian Education, and authorized the *Journal of Religion*. It is a credit to the Church, and is ably edited by Dr. C. W. Abington of Dallas, Texas. It enjoys a large family of readers.

Dr. E. C. Hatcher of Alabama has been Editor of the *Southern Recorder* since 1940, when Dr. Clayborne was defeated and refused to offer again for the Editorship. He is a gifted evangelist, and travels the Church very extensively. His subscription list is large.

The Sunday School Union publishes Sunday school literature: quarterlies, cards, and lesson helps. It carries supplies for Church schools. Without a doubt the Union is the most outstanding monument to the constructive genius of the Church in the field of business. It was built largely by Ira T. Bryant. He was elected to the Secretaryship at Norfolk in 1908 over W. D. Chappelle, who was considered for the Bishopric. He had served eight years, following the first, and founder, Dr. C. S. Smith, elected a Bishop at Columbus, Ohio in 1900. Bryant built wisely upon the foundation laid by his predecessors. Being an expert printer, he was prepared to do the work efficiently. Bishop Smith says:"From the standpoint of concrete constructiveness, Ira T. Bryant is to be credited with the noblest achievements in the development of the Sunday School Union." The plant covers more than a block of strictly modern brick buildings that face a quadrangle. It is well-equipped to print anything from a card to a book. Scores of young people are employed there. This Department is solvent, a going concern. The Secretary-Treasurer is Professor Eustace A. Selby. He defeated Mr. Bryant, who had been the object of discussion for several years, in 1936. While Bryant was building a lucrative publishing plant he became a severe and relentless critic of the Bishops of the Church. To many of them he became persona non grata. Especially was this true in Louisville in 1924. The objects of his assaults were Bishops Wm. H. Heard, John Hurst, A. J. Carey, Joshua H. Jones, and Wm. A. Fountain.

When the time for election of General Officers arrived, and the vote was to be taken for the Secretary of the Sunday School Union, the presiding officer was Bryant's friend, Bishop W. D. Chappelle. The strategy was to have a special blue ballot. During the night someone apprised Bryant of the scheme to defeat him. He had some ballots printed of the same color but with his name on them. When the voting began and was in progress, those who wished his defeat were jubilant when they saw so many blue ballots being put into the box. But when the tellers began to read, the story was different. Bryant was re-elected.

The feud continued at Chicago in 1928, but Bryant was stronger than ever. He played a strong part in the removal of all the Bishops who had served on Districts eight years or more. The real leader was Bishop Reverdy C. Ransom. He had written several articles to the Church papers about conditions which ought to be remedied. His was a voice crying in the wilderness. At Cleveland in 1932, Bryant was still powerful. He was respected and feared. His paper, the *Young Allenite*, was widely read. By the time the General Conference delegates met at New York, the tide turned against him. He committed the blunder of publishing his attacks in the Sunday School literature. Many of his erstwhile friends resented this. Bishop R. A. Grant of Florida and Alabama was against him. His only episcopal friends were Bishops Ransom, Flipper, and H. Y. Tookes. When the balloting was over, he had lost to Professor Selby. So long as he, Dr. John R. Hawkins, and A. S. Jackson remained together he was formidable. The former was Financial Secretary, and the latter Secretary of Education. Bryant had parted with them, two of the strongest laymen in the Church. So instead of turning over the office, building and equipment to Secretary Selby, Bryant elected to fight the edict of the General Conference.

Selby had to begin having his literature printed at the Book Concern, and later in Nashville by private business houses. The Church was divided, and many pastors and Sunday school superintendents patronized Bryant, who had a rival business of his own.

The new Department of Christian Education was hampered. The officers were Dr. Abington, Editor of Religious Literature, and S. S. Morris, Secretary of the League.

Interminable lawsuits ensued. Selby was forced to resort to the civil power for redress. Time and time again the Church lost, but kept steadily on her course. A Legal Redress Committee was appointed to handle the interests of the Church. The case was tried in several courts including the Supreme Court of Tennessee, the District Federal Court, and finally in the Federal Court which sat in Cincinnati. There three judges decided an appeal in favor of the Church. There was again a suit to restrain Bryant from using the name of the Church on his building and literature. The Church won. There was another suit for an accounting. The Church won this also. Thus after thirteen years, the Sunday School Union is the undisputed property of the Church, and Bryant had to pay in the neighborhood of $100,000. This phase of our story will be treated in more detail in a subsequent chapter.

The second phase of educational effort was manifested in the Annual Conferences, and later in the General Conferences. Definite signs did not appear until about 1842 when the Philadelphia Conference passed the following resolution:

> That the Elders and Deacons of the Connection make
> use of all the means in our power from henceforth to
> cultivate our minds and increase our store of knowledge.

"Indefatigable study" was recommended, following a strong preamble. The resolutions, introduced and read by Daniel A. Payne, were the first strong, entering wedge to rive the mass of general ignorance and force the ministry of our Church to a higher plane of intellectual culture.

As the organization of the Church is to be thought of in terms of Allen, and the progress of the western work in terms of Quinn, the intellectual advance must be in the activities of Payne. Rightly has he been called "the Apostle of Education." His entire life was cast in that category. If ever a man's work was born with him, it was true of this son of London and Martha Payne. His life was so epochal and his work so colossal that some space must necessarily be devoted to it.

Payne was born in Charleston, February 24, 1811. His parents died when their son was only ten years old, but the father had taught young Daniel the alphabet when Daniel was five years of age. Later he studied two years at the Miner School, established 1803 by the Miner's Moralist Society. While quite young, Payne manifested keen intellectual interests. He learned French and Latin without a teacher. When his day's work was done he would study until near midnight; rising early in the morning he would be at his books from four until six. At the age of fifteen he joined the Church, and was converted at eighteen. At twenty-one, Payne began a day school with three pupils, and received fifty cents each. He taught adult slaves at night for three dollars per month. His school activities developed rapidly until he had a building erected in which he taught until 1835, when the state of South Carolina passed a law making it a crime to instruct Negroes. His school was so popular that it was said by one of the leading journals of the city: "Payne is playing h—— with the n—s." Consequently the young schoolteacher was compelled to close his school and leave the city for the North.

When Payne sailed away from his native Charleston he went to New York. Later he entered the Lutheran Seminary at Gettysburg. At the outset he did not join the African M. E. Church, because of prejudice against educated ministers.[4] He was ordained in the Synod of the Lutheran Church. His services were in demand and he was invited to pastor by the Presbyterians. He accepted a church at East Troy, New York. The lofty bent of his mind is evidenced by his refusal of an offer of $300 by The American Antislavery Society to travel with all expenses paid. He believed with the great campaigner for Christ, "This one thing I do." A minister should do nothing but preach the Gospel. Payne was very zealous, and one of the strictest men the Church has ever had within its ranks. He was very rigorous in speech, and later abused his throat to the extent that he was compelled to use a slate for communication. His interest in education manifested itself wherever he went. In Philadelphia he formed a private school, and began with three pupils. It grew to sixty. In 1841 he united with the African M. E. Church — one of the most significant events in the annals of the denomination. For he gave tone, dignity

---

4.   Josephus R. Coan, *Daniel Alexander Payne*, 50.

and trend to it. He was always interested in the things of the intellect, literary societies, journals, magazines, and studies. The emphasis that the Church places upon the things of the mind goes back to Payne.

The Conference Course of Studies with which all preachers are familiar, stems from Payne. He was the author of the resolution which established it. This was in the General Conference of 1844. It created consternation, and the bitterest opposition. Men called him "a devil," and said all manner of evil things about him in private. Others said his epistles were "infidelity in its rankest form. . . . Infidels can do no more. . . . Full of absurdity. . . . Reckless slander on the general character of the Connection." So great was the fear that some thought the Church would be torn asunder, and divided over the issue. Payne felt that he was about to be destroyed and decided not to attend the General Conference, and tendered Morris Brown his resignation. He said: "Son, that is the very thing they want you to do. They don't want you to be at the General Conference; so you must go."

The resolution was presented and immediately pandemonium broke loose. The house was thrown into confusion, so much so that it adjourned of itself. Next morning at the reading of the journal a motion to reconsider was offered. Bishop Morris Brown, himself not a school man and whose English was very poor, had the vision to see the need of a trained ministry. He made an eloquent address in favor of the proposal. It was impassioned, and melted the hearts of the men to the extent that before he was through, there were cries: "Give us the resolution! Give us the resolution!" The same men who stormed, and broke up the Conference on the previous day, voted to the last man for its passage. This was a monumental achievement on the part of Payne, for the Course of Studies has influenced more men than anything else which Payne ever did.

In 1852 William Paul Quinn was the only Bishop at the New York General Conference. The Reverends M. M. Clark, Alexander W. Wayman, and E. C. Africanus were elected Secretaries. The Reverends John Cornish and Levin Lee were the Assistants to the Bishop. The Episcopal Address was read by Secretary Wayman. As the morning session drew near its close, Bishop Quinn talked with Reverend Wayman about a suggestion made at the previous General Conference that a special sermon be preached. He suggested Dr. Payne, and Reverend Wayman agreed; so he was scheduled to preach at four o'clock in the evening. When he was apprised of the intention of the Bishop, he claimed that he was not prepared for so great a responsibility, but Bishop Quinn insisted. With only two hours to prepare it, Payne delivered a sermon from the text: "Who is sufficient for these things?" The great Biblical scholar Dr. James Moffatt renders the passage: "And who is qualified for this career?" He closed his discourse with the following: "Who is sufficient to preach the Gospel of Christ, and govern the Church which he has purchased with His own blood? Who is sufficient to train the host of the Lord? Who is sufficient to guide it through the war against principalities and powers, against spiritual wickedness in high places, against all the hosts of earth and hell, and place it triumphant upon the shining plains of glory? Who is sufficient? I answer, the man who makes Christ the model of his own Christian and ministerial character. This man, and he alone, is sufficient for these things."

When the hour arrived for the balloting in the election of Bishops, it was discovered that the outstanding men for the office were Daniel A. Payne, A. R. Green, Willis Nazrey, and Richard Robinson. The first-named was the acknowledged intellectual leader of the Church. He was regarded as a scholar and an educator. It has already been stated that four years previously he was maligned and vilified because he emphasized the need for a trained ministry. He had been called an "atheist" and an "infidel." His ability and loyalty to the Church caused the delegates to consider him seriously for the Episcopacy. Dr. Green was known as the able editor of the *Christian Herald*, and as a legislator. The older men favored Nazrey, and Robinson, who had been a missionary to Haiti. They believed them to be good, Christian men. Nazrey was scheduled to preach at night, but upon the advice of his friends, he excused himself. When the balloting was over, he and Payne were elected Bishops.[5]

Many regard the purchase of Wilberforce by Payne as his most outstanding contribution to the Church. Truly it was a daring act of faith, to buy an institution with 152 acres of land for

---

5. A. W. Wayman, *My Recollections,* 49 ff.

$10,000 when having no capital. For years it stood as a towering monument to the genius and capability of African Methodists to educate themselves. It was the pride of the race, a star of hope for descendants of slaves. The mammoth Shorter Hall was built under the inspired leadership of Bishop Joshua H. Jones. In 1945 its debt was liquidated during the presidency of Dr. Charles H. Wesley, and the Bishopric of Reverdy C. Ransom. The institution, of which Payne was the first President and Dean, is now divided between the Church and the state of Ohio. The dividing line is the old ravine. It is fervently hoped that a way will be found in the future to heal the breach.

Antedating the founding of Wilberforce was a movement by the Ohio Annual Conference in 1845 at Columbus when it created "the Union Seminary of the African Methodist Episcopal Church." A committee selected a tract of land comprising 172 acres in Franklin County, twelve miles west of the capital city. The price was $1,720, to be paid in installments.[6] The first Principal was the Reverend John Mifflin Brown, a product of Oberlin College. The school did not prosper, for obvious reasons. Its maximum enrollment was 62, and its minimum 34. The Principal reported having received as salary for one year the sum of eighty-five dollars. The property was finally ordered sold when Wilberforce was purchased for the Church. "By a vote of the Ohio Conference, it was abolished, and the property ordered sold for the benefit of Wilberforce." By poor management this project was allowed to slip from the Church, and Wilberforce received little profit from the sale. Thus, long before Emancipation and the Tuskegee idea, the Fathers of the African M. E. Church introduced the concept of industrial education, by affording an opportunity for young men and women to earn support for themselves while attending school.

In attempting to meet the needs of the people who lived in areas where equal educational facilities were denied them because of color, there was developed a system of schools and colleges, chiefly in the former slave states. These came into existence during the period of Reconstruction. Many have done remarkable work, and gained recognition by accrediting Boards of Education.

6. C. S. Smith, *History of the A. M. E. Church,* 347 ff.; Payne, *op. cit.,* 422 ff.; J. W. Cromwell, *The Negro in American History,* 15 ff.

Perhaps the most notable are Morris Brown and Allen University, since the schism at Wilberforce.

There are several theological schools, but the most ambitious efforts are Payne Seminary, and Turner at Morris Brown. The Church has yet to get squarely behind a unified program of religious training and to prosecute it vigorously. The perpetuity of the Church depends largely upon the thorough training of her own prophets. This cannot be left to others. Through the years the Church has concentrated on secular education, but with the Federal government, and the individual states approaching the level of equality in the appropriating of educational funds, the Church must direct her resources more in the direction of ministerial efficiency.

Some of the most brilliant scholars of the race have been connected with Wilberforce University. Dr. William S. Scarborough was an eminent Greek student, and published a text in the field: *Aristophanes and "The Frogs."* It received high acclaim. He was once President of the institution. Gilbert Haven Jones received his Ph.D. degree from Jena. His dissertation was on "The philosophy of Borden Parker Bowne, and Lotze." For years he was President, and served as Dean of the College of Liberal Arts. F. H. McGinnis, Dean, received his doctorate from Ohio State University. Bishop R. R. Wright, Jr., is a Ph.D. scholar from The University of Pennsylvania, and served as President. He is now Bishop of Arkansas and Oklahoma. D. Ormonde Walker holds a Master of Arts degree from Western Reserve, and S. T. B. from Boston. He was elected to the Episcopacy in 1948 at Kansas City, Kansas. Charles H. Wesley holds a Ph.D. from Harvard. He was at the head of the institution at the time of the split, and now heads the state institution. He was succeeded by Charles L. Hill, Ph.D. from Ohio State University, a learned scholar in the field of philosophy and linguistics. The internationally recognized Dr. W. E. B. Dubois once taught at Wilberforce. The number of faculty members with high scholarship, degrees, and many graduates of the institution is legion: Milton J. Wright, Upthegrove, Woodward and others.

At the close of the Rebellion the Church spread to the South, and West. Numerous high schools and colleges came into being. Classes were taught weekdays in churches, and services held in the churches on Sundays. Annual Conferences sponsored high schools, and academies. By 1884 the Connection was divided into four Educational Districts. Ministers were encouraged to provide schools for the people. Twenty-five cents out of every dollar collected for education was sent to the Connectional Secretary of Education, and the balance was sent to a District Secretary. The schools reported by the Board of Education in 1884-85 were:

Wilberforce University, Greene County, Ohio, founded in 1856

Allen University, Columbia, S. C., founded 1870 at Cokesbury, S. C.

Divinity & Industrial School, Jacksonville, Fla., 1883

St. James Academy & Industrial Seminary, New Orleans, La., 1882

Morris Brown College, Atlanta, Ga., founded 1884

Kittrell School, formerly Johnson, Kittrell, N. C., 1886

Quinn College, Waco, Texas founded, 1872

Dickerson Memorial Seminary, Portsmouth, Va.

Turner College, Hernando, Miss., founded 1881

Western University, Quindaro, Kansas

Garfield University, Alabama (projected)

Campbell Institute, Projected at Shelbyville, Tenn.

Mission Schools in Haiti, Africa, and the British Dominions

District Schools:

Selma Institute

School of the Rev. R. Brooks, Jefferson, Ga.

A. M. E. School, Port of Spain, Trinidad

The Abbeville School, Abbeville, S. C.

Sumpter District School, Sumpter, S. C.

Payne High School, Cuthbert, Ga.

Normal and Preparatory School, Cartersville, Ga.

It is quite evident from the above report that the Church was trying desperately to meet the educational needs of the recently emancipated slaves and their children. They had been set adrift with nothing. In slavery they did not even own their bodies. When freedom came, they had no tools, land, or capital. They had no organized Churches in the former slave country, no schools, or intelligent instructors. They had to take whatever they had and make whatever they wanted, literally lifting themselves by their own bootstraps. The marvel of the centuries is how these people oriented themselves, and canalized their efforts in a way that made for racial uplift. From 1886 to 1890 the Church raised for education $48,976.60. According to the *Christian Recorder* of July 7, 1949, Bishop R. R. Wright has raised during one year in Georgia alone, $243,000, and The First Educational District, comprising the First, the Third, Fourth, Fifth, and Thirteenth Episcopal Districts, will this year raise a budget of $185,000 for Wilberforce. Morris Brown has a cash endowment of a half-million dollars, and Allen University is worth two million. The total value in cash of all the educational institutions will run high into the millions.

This is remarkable for a people whose ancestors were enslaved for a century and a half, and whose progeny have tasted the fruit of freedom fourscore years. It augurs well for the future. The distance traveled along this way is long, since the first voice was raised for education in the Philadelphia Conference in 1835, and in the Baltimore Annual Conference until the present. The amount invested for the benefit of boys and girls who otherwise would not have had a chance to unfold, exfoliate, and develop cannot be actually estimated.

In spite of the large sums raised for education, standardization has suffered because of multiplicity. In 1932, Dr. Arthur S. Jackson, Commissioner of Education, presented a brilliant report to the General Conference, and recommended a merger of colleges. It was idealistic and correct, but local pride, loyalties, and District Boards of Trustees stood squarely in the way. However, Bishop S. L. Greene in the Eighth District merged Lampton College in Louisiana with Campbell at Jackson, Miss. In 1948, Bishop D. Ormonde Walker had the Noah W. Williams School of Religion merged with Payne Theological Seminary, and Bishop L. H. Hemmingway had the foresight and courage to close Kittrell in North Carolina. In the future it may be merged with Allen University — the logical course. For the further consummation of such an advanced program, the Church will have to wait for time and an enlightened people. Finally they will rise

96   *The Romance of African Methodism*

up and demand it. Bishop Wm. A. Fountain merged Payne at
Cuthbert, Ga. with Morris Brown, and Central Park at Savannah.
Turner College in Tennessee was closed. In every event a merger
has spelled progress and increased strength. Flipper-Davis was
merged with Shorter in Arkansas. The former was in Oklahoma.
This was easy because the two were in the same Episcopal District.

Florida has Edward Waters College and the B. F. Lee Semi-
nary. The state is presided over by Bishop John A. Gregg, a
veteran school man and former President of Wilberforce Univer-
sity. He was the first man of color elected to the presidency of
Howard University. He elected to remain with the Church. Payne
Junior College is in Alabama. The theological school is the
Nichols Seminary, named for the father of Bishop D. Ward
Nichols. The Bishop is S. L. Greene. Campbell College is at
Jackson, Miss. The Seminary is called Lampton for the late Bishop
E. W. Lampton. The District is presided over by Bishop M. H.
Davis. This school has over six hundred acres of rich delta land
at Mound Bayou. It is being cultivated. The Seminary Dean is
Dr. J. S. Morant. Shorter College with Jackson Seminary is in
North Little Rock, Ark. In 1948, Bishop G. W. Baber purchased
a tract of land adjacent to the school property. Bishop Fountain
greatly developed the college. It was under his Episcopacy in
Georgia, and President W. A. Fountain, Jr. that a quarter-of-a-
million-dollar stadium was built, and student apartment dormi-
tories at Morris Brown. Paul Quinn College is at Waco, Texas.
This is the institution where the writer spent two of the most
productive and fruitful years of his life. Within that brief period
the school was accredited, and the student body increased to
hundreds. The Presiding Bishop is Dr. Joseph Gomez. The Seminary is named for the late Bishop Young. Bishop J. H. Clayborne
is over the Thirteenth District of Tennessee and Kentucky. There
is the Wright School of Religion, organized by Bishop R. R.
Wright. The Dean is Dr. M. Milton Mickens. In addition to the
schools in the United States, there are those in Africa, South
America, and the Islands. Wilberforce Institute is in South Africa,
where Bishop I. H. Bonner presides. Bishop W. R. Wilkes is over
South America, Cuba, and the Islands.

Bishop W. Sampson Brooks was elected a Bishop in 1924 at
St. Louis. He was assigned to West Africa. He was a great finan-

cier and possessed of a wealth of personal magnetism and charm. While Pastor of Bethel, Baltimore, he raised $33,000 in one effort, a record for the Connection, and burned the mortgage. An unforgettable address was delivered by Reverdy C. Ransom on the occasion of the mortgage burning: "And the Egyptians shall hear of this, and they will tell it everywhere!" It was brilliant and moving. That was in February, and in May, Brooks was made a Bishop. He carried the same kind of zeal into his episcopal office. Immediately after his election he began collecting funds for his African assignment. In Liberia he erected a modern, fireproof school building. He traveled the country from border to border. His appeal was irresistible. Men threw their watches into the collection plate. Women gave their rings, earrings, and bracelets. Graphic was the picture which he painted. He spent eight years in Africa. When he was returned home he was sent to Texas, where he redeemed Paul Quinn College. He attended the Council of Bishops at Jackson, Mississippi. While sitting in the hall after the service of worship I drew near to him. He asked me for a dollar, and had me call several men to his side. As they came he requested a dollar for his school. Each responded. It was a pleasure and privilege to give money to Bishop Brooks. He said to me: "Come on, and help me, son. Soon you will be up here, and carry on as I am trying to do. God will bless you." Sitting in one spot we collected a large sum and I put it into his hands. We parted and a few days later the following surprising letter was received:

Feb. 12, 1934

The Rev. George A. Singleton, D.D.
622 E. Mason Street
Springfield, Illinois

MY DEAR BROTHER:

This comes to thank you for the real, genuine help that you gave me at the Bishops' Council. I can never forget it. . . . Come to Texas at any time and regard yourself as our guest.

Thanking you again for your splendid service rendered, I am

Sincerely yours,

W. SAMPSON BROOKS

He literally wore himself out in the cause of Christ. His tall, muscular, robust frame could stand no more, and his spirit passed in St. Louis in the midst of a drive for Paul Quinn. Dr. Breedlove on Cook Avenue gave him the best of medical care, but God knew best. The funeral was largely attended. The principal eulogy was delivered by Bishop Ransom from Malachi 2:7. "The priest's lips shall keep knowledge." It was unique. The brief tribute by Bishop H. B. Parks was eloquent and fitting. A great educator had passed into the great beyond. The Texas delegation headed by Lucy M. Hughes and C. W. Abington, sang one of the favorite numbers of the deceased:

> It may be the best for me,
> And it may be the best for me;
> The Lord knows the way, and I'll obey,
> And it may be the best for me.

The choir of St. Paul was represented by a soloist who sang very feelingly: "When my soul reaches home. All my trials will be over, when my soul reaches home."

A few days afterward the following tribute appeared in the *Christian Recorder*:

Bishop W. Sampson Brooks

He was a noble member of his race,
With strong physique and well-inspired within;
With will to climb and take an honored place—
Of leadership high in the ranks of men.
He worked undaunted while in foreign fields,
To render service as he saw it best;
His spirit was the kind that never yields
When facing danger or when sore oppressed.

The gallant hero went where duty called,
Both friend and foe he summoned to his aid;
In difficulties he was not appalled,
He took his leave just as his Father willed;
The place he left can never quite be filled.

—THE REVEREND WILLIAM MARTIN
Dallas, Texas

The schools of the Church represent a state of mind. They are soul and spirit. They may lack "standard" equipment, but they are eternally rich in personality-producing power. The students get something which cannot be duplicated or found anywhere else. They are taught racial self-respect, and racial self-esteem. Without these elements education for Negroes becomes a hollow mockery. The ideal is self-help. The motto is "We teach the mind to think, the heart to love, and the hands to work." The schools of the Church represent determination and ambition to march forward out of darkness into light in spite of handicaps. The echoing cry is to know, "To know!"

In 1930 the average expenditure for every pupil throughout the nation was $90; the expenditure for white children in the South was $44.21, less than half the national average; the expenditure for Negro children was $12.57, only about one-fourth that of southern white children, and about one-eighth that of the average pupil in the nation as a whole. The Church operates its schools in the South, with the exception of Wilberforce University, and Payne Theological Seminary, where these gross inequalities exist. Georgia expends an average of $35.42 for each white pupil, and $6.48 for each Negro; in Mississippi the figures are $45.34 for each white child, and $5.45 for each Negro child. The Negro teacher receives only 47 percent of the salary amount that the white teacher receives. In 1913 in Montgomery County, Alabama, $14.50 per pupil went for Negro teachers. In 1931 the figures were respectively $28, and $4. The value of school plant equipment for each white child in the South was $157, and for each Negro pupil $37.[7] These figures may be revised upward in the light of the strenuous fight led by the N.A.A.C.P. for the equalization of salaries throughout the South. In most instances signal victories have been won, and a parity exists, but the fight has been in no wise completely won. So in the face of these incontrovertible facts, the Church is justified in carrying on a program of education. There is still a role for the denominational school to play. Leaders inspired to independent thinking must be trained. The venture of the Church in education has been fully justified, and the movement continues.

---

7. The Rosenwald Fund (Chicago), *School Money in Black and White.*

CHAPTER IX

Advancing Frontiers

I seek my brethren. — GENESIS 37:18

Where there was strife
Let union be;
Where bondage was —
Liberty.
            —JOHN DRINKWATER

Four years of bloody, costly, fratricidal war came as the result of two and a half centuries of the most iniquitous and diabolical system of human chattelism mankind has ever known. Like the ancient Israelites under the slave system of the Egyptians, the bondsmen were not permitted to go until the destroying angel had passed through the land, and drenched it in the blood of its first-born.

Slavery had circumscribed and prevented the growth of the Church in the South and Southwest. Very early in the nineteenth century African Methodism was forced to haul down its flag in the cities of Mobile and Charleston. From the latter place Payne was forced to leave in 1835, because he was instructing his people in the rudiments of knowledge.[1] But he prophesied his return. The period from that date until the Rebellion constitutes one of the most intensely interesting chapters in American history. It is ironical that immediately after the downfall of the slave power in 1865, exactly thirty years later, Payne returned to his native city and state as an ambassador of Christ — to the city where the first shot was fired in the war.

The coming of Payne was the first step in the frontier advance in the South. The land had felt the impact of ravaging war. Destruction and poverty were everywhere evident. A greater opportunity for missionary work had never faced the Church. The

---

1. John Wesley Cromwell, *The Negro in American History*, 117.

Macedonian call was heeded. In 1863, Bishop Wayman received information that the colored people, members of the Bute Street M. E. Church, South, in Norfolk were left as sheep without a shepherd, and desired to unite with the Baltimore Conference, if he could come down and see them. Previously the necessity of sending missionaries to Africa and Haiti had been discussed in the conferences presided over by the Bishop. He said he would never consent to go, or assist in sending anyone over there, until he could go all over the South and see his brethren. Several years previously he had selected the text he would preach: "I seek my brethren" (Genesis 37:16). At last his opportunity had come. He seized it, and went to Norfolk. On Sunday night he preached his long-desired sermon to a very large crowd, and again on Monday afternoon when his text was: "We are journeying to a place of which the Lord said, 'I will give it thee; come thou, and go with us, and we will do thee good.' " It was found in Numbers 10:29. The Board met at night, and adopted an agreement drawn up by the Bishop. On Wednesday night he spoke again from the text: "We will go with you, for we have heard that the Lord is with you" (Zechariah 8:23). The secretary read to the congregation what the Official Board had done, and the action was agreed to. Bishop Wayman had the joy of preaching his text and taking into the fold of African Methodism eight hundred members and five ministers.[2]

Having promised the people that upon his return he would bring Bishop Payne, he wrote to the Bishop and arranged a trip to Norfolk. The party of pioneer missionaries was composed of Bishops Payne and Wayman, and the Reverend John M. Brown. While walking down one of the principal streets, one man was heard to say: "Here comes the Bishop, and his staff." They visited the Sunday school in the morning. Bishop Payne preached at three o'clock in the afternoon, and John Brown at night. Bishop Wayman journeyed over to Portsmouth to seek his brethren there. A few days afterward, Bishop Payne took them into the Church of Allen. John M. Brown was appointed by Bishop Payne to Norfolk. Thus the Church entered the Old Dominion, and the frontier began to advance with signs of victory for Union arms.

Great prophetic insight was not necessary for one to see that

---

2. A. W. Wayman, *My Recollections*, 91.

the fate of the slave power was written in the stars. The successful military exploits and achievements of General Grant and General Sherman presaged the certain outcome. The Emancipation
Proclamation weakened the South and strengthened the North.
The labor supply of the cotton kingdom was free to leave the
plantations. These millions of laborers would constitute the
Church along the advancing frontier. Such a glorious opportunity!
A mighty challenge for Christian missionaries to enter the war-
torn section of the country, and tell the story of the Cross to their
people; to set up their own Church which knew no man after the
color of his skin!

The Church was equal to the task, for in the winter of 1864-65,
the Reverend James Lynch, missionary to South Carolina, sent
out a call for help. On Wednesday, March 15, 1865, Alexander
Wayman and Elisha Weaver sailed to Helena Island. When they
arrived and inquired for James Lynch, they discovered that he had
gone to Savannah. They sailed to Savannah, as their passes were
from New York to that city. After viewing the destruction
wrought by General Sherman in the famous city by the sea, they
found the house of the Reverend Charles L. Bradwell, through
the kindness of a Baptist minister. The Reverend Lynch was there,
and had already set up the banner of African Methodism in the
city of Savannah.[3] Old St. Phillips Monumental stands today on
Hull Street, an eloquent testimony to his labor. Lynch had piercing black eyes, and a forehead of immense breadth, jet-black
hair, and possessed unmatched eloquence, with a persuasive
manner.

With the coming of the night a multitude assembled at the
place of worship, and Bishop Payne delivered his soul with unction and power. His text was "My presence shall go with you, and
I will give thee rest" (Exodus 32:14). In company with the
Reverends Lynch and Weaver, Bishop Wayman held a large
educational mass meeting at one of the Baptist churches. One
day he visited one of the day schools that was being held in what
was once a slave-pen. In one of the table drawers he discovered a
bill of sale of human beings that the owner had left posthaste as
Sherman's army of deliverance fell upon the city.[4] From Savannah

3. *Ibid.,* 104.
4. Wesley J. Gaines, *African Methodism in the South,* 5.

the missionaries returned to Hilton Head and Charleston. Wayman met the people at a sunrise prayer meeting, and addressed them. At three o'clock in the afternoon he preached his famous text: "I seek my brethren." The service was held in the largest brick building, known as Zion Presbyterian Church. On Monday night a meeting was called and a vote was taken to unite with the African M. E. Church. Less than a hundred yards from where Wayman stood that afternoon and preached, now stands Emanuel, the largest, and mother church of the denomination in the South. A few days after these events the organization was perfected by the Reverend James Lynch.

Back to the activities of Bishop Payne.[5] Early in May, 1865, he visited the rooms of the American Missionary Society, and arranged for the partial support of the missionaries in South Carolina. Two days later he sailed for the Palmetto State. Accompanying him were Elder James A. Handy, and Licentiates James H. A. Johnson and T. G. Steward — missionaries to the freedmen of the South. These men were all destined to become great leaders in the Church. The first time that Bishop Payne heard Handy preach, as a local preacher, he remarked that he would never make a preacher, would not live long, and would never be able to hold a charge in Baltimore. The good Bishop said that Handy began in an error, continued in an error, and concluded in an error. No one is able to predict with certainty the outcome of a human personality. Payne dubbed Handy a failure, but a few years later the prophecy's "failure" accompanied him as a missionary to South Carolina, and helped in laying a permanent foundation of the Church in the state. Handy became one of the leading pastors in Baltimore and the Connection, and wrote a valuable volume of history of the Church. In 1892 he was elected one of the Bishops, at Philadelphia. Finally, he lived a long and useful life, which was a benediction.

Bishop Payne, like most geniuses, was very eccentric. He always wore a large, heavy overcoat. Bishop J. S. Flipper told the writer that Payne would not sleep in a room unless it had a stove in it. The late Dr. H. P. Jones, of Philadelphia, while Pastor of "Mother Bethel," related the following incident: Once Bishop Payne was holding an Annual Conference, and on Sunday morn-

5. Wayman, *op. cit.,* 104.

ing when he was in the act of ordaining a class of preachers to the ministry he came to a brother and stopped. He said to him: "Get up from there; go home and comb your hair. Do you think that I am going to lay my holy hands upon those n-ps?"

The *Arago* on which the missionaries sailed, landed at Hilton Head. They visited the church founded there by James Lynch, then continued their journey to Charleston. On Monday, May 16, 1865, Bishop Payne organized in the Colored Presbyterian Church, the South Carolina Conference, assisted by Elders James A. Handy and James Lynch; two itinerant Licentiates, Theophilus G. Steward, later to serve as a Chaplain and be retired from the United States Army, and James H. A. Johnson. William Bently was the local preacher. These were the only persons present at the time of the organization.[6] Several days after the opening, Elders Richard Harvey Cain, one of the first graduates from Wilberforce University, A. L. Standford of New York and Philadelphia, and George A. Rue of the New England Conference, came and joined. The native southern preachers were Charles L. Bradwell, N. Murphy, Robert Taylor, and Richard Vanderhorst, subsequently a Bishop in the C. M. E. Church. At the time of its organization the Conference embraced fully four thousand members, a Pentecostal number. It covered the states of South Carolina, North Carolina, and Georgia. It raised for contingent expenses $48.48; for Sunday schools, $16; for Pastors' support, $150. This last was paid to William Bently. James Lynch received no appointment as he was made Editor of the *Christian Recorder*. He finally left the A. M. E. Church for the M. E. Church, and shortly thereafter died.[7]

Thus at the close of the year 1865, the frontier of the Church had moved southward to Norfolk; Wilmington, N.C.; Georgetown, Charleston, and Hilton Head, and to Savannah. Precious seed had been sown by heroic men, in a field which for two and a half centuries had known only the labor, groans, blood, sweat, and tears of slaves. The seed has borne abundant fruit, and the end is not yet. The time of rejoicing is yet to come, when those of other generations will garner and bring in the sheaves.

The following year the South Carolina Conference was held

6. James A. Handy, *Scraps of A. M. E. Church History*, 236.
7. Gaines, *op. cit.*, 6.

in the city of Savannah, May 14, 1866, and continued in session nine days. The name of Henry McNeal Turner appears on the roll as having been transferred from the Baltimore Annual Conference. Time has proven this a most significant event in the history of the Church. Wesley J. Gaines, related to General Robert Toombs, of Wilkes County, Georgia, was admitted on trial. Five of the members of this first Annual Conference to be held in Georgia became Bishops: Richard Vanderhorst, later a Bishop in the C. M. E. Church, Henry McNeal Turner, Wesley J. Gaines, Richard Harvey Cain, and James A. Handy. There was collected for contingent purposes, $10.30; Pastors' support, $3,371.00; Sunday schools, $112.85; Missions, $339.04; Book Concern, $2; support of the Bishop, $85.00; superannuated Bishops and Preachers $1.00. There were 18 Elders, 13 Deacons, 15 Local Deacons, and a membership of 22,338.

William Gaines, the brother of Wesley J. Gaines, was the first missionary to the northern and western parts of Georgia. He planted the Church in Macon, Atlanta, and Columbus. James Lynch, who labored so faithfully and successfully in South Carolina and Savannah, and became the Editor of the *Christian Recorder,* took in the Church at Augusta. When William Gaines died in Columbus on November 20, 1865, he was succeeded by the Reverend H. M. Turner. Through his burning zeal and untiring efforts the Church was extended greatly in the state of Georgia. Once he was Presiding Elder of the entire state. It is said that he told the recently emancipated freemen that Abraham Lincoln wanted them to join the African M. E. Church.

When the Annual Conference met at Savannah in 1866, it set apart forty-six persons for the ministry.[8] An eyewitness describes the scene as one never to be forgotten by those whose privilege it was to be present. From the slave-pens to the Gospel Ministry of Jesus Christ! Yesterday they were mere things who did not even own their bodies, today they are told: "Take thou authority to preach the Gospel in the Church of God." "Go, and as ye go, preach!" until the kingdoms of this world are become the Kingdom of God, and His Christ. For years their mothers and fathers had prayed earnestly for such a day, but died without the sight.

The Church literally leapfrogged southward and southwest-

8. *Ibid.,* 4 f.

ward. Eacn succeeding year the advancing African Methodist
cohorts pushed forward. To such an extent had the Christian
Army grown that Georgia, Florida, and Alabama petitioned to
be set off as separate Conferences. The petition was recognized
by Bishop Wayman, who was presiding in the stead of Bishop
Payne, absent. The result was far-reaching. The Georgia Conference met for the first time on March 30, 1867, shortly after
the adjournment of the mother Conference in South Carolina, and
before the General Conference of 1868, which met in Washington, D.C. It was fitting that the first General Conference after
the war should be convened in the capital city of the nation.

How the hearts of the two hundred members of the General
Conference must have palpitated with humble pride as they made
their way to Washington to celebrate the Divine favor! The
Union was preserved, and the birthright of a people restored.
Washington was the logical place. Three Bishops were elected:
James A. Shorter, Thomas Marcus Decatur Ward, and John
Mifflin Brown.

Bishop Wayman organized the Virginia Conference on May
10, 1867. The same year on June 8 he organized the Florida
Annual Conference at Tallahassee. Bishop John M. Brown organized the Alabama Annual Conference at Selma, on July 25, 1868.
He was an able man, and brought to the Episcopacy fine scholarship, amiability, firmness, and sympathy, which won for him the
love and respect of the men for his gentlemanly ways. He was a
product of Oberlin College, and the very embodiment of dignity.[9]
Bishop Ward was one of the greatest orators that this country
has ever produced. He was richly endowed with an innate gift,
untouched by the schools. He possessed a vivid imagination, was
eloquent to the nth degree, and a master in the art of word picture
painting. His power of description is at once realistic, graphic,
and overmastering. Ward was a prodigy. More will be said about
him in a later chapter.

African Methodism had been known to exist in Mobile as early
as 1820, four years after the formation of the Church in Philadelphia, but "the walls of slavery were towering high, therefore the
little band had to bow low." In 1864 Bishop Jabez P. Campbell,
and M. M. Clark, who was Editor of the *Christian Recorder* in

9. *Ibid.,* 20.

1852, came to the city, and were received coldly. However one of the "old white colleges" opened its doors, and permitted the two distinguished ministers to preach the Gospel.

At the time of the organization of the Alabama Conference, Bishop Wayman gave appointments to Louisiana.[10] Then on November 1, 1865, the Louisiana Conference was formed in St. James Chapel on Roman Street with Bishop Campbell presiding. Heretofore this church had been a part of the Missouri Annual Conference, which was organized by Bishop William Paul Quinn in Louisville, September 13, 1855. Louisville was then a stronghold of slavery. But there were giants in those days!

Like a mighty army the forces of African Methodism had marched from the banks of the Potomac to the Land of Flowers and the Gulf of Mexico in the South and to the "Father of Waters" in the West. From thence the advance was onward into Texas, Arkansas, Kansas, Oklahoma, beyond the Rocky Mountains to the Pacific Coast. Nothing could stand in the way of the veterans of the Cross and the campaigners for Jesus Christ. Bodily peril and danger meant little or nothing to them. Like their great Bishop, they desired to "seek their brethren." The work of advancing the frontiers of the Church was accomplished at a tremendous sacrifice. But these men were cast in an uncommon mold. They were incomparable heralds of a passion, and followers of a gleam. They were burdened with a deep sense of their mission. It was a joy in some measure to fill up that which was wanting in the sufferings of their Lord. Their one paramount and consuming end was to carry the simple story of the Cross to their recently emancipated brethren, and bring them to a saving knowledge of the Christ.

These grand and noble men now sleep in the dust of the increasing years. Many repose in unmarked graves in forests, beside streams, on hillsides, in valleys deep, and out upon the rolling plains of the West. But their works do follow them, and other generations have entered upon their labors.

Before the Church began its significant advance into the South and West, the northern boundary had been crossed into Canada, the land of Freedom, as early as 1834. Canada being the terminus of the Underground Railroad, large numbers of Negroes

---

10. *Ibid.,* 225.

trickled through the northern states from the slave states. Many were there who had been born free and knew nothing of the slave system. Canada was a haven for the oppressed. The Canadian Conference was organized by Morris Brown, July 21, 1840, at Toronto with twelve members. It grew. The first step was taken to organize the British M. E. Church at Chatham in 1855 when the Reverend Benjamin Stewart introduced a resolution petitioning the General Conference of 1856 to set aside the work in Canada as an independent body. It was startling, but the resolution was adopted. Bishops Quinn, Payne, and Nazrey were present. Bishop Quinn was apparently elated.[11] He talked about removing to Canada. It can be easily seen why he felt that way; because of the Fugitive Slave Law. It was a bitter pill. Many Negroes went to Canada to buy homes and settle down. There was a dispute over the name. Many of the settlers had married Canadian wives, and they objected to the designation "African." Such a title in the name of the Church would make a distinction not cognizable under the British flag, and by British law. At Buxton alone, there were about forty men in the settlement whose wives were in this category, and they would be cut off from membership because they were not Africans.

These reasons were set forth by Elder William H. Jones, a leader second to Bishop Nazrey, who took charge of the work, October 7, 1856, at Toronto.[12] Bishop R. R. Disney succeeded Nazrey. He tried to force union of the B. M. E. Church in 1880, but without success. Five years previously, on August 20, 1875, Morris Brown was fatally stricken with paralysis and was brought from Shelbourne, Nova Scotia, to Philadelphia by the Reverend Noah C. W. Cannon. He passed away shortly thereafter.

Canada's great gifts to African Methodism have been John Albert Johnson and Charles Spencer Smith, who became Bishops. For years the efficient official stenographer of the General Conference has been the Reverend Dr. S. E. Churchstone Lord of Amherst, Nova Scotia. One of the leaders of Canadian African Methodism is Dr. W. C. Perry. Dr. L. L. Berry, Secretary of Missions, has been interested in uniting the B. M. E. Church with the African M. E. Church. Through the years there has been a

---

11.   Payne, *op. cit.,* 361; C. S. Smith, *History of the A. M. E. Church,* 27 f.
12.   Payne, *op. cit.,* 128 f., 384 ff., 390.

close relationship of a unique nature. Canada is a fertile field. Bishop G. W. Baber of the Fourth District is carrying out a missionary plan of subsidizing the work in the Canadian Conference, and having the Conference Branch Missionary Societies of the Fourth Episcopal District assist in supporting five young men who will be sent to help develop the field.

CHAPTER X

Unsung Heroes

Of whom the world was not worthy. — HEBREWS 11:38

Full many a gem of purest ray serene
The dark unfathomed caves of ocean bear:
Full many a flower is born to blush unseen
And waste its sweetness on the desert air.
                                                    — GRAY

The years continue to take their unerring and certain flight into the night of the centuries, leaving in their wake the heroic deeds of bold pioneers who by the grace of God laid an enduring foundation of the Church. Their labors were circumscribed by the slave power, but after the war was ended in 1865, these God-intoxicated men extended African Methodism into Florida, to the southern limits of the country where its shores are washed by the warm waters of the Gulf of Mexico, and onward to the West and the peaceful Pacific. Humble messengers of the cross they were — men of the upturned eye and sensitive heart, with souls aflame and a burning passion for the kingdom of God. Across the wind-swept centuries they heard the command of their Lord from the Ascension Mount: "Go ye, into all the world, and preach." It was just as imperious to them as it was to those other apostles who saw and heard him. As Paul lifted Christianity out of its narrow, nationalistic, chauvinistic, and racial mold, the prophets who rallied to the ensign set up by Richard Allen, and those upon whose shoulders their mantles fell, lifted American Christianity out of the category of caste and color prejudice, purified it and sent it forth to bless all the people everywhere. They demonstrated for the centuries that color lines have no place in the Church of God, and that all men are to be regarded in the light of their latent possibilities. The reaction of the founders of the African Methodist Episcopal Church against segregation and Jim Crowism in

110

the house of God constitutes one of the most thrilling and inspiring chapters in the long history of the Christian Church. There is excellent material for a supplement to the Acts of the Apostles.

The African Methodist Episcopal Church is not a segregated or Jim Crow institution, although its membership is preponderantly Negro. Richard Allen described the revival of 1789 in a letter to Bishop Francis Asbury: "Our congregations nearly consisted of as many whites as blacks. Many that never attended any place of worship before came, some through curiosity, and many of them are awakened and joined the society, so that nearly as many whites as blacks are convinced and converted to the Lord."[1]

On the other hand, the African M. E. Church is a protest against segregation. Within its ranks are all colors and diverse races. Years ago one of the prominent members of the Church of which the writer is now the minister, was a wealthy white lady. Two years ago he took into the same Church a very fine white lady of wonderful preaching ability and evangelical power. At the Annual Conference she was recommended for Evangelist papers and was handed the same by Bishop H. B. Parks, the Presiding Bishop. She is loyal and faithful to her Church, and while away on evangelistic campaigns, sends to the Pastor her quota of the Church obligations, both local and general.[2] She is a good woman, pious, devout, and full of the Holy Ghost. The Reverend J. F. A. Sisson of Georgia and later of Arkansas, was a white man, and a fine spirit. His name appears as the Recording Secretary of the General Conference of 1872.[3] The writer knows of several white Churches that have Negro members, but the present purpose is to show by incontrovertible facts that the A. M. E. Church draws no color line in its constituency. It believes and practices with John Wesley, the founder of Methodism: "If thy heart be as my heart, then give me thy hand." Its motto has real and vital meaning: "God our Father, Christ our Redeemer, Man our Brother." According to Bishop Bonner, churches at Bloemfontein, Orange Free State, Worcester, Cape Province, and Victoria, West Cape in South Africa all have several

1. Charles H. Wesley, *Richard Allen, Apostle of Freedom*, 120, 252.
2. Evangelist P. Harrell, St. Paul A. M. E. Church, Springfield, Ill.
3. B. W. Arnett, *Budget, 1885*, 75; T. G. Steward, *Fifty Years in the Gospel Ministry*, 69.

white members. At Worcester a white lady is a stewardess and a member of the missionary society. When the Cape Colony Annual Conference met at this place she was foremost in entertaining. The Rev. D. P. Gordon is Pastor.

Of the freedom-loving men who associated themselves with Richard Allen in the Organizing Convention of 1816, when human slavery hung over the land like a pall, only one or two of the sixteen, representing five Churches, are remembered today. They did not, however, waste their fragrance on the desert air. Their names may not be known or mentioned but their accomplishments will be appreciated increasingly as the years pass.

At the head of the list of African Methodist heroes stands the founder, Richard Allen. His majestic figure stands like a colossus commanding the ages. In the history of Christianity he is next to St. Paul, in that he challenged the hydra-headed monster of race prejudice and rather than submit to humiliation in God's house he went out and erected a temple wherein he and his people might serve and worship according to the dictates of their own conscience, none molesting or making afraid. Not one of the Patristics of the early Christian communities, not a saint in the Middle Ages, not one of the Protestant reformers, not a single prophet through the stirring centuries in England when the Eighteenth Century Revival swept over the isles, fronted and faced what Allen had to combat. He was a mystical pragmatist, a religious genius, but more than all things else, he was a man from the crown of his head to the soles of his feet. When his people had no rights and no control over their own bodies, Richard Allen had the vision and courage to point the way of racial manhood and racial self-esteem.

Richard Allen was not a learned scholar, but a slave. He said the system was "a bitter pill." By industry and thrift he worked on his own time and saved enough money to purchase his freedom. In the course of time he became wealthy. Often he came to the rescue financially of the Church which he advanced means to purchase and erect. Richard Allen's first wife was named Flora.[4] This was in 1791. In the year 1805 his wife's name was Sarah. She lived to the year 1849 or 1850, about twenty years after her distinguished husband's spirit had passed. They were the parents

4. Arnett, *Budget, 1900,* 86.

of six children. The name of Richard Allen, Jr. appears as Secretary of the Organizing Convention of 1816, and of the first Annual Conference that met in Baltimore the next year. This was because he was more capable than the older men who were members. The other children were named: Peter, John, Sarah, Ann, and James. John lived several years in Haiti, and became proficient in the French and Spanish languages. He could speak and translate them with facility. In later years the Bishop carried on a boot and shoe store. He had learned the business early in life. Shortly before his death he retired. When he passed away his estate was worth between thirty and forty thousand dollars, all of which had been accumulated by his own intellect, industry and thrift.

Richard Allen "was a man of mixed blood, his mother being a mulatto and his father a pure African; this gave his complexion a soft chestnut tint, as is shown in the fine oil portrait of him, now in possession of his oldest daughter, Mrs. Sarah Wilkins. The expansive forehead and the fullness of the lower eyelids indicate expansiveness of intellect and a ready command of language."[5]

DANIEL COKER

The real name of Daniel Coker was Isaac Wright. He was the son of a white Englishwoman, and a slave whose name was Coker. He was born on Eastern Shore, Maryland, a region which through the years has given to the Church many outstanding leaders. Coker assumed his name to hide his identity when he ran off from slavery to the state of New York. He was ordained by Francis Asbury, and when he returned to Baltimore he remained in seclusion until his friends had purchased his freedom. Coker was a man of uncommon talent and ability. He was a powerful preacher and very eloquent. He was fair of complexion, and quite handsome, with well-formed features, full eyebrows, and lashes that protected eyes that bespoke a deep sincerity. His nose was prominent and sharp; mouth beautifully shaped which gave evidence of eloquence. His chin was that of a man born to command. Coker stood erect, a perfect picture of gentility and man-

5. D. A. Payne, *History of the A. M. E. Church,* 85 f.

hood. He was one of the first authors of the race in America, and wrote *A Dialogue Between a Virginian and an African Minister.* He also wrote a little work on Liberia called *The New Republic.* In 1820 Coker left this country among the first emigrants, to find a home in the freedom of Africa.[6]

While Richard Allen was laboring in Philadelphia, and the country roundabout, Coker was inspiring the people in Baltimore and Maryland. To his genius and ability very largely we are indebted for the organization of the Church, for he was brilliant. The high esteem in which he was held by his brethren was expressed in his having been the first choice for Bishop when the Church was organized. The following day he got out of the picture and Richard Allen was settled upon as the first Bishop of the African Methodist Episcopal Church. What marks Coker as a man of rare spirit is his co-operation. He brought Maryland into the fold of the infant Church, and when he was not set apart for the Episcopacy, lent his all to the good of the cause. His having gone to Liberia, West Africa, and Sierra Leone, constitutes him the first missionary, even though he was not traveling in that role.

MORRIS BROWN AND ASSOCIATES

While Richard Allen and Daniel Coker headed the movement in Philadelphia and Baltimore, the Reverend Morris Brown was active in the city of Charleston. By 1822 the African Methodists in the "city by the sea" numbered about four thousand. Unsung heroes associated with Brown were Henry Drayton, Charles Carr, Amos Cruickshanks, Marcus Brown, Stewart Simpson, Harry Bull, John B. Matthews, James Eden, London Turpin, and Aleck Houlston. The Church had its own cemetery, or "field of graves." A lot was purchased and a church erected. An uprising of slaves in 1822, in an attempt to throw off the yoke of bondage, resulted in the suppression of the religious movement. None of the leaders of the Church were implicated in the uprising. But rather than be denied the right of free worship, Morris Brown, Henry Drayton, Charles Carr, and Amos Cruickshanks went to the city of

---

6. *Ibid.,* 88-91.

Philadelphia, and joined with Richard Allen. James Eden, with a majority of the Brown followers, united with the Scotch Presbyterian Church. Eden finally sailed with the first emigrants who went from Charleston to Liberia. This shows conclusively the passion on the part of the colored people for freedom. Rather than live as slaves they preferred to die free men, and attempted to revolt. Rather than remain in a land of bondage those who were able would leave and return to Africa.

A GLORIOUS COMPANY

William Lambert, a licentiate, was sent to New York in 1819 to secure an opening for the African M. E. Church. Scipio Beans was chosen by the Baltimore Conference to be a missionary to Haiti in 1827, seven years after Coker sailed to Liberia. In 1830 the Ohio Conference was formed at Hillsboro, Ohio. Some of the pioneers were the Reverend John Charleston, John Boggs, Wiley Reynolds, Austin Jones, Jeremiah Thomas, James Bird, Thomas Lawrence, and William Paul Quinn.

John Charleston was a burning and a shining light. His labors were abundant and fruitful. Seldom does such a spirit appear amongst men. In another place more will be said about him. Bishop Campbell is the authority for the statement that John Boggs went to Africa as a missionary as early as 1824, eight years after the organization of the Church.[7] Two things need to be stated. He went as an accredited missionary, the first to represent the Church officially, because Coker seems to have gone on his own accord, but took advantage of his voyage to form an A. M. E. Church among the passengers while aboard ship. The second is that the Church was soon to see the need of missions. The ties that bound them to the fatherland and their kindred were strong.

Shadrack Basset, Peter D. W. Schureman, and Rev. W. D. W. Schureman were great trail blazers in Maryland. The story of Noah C. W. Cannon is typical of a servant of God. He was often in peril for his life, but undaunted he pressed forward. Jeremiah Miller was put in prison at Easton, Maryland. He predicted that the Lord would shake the town that day. In the afternoon a

7. C. S. Smith, *History of the A. M. E. Church,* 155.

great storm arose. The sheriff ordered him freed. Anthony Campbell, father of Bishop Jabez P. Campbell, was preaching at Cecil Cross Roads, or Cecilton, when the church was surrounded by some who came to take him. He put on a lady's shawl and bonnet, got out at the back window and walked away. The influence and power of slavery was felt keenly by the early Fathers of the Church, but in their zeal for the kingdom they blazed paths where highways never ran. They are unknown to the present generation but their sacrifices of tears, beatings, imprisonments, insults, and untold hardships were not in vain. They have answered the summons that calls all earth's children across the mystic stream. God buries His workmen, but His work goes on.

WILLIAM PAUL QUINN

The glorious labors and deeds of William Paul Quinn were so fruitful and Herculean that he overtowers all his compeers. As a pioneer of the Church he was the St. Paul of African Methodism. As a young lad he was present at the Organizing Convention. He was the first to mount a horse and cross the Allegheny Mountains; he was present when the Western or Ohio Conference was organized in 1830. This rugged, itinerant prophet went everywhere preaching the Gospel and establishing Churches in the frontier region. He braved dangers; was in peril of his life often. Many times he was compelled to engage in physical combat when his services were interrupted by rowdies. He would whip them, and continue his task of beating the devil. Paul Quinn was endowed by God with a large, strong body, that fitted him for his Herculean task. It was this fearless, intrepid ambassador of the Lord who led the advance of the Church in the wilderness through the western country to the far shores of the Mississippi. Associated with William Paul Quinn were several sacrificing men and women of God whose names will never be read by mortal eye, but are recorded in the Lamb's Book of Life.

T. M. D. WARD

Before the sun of William Paul Quinn had set in a cloudless

sky, there appeared another preacher of might and power, an apostolic campaigner for Christ — Thomas Marcus Decatur Ward. The torch that fell from the hands of Quinn he caught and carried all the way to the Pacific Coast. His way was prepared in California by a local preacher, Charles Stewart, who was the first to sow the seed of African Methodism in California in the year 1852. Six months after Brother Stewart left there came Reverend Ward. He did for California during the gold rush days what William Paul Quinn had done in Ohio, Indiana, Kentucky, Illinois, and Missouri. Those were the days of the typical rough-and-ready, up-and-coming mining campers immortalized in literature by such writers as Francis Bret Harte.[8] But Ward was fully equal to the occasion. He was the most outstanding preacher the Church had produced up to his time. Certainly he has not been surpassed in oratorical power and facility of speech. Vivid and graphic description reached its highest levels in his superb eloquence. His gestures were noble, his voice sonorous, thunderous and rolling. Ward's figure was tall, and heavy-set. He was described as having "an eagle eye," with a penetrating gaze which was irresistible. According to the late Dr. L. R. Nichols, who knew him, his "hands were like hams." Whenever he raised them his hearers would rise, scream, and shout. Congregations could not bear to sit under the spell of his utterances over fifteen minutes.

It has always been my good pleasure and profitable habit to seek out the oldest men at Annual Conferences or public gatherings and listen as they talked about the early makers of African Methodism: Bishops H. B. Parks, Joseph Simeon Flipper, John Albert Johnson, and William Henry Heard; Drs. John M. Henderson, M. T. Robinson, J. G. Robinson, and R. S. Jenkins. Of that coterie only the last is alive. After sixty-eight years of traveling he is retired at Dallas, Texas. Bishop Parks's great delight was talking about Thomas Marcus Decatur Ward, and he referred to him as "the old man eloquent." What follows is a sample of his style and eloquence (from Stockton, California, he wrote Editor John M. Brown of *The Repository of Religion and Literature*):

> I sincerely ask the prayers of the Church on the other
> side of the continent that the arms of my hands may be

---

8. Bret Harte, "The Luck of Roaring Camp."

made strong by the hands of the mighty God of Jacob. I have endeavored for more than five years to preach a free and whole gospel, that gospel which is not in the word but in power, and in the demonstration of the Spirit. I have aimed to bring the Church up to a higher state of moral and spiritual excellence. How far I have succeeded, time alone must tell.

I shall continue to pursue that course which has largely brought me the inheritance of penury, reproach and loss; but amid all, my heart has been strong in the strength which God supplies through His Eternal Son; and now let come losses, slanders, and toils, I will press forward until I reach the land of promise. . . . Truly the wilderness doth blossom as the rose, and the rippling streams break out in the parched and arid desert.

The Quadrennial Sermon of 1880, when the General Conference met in St. Louis, was delivered by Rev. Ward, who had been elected to the Episcopacy in 1868. He used as a text Acts 20:18; as theme, "The Shepherd and his flock." The following excerpt will allow him to speak for himself:

Brain power will be supreme. Encourage learning and you will live; despise it and you will die. An enlightened ministry, whose talents and calling have been consecrated to God, will make an intelligent, large-hearted Church. "Like priest, like people." We should select books that contain within as small a compass as possible the pith and marrow of the best authors upon such subjects which most interest and concern us. No man can learn everything, but what any other man has done, we can do. Master whatever you take in hand. A knowledge of the classics, and especially of mathematics, will be great aid in the interpretation of the doctrines of the gospel.

Such was the advice of a man who was uneducated. His peroration and conclusion are samples of sustained and moving eloquence:

Ye who come from the different sections of our ocean-bound Republic, our country made one by the blood of a million men — a nation whose domain extends from sea to sea purified in the hot furnace of civil war, is now rising into greatness, not through her vast possessions only, but by her respect for the rights of men. This nation, with her feet dripping in the waters of the Gulf, her head reclining on the granite peaks of Alaska, to such a country we reaffirm our unswerving allegiance. Men who come from the sunny savannahs of the flower-spangled South, and from the rolling, teeming prairies of the West, as well as from the sunset land where Mounts Shasta, Hood, and Baker lift their white shafts to the clouds — to one and all, we say, be loyal to God, be true to yourselves, to your Church, and to your race. Avoid pedantry of learning.

Crush out the imps of ignorance, vanity, ambition, treachery, political trickery, and hell-born caste, always placing true and tried men over the flock. Do all these things and we shall be a polestar to the colored Methodists of America. Africa, long shrouded in pagan night, shall catch the silvery beams that stream from Bethlehem's star; Ethiopia, long despised, forgotten, and forsaken, shall stretch forth her hands to the Heavenly Shepherd, who today is ranging the cold, barren mountains of paganism, seeking the millions who have been torn by the wolves of superstition and idolatry.

Another sample of Bishop Ward's style may again be seen in his matchless tribute on the Fortieth Anniversary of Bishop Daniel Alexander Payne. He rose to great heights and said: "We who have followed him for twoscore years as a Bishop, crown him as our leader and place fresh laurels upon his brow. Great chieftain, at the end of fourscore years and one, the golden sunset throws its radiance around thee. Thou need not fear, for thou shalt see that sunset rise amid the blaze of glory of the city of God."[9]

The following letter to Dr. B. T. Tanner, then Editor of the *Christian Recorder* reveals "the old man eloquent" in his true character: _____

9. C. S. Smith, *op. cit.,* 194.

San Francisco
December 15, 1856

MY DEAR BROTHER IN THE LORD:

You wish to know where I was educated. If you have ever been in Center County, Penna., you have seen a little valley called after the founder of the Keystone State. To the west of this valley are the Allegheny Mountains bathed in the golden glories of the setting sun. On the north are the Tusca Mountains, on the south are the Whitney Mountains. Amid the winds that sweep over these pine-clad mountains, the forked lightnings that leap from mountain cave to valley deep, the thunder drums that mingle their sounds with the voice of the storm — from these I learned the lessons of God's power, the vengeance and wrath of his ire. My soul was humbled when I heard God's thunder-horn summoning the armies to battle.

The walls of those stately mountains, the sunlit and star-paced heavens, and the grass-clad earth were my alma mater. My books were the sweeping river, the opening rose-bud, the babbling brooklet, the brilliant apple blossoms, the thunder-riven oak, the russet peach, the flaming stars, the sparkling, limpid spring, and the soft whispering zephyr. The warbling of nature's feathered harpers often reminded me of the music which is heard in the city of God, the New Jerusalem. The frostbloom of winter and the green of summer all reminded me of the mutability of life. Thus in passing through life I have found a gem of thought from this and the other Book. The only positions I have filled have been those of plow-boy and Methodist preacher. Twenty-four years I have been an officer in the army of the African Methodist Episcopal Church, and such I hope to be until my feet shall touch the other shore — the Edenland where with crown and harp, robe and palm, I hope to spend a sun-bright day, cloudless noon and an ever-opening morn.[10]

On June 10, 1894 the hope of "the old man eloquent" was realized, and he slept with the Fathers.

---

10. *Ibid.*

So live that when the mighty caravan,
Which halts one nighttime in the Vale of Death,
Shall strike its white tents for the morning march,
Thou shalt mount onward to the Eternal Hills,
Thy foot unwearied, and thy strength renewed
Like the eagle's for the upward flight.

JOHN MIFFLIN BROWN

John M. Brown was one of the heroes of the Church in the early period. He was one of God's noblemen, every inch a gentleman. His Oberlin training caused him to stand out in a day when literary preparation was rare. He was a type that drew a large circle of admirers to him. He had the happy faculty to make and keep friends. At the close of the War of the Rebellion he was assigned to Portsmouth, Va. as Pastor by Bishop Payne. The assignment was made because in the judgment of the Bishop a trained man in the doctrines, usages and policy of the Church was needed at that point. He served with distinction, but his work in New Orleans at the St. James Chapel brings to light the character and mettle of the man. This was an aristocratic charge, attended by freemen. Often slaves came to hear the Word of God expounded, and it caused dissension. Five times was the minister imprisoned, not because of enmity on the part of the whites, but because of the jealousy of his own people. This prophet stood firmly for the right, and in the end conquered. His work so impressed the Church that when the General Conference of 1868 met in the city of Washington, D.C. he was elected to the Episcopacy in the class of James A. Shorter, and T. M. D. Ward. Bishop Brown was very active in the organization of the Annual Conferences in the South. He was deeply interested in education, and was the Principal of the first school owned and operated by the African M. E. Church — Union Seminary, a few miles out from Columbus, Ohio. Bishop Brown presided over the Columbia District Conference which met at Newberry, S.C. on July 29, 1870, when a resolution was adopted to purchase one hundred and fifty acres of land at Cokesbury, S.C. — the beginning of what is now Allen College, Columbia, S.C. Bishop Payne was the general superintendent in 1871 when the deal was consummated and the school was named Payne Institute. For some unknown reason the proposition was opposed by Judge J. J. Wright, a Negro Justice of the State Supreme Court.[11] Bishop Brown played a large part in the founding of Wilberforce University in Ohio.

DANIEL ALEXANDER PAYNE

But of all the heroes of the Church, *Daniel A. Payne's* name must be written first in letters of gold. When he fell asleep, it might have been acclaimed in the words of Elisha upon the translation of Elijah: "My father, the chariot of Israel and the horsemen thereof." Payne was not an unsung hero, for the story of his life and deeds is forever inscribed in the annals of the Church which he loved. They shall forever endure on the scroll of fame while Time her record keeps. He was at once the Augustine, Luther, and Calvin; educational reformer, linguist, man of letters, historian, teacher, prophet of far vision, and preacher by the grace of God. No man more than he gave direction and trend to the African M. E. Church. It continues until this day to move in the paths blazed by him.

Bishop Payne had an infinite capacity for work. In every sense of the word he was a Methodist, like his prototype, John Wesley. Everything must be done decently and in order. He was careful and exact in every minutia. A distinguished gentleman whose acquaintance he had formed abroad visited him once at his Tawawa Springs home. When the visitor entered the home, he placed his hat on a chair, Payne deliberately sat upon it, keeping his seat throughout the conversation. Finally, when the gentleman rose to go, Payne extended his hand and gave him his battered and crumpled hat with sufficient money to purchase a new one in the nearby town of Xenia. The Bishop treated his guest in this wise because racks, and not chairs, were made for hats. He was called eccentric. It is said that he would not stay in a room in which there was not a stove.[12] But withal he was a high type of a gentleman. Whatever idiosyncrasies he might have had were due to genius.

From the beginning of Payne's active career at Charleston, his

---

11.   "Historical Statement," *Catalogue of Allen University*, 1936, 15.
12.   Bishop J. S. Flipper, 488 Houston Street, Atlanta.

chief interest was education. In early life there he was a school-teacher. Mental training was his master-passion until his fruitful life closed. Unborn generations will read and attend the story of the Wilberforce University venture with rapt attention. It was he who inspired the publication of the *Christian Herald* (later the *Christian Recorder*) in 1848, the work missions as embodied in the Parent Mite Missionary Society, the Conference Course of Studies, and the system of education for the Church. Great as he was, he remarked once that he would give the A. M. E. Church twenty-five years to live after his death.[13] This was evidence of a weakness to which all flesh is heir. In spite of his prediction, the army of African Methodism continues its onward march down the centuries, and will continue to fulfill its Divine mission of racial and world redemption. After attending, and presiding over one of the sessions of the World Parliament of Religions in Chicago in 1893, Payne returned to his Ever Green Cottage home at Tawawa Springs, Wilberforce. He prepared to go to Florida for the winter, which was his usual custom, but on the day before his anticipated departure for Jacksonville, the throne of God came down, and his spirit went up to meet his God. "The appearance of Bishop Payne was that of a chronic invalid; thin almost to emaciation, below the average in height; features sharp; keen, penetrating eyes; voice, sharp and shrill; but with an ample fore-head indicating intellectual strength and refinement."[14] Another describes him as "a small shriveled figure, deep-lined face and sunken cheeks."[15]

HENRY MC NEAL TURNER

There was already amid the ranks of the African Methodists a very rugged, intrepid, and unique character who was destined to "rock two continents," Henry McNeal Turner. He was born on what is now Hannah Circuit, near Newberry, which was then in Abbeville County, S.C. I have been to the site of the old slave mansion which stood upon a red clay hill, and picked up pieces

13. The Reverend George Brown, presiding elder, Illinois Conference, 1308 E. Monroe Street, Springfield, Ill.
14. John Wesley Cromwell, *The Negro in American History*, 125.
15. James Weldon Johnson, *Along This Way*, 58.

of broken pottery. Turner was "bound out" to the hardest kind
of labor in the cotton fields and the blacksmith's trade in Abbeville until his manhood. He possessed an insatiable craving for
knowledge. In some way he procured an old Webster's Blue Back
Spelling Book. An elderly white lady and a boy with whom he
played taught him the alphabet and to spell as far as two-syllable
words, but he got no farther then as he was discovered in the
act. He found an old colored man who did not know a letter, but
was a prodigy in sounds and could pronounce anything spelled
to him. This helper was removed to another plantation, and he
was again left to his own resources. His mother hired a white
lady to give him lessons every Sabbath, but the neighbors were so
indignant that they threatened to have the law on her, as it was
then against the law to teach a Negro the alphabet.

Three years later, at the age of fifteen, he was given work
in a lawyer's office at Abbeville Court House. The men in the
office were impressed with his excellent memory and taught him,
in defiance of the law, to read accurately, history, theology, and
even works on law. He continued to pursue his studies alone, and
later went to New Orleans, thence to Missouri, and still later to
Baltimore, where he had charge of a small mission. Here he studied grammar, Latin, Greek, Hebrew, German, and theology
under eminent teachers.

Turner joined the M. E. Church South in 1848, while but
a boy, and was licensed to preach in 1853. He was ordained
Deacon in 1860, Elder in 1862, and was consecrated a Bishop in
1880. He received the degree of LL.D. from the University of
Pennsylvania in 1872. At the beginning of the War of the Rebellion he was commissioned by President Abraham Lincoln as the
first Negro Chaplain in the United States Army, and served with
distinction throughout.

At its close Chaplain Turner went south and met the South
Carolina Conference which convened at Savannah, May 14, 1866.
He came from the Baltimore Conference. Bishop Wayman gave
him the sobriquet of "Plutarch" because of his ability as a historian. He bore it with dignity. Turner was a "type." His kind
seldom makes their advent among men. Turner stirred and mar-
shaled the entire forces of the Connection along a far-flung front.
He did more than any other one man to extend the Church in

Georgia. In fact, African Methodism in that state must be thought of in terms of him. Certainly there were other good men, tried and true, who labored with him, but he stands out head and shoulders from the crowd. The days of Reconstruction immediately after the war were times that tried men's souls, and called for great fortitude. Turner possessed it in a remarkable degree. He feared neither man nor devil. In 1876 he was chosen to edit the *Christian Recorder*. Four years later, in St. Louis, he was elected to the Episcopacy. For a long time he was one of the outstanding and commanding leaders in the Church. Turner had a consuming passion for Africa. For a long time he advocated that the race return to the fatherland. In reality he chafed under the unjust treatment his people received in the "land of the free and the home of the brave." It is easy to see how a good, loyal citizen, who has risked his life for the flag in time of national peril, should feel when in the time of peace and freedom he is not accorded decent and just treatment. It is the irony of history. Turner was Vice-President of the African Colonization Society, and pleaded that aid should be given by Congress, that "we may return to our fatherland." This was in the Georgia Conference that met on January 18, 1877, at Bainbridge, Georgia. One who did not agree with him said, in an account of the speech: "The Bishop may yet go there, and if he does, it will be the wish of his many friends that he be made president or king of the whole country."[16] Both Turner and his critic subsequently became Bishops in the Church. Bishop Turner founded the *Southern Christian Recorder* and the Women's Home and Foreign Missionary Society, but his monumental achievement was the bringing into the Church of the South African Conferences through J. M. Dwane, "delegate from the Ethiopian Church, July 12, 1896." In the interim of the General Conference, the Secretary of Missions, Rev. H. B. Parks, now Senior Bishop in the Church, and J. S. Flipper, also a Bishop, introduced the Reverend Dwane to Bishop Turner in Bishop Turner's Atlanta home.[17] He was a member of the Georgia Legislature and an author who made a lasting contribution to the literature of the Church. Turner was a fearless champion of the rights of his people. He was uncompromising, but undaunted. Once he

---

16. Wesley J. Gaines, *African Methodism in the South*, 71.
17. B. W. Arnett, *Budget, 1900*, 245.

got into bed in the daytime with his boots on to escape the Ku Klux Klan, after having ridden the tender of a railroad train. Elder Wayman gave him the sobriquet of "Plutarch" because of his knowledge of history. By that name he was known to the Church of his generation. The Church will yet see Turner in his true light as the perspective of his time lengthens. He will be silhouetted against the background of the centuries as one of God's noblest servants, a true knight of the Cross, about whom Bishop William David Chappelle said: "He lived fifty years ahead of his people." He was indeed one of the mightiest oaks in the forest.

OTHER LEADERS

The record of all the known heroes in the early days of the Church cannot be mentioned in such a treatise as this. There were many "smaller men" with large influence, saints of God who toiled amid hardships in obscure places, and obtained a good report. To every overtowering man like Elder Alexander Wayman, the hero of Eastern Shore, there were scores of others whose names have escaped the Church chronicler. They went everywhere along seldom-frequented trails, bypaths, rugged roads; they walked foot-logs, forded streams, swam rivers, climbed mountains, went through the valleys, threaded their lonely way through dark and dismal swamps, struggled against the Ku Klux Klan, preached in fields, camp meetings, brush arbors, in log cabins, and proclaimed the good tidings of great joy. Some were imprisoned and beaten with stripes and driven out of town. But they counted not their lives dear unto themselves, only that they might make full proof of their ministry and finish their course with joy. Like true and bold knights of the Cross they sallied forth and quitted themselves like men. They walked long circuits. One of the writer's relatives, by the name of "Uncle" Henry Jones, was a member of the South Carolina Conference at its second session. He often said that he walked ninety miles frequently, in fact weekly, from Wilmington, N.C. to Conway, S.C. to preach and help lay the foundation of the Church. No night was too dark or stormy for these evangels; no stream too turbulent or wide that it could not be crossed; no mountain too high, or vale too deep to be climbed and passed through. In heat and cold, rain or shine, sleet or snow, afoot, astride horse, mule, ox cart, road cart, or buggy, these circuit riders kept on the go. They sought their brethren until the hills and plains re-echoed with the gladsome song of the re-deemed.[18] In the last day when the children of men shall stand before the bar of God to be judged according to the deeds done in the body, these heroes of the faith who suffered, hungered, under-went privations, were opposed by race haters, foes within and foes without, having washed their robes and made them white in the blood of the Lamb, will hear the happy words of the Saviour: "Well done. Enter thou into the joys of thy Lord. Thou hast been faithful over a few things, I will make thee ruler over many."

Bishop William H. Heard was born a slave in Elberton, Ga. He raised himself by his own bootstraps, became a metropolitan pastor, a powerful Methodist preacher, member of the South Carolina Legislature, and Bishop in the Church. His epigrammatic utterances have lasting value: "A divided interest will suffer." "A two-headed thing is a monstrosity." He said once: "I do not preach like Singleton, or lawyers who have been to school. I 'tact the text!" His famous closing of a sermon was beautiful and typical: "Fifty-odd years ago I unsheathed my old Damascus blade down in old Elberton, Ga. and I expect to wield it until I come to the end. And on the up-lifted plains, where Jesus rides at the head of the army, I'll stick it in the golden sands of time, and study war no more!" When he reached that climax, the house was stirred. He could move any congregation. He often remarked that "Methodism is religion in earnest."

The Gospel writers refer to "certain other women," who ministered unto Jesus, in addition to Mary, His Mother, the sisters of Lazarus, Mary of Migdal, and Salome. There must have been a large number who heard and followed Him. Of the men, the names of "twelve," and a few others are mentioned. One sheet of tablet paper would hold the names of all, who according to the record participated in the great drama. Add to them Paul, Stephanas, Luke, Titus, Timothy, Silvanus, Barnabas; Dorcas, Eunice, Lois, Euodias, Synteche. So the members of the Prayer Band of forty-two who met with Allen are unknown; so the

18. C. S. Smith, *op. cit.,* 182-84.

Upper Room host on the Day of Pentecost. And there were "certain other" men.

George Hogarth, Editor of the *A. M. E. Church Magazine* in 1841, was born at Annapolis. He died in Brooklyn, in 1850. Augustus R. Green was a Virginian, and Editor in 1848 of the *Christian Herald*. He later resigned after four years and returned to the pastorate. He went to Canada and became a Bishop in the Independent M. E. Church. In May 13, 1878, he resigned his office, and came back to the Church as a Pastor and Elder. He fell at his post in Vicksburg, Mississippi, in a yellow fever epidemic.

An outstanding early character in the Church was Molston M. Clark. He was born at Canonsburg, Pennsylvania in 1807, and was trained in the college there. In 1844 he was elected Secretary of the General Conference, and Traveling Agent for the Book Concern. He resigned, went west, and then to England to attend the Evangelical Alliance. Upon his return home he was elected Editor of the *Christian Recorder* in 1852. A few years later he resigned and joined the M. E. Church, and was made Principal of the Monrovia Academy in Africa. Upon his return to America he was Pastor of St. James in New Orleans, and Quinn Chapel in Louisville. He answered the final summons at Alton, Illinois.

Out of the past looms Jonathan Tudas, a layman of Philadelphia. He was born at Salem, New Jersey, and when quite young went to the Quaker City. He was present when the Church was organized, and witnessed the "consecration" of Richard Allen. James Fitz Allen Sisson was a white gentleman from Fall River, Mass. He was admitted to the Baltimore Conference in 1860, and was the first missionary to Suffolk, Virginia. His work was along the frontier in Arkansas, and the Indian Territory. Sisson served as one of the secretaries of the General Conference. He was a delegate in 1872, 1876, 1880, and 1884. In 1872 his name appears with the Georgia delegation as Recording Secretary. Hiram Revels of Fayetteville, N.C. was born about 1822. He left the state and went to Indiana, and became a prominent minister in the Church. He left the denomination and joined the Presbyterians, and was Pastor of Madison Street Church, Baltimore. He returned to African Methodism, and while Pastor at Natchez, Mississippi, was elected the first United States Senator of color in the history of the nation. This was on March 11, 1870. It was indeed ironical that his seat in the Senate Chamber should be the one which had been occupied by Jefferson Davis, president of the Confederacy.

Reverend William G. Steward of the East Florida Conference served as Postmaster of Tallahassee for eight years, and gave general satisfaction. Presiding Elder Robert Meacham of Florida was a State Senator for many years. Bruce H. Williams of Charleston, S.C., was an aristocrat, and of impressive bearing. He was a member of the South Carolina Legislature. His Conference relationship dates from 1867. Richard Harvey Cain was a Wilberforcean. He helped to organize the Church in South Carolina, and was a member of the State Legislature. He was the moving spirit in founding Paul Quinn College. Cain was elected a Bishop in 1880.

The Reverend Charles H. Pearce was born a slave in Queen Anne's County, Maryland. He purchased his freedom, and was licensed to preach in the M. E. Church. In 1852 he was admitted into the New England Conference. From there he went to Canada and remained until the Rebellion War ended. He returned to the United States, and went to Florida. He organized the African M. E. Church there. He was a rare jewel, and served in the Florida State Senate.

No man in the history of the Church has a more illustrious place than Benjamin W. Arnett. No one made a more lasting contribution. He was born at Brownsville, Pennsylvania, had a penchant for gathering facts, and was a natural-born statistician. As Financial Secretary of the Church he dignified the office, and produced several invaluable volumes of *The Budget,* packed with facts and figures. He was a hard worker. For several years he was a member of the Ohio Legislature and was a leader in accomplishing repeal of the Black Laws in the state. Bishop Arnett was elected a Bishop in 1888 at Indianapolis. His one-time residential home at Wilberforce, called "Tawawa Chimney Corner" is owned by Bishop Reverdy C. Ransom, who worked for him while a student at Wilberforce University.

It was Harry Stubbs who raised the flag of African Methodism in Alabama. He was born in Georgia at Columbus. At an early age he entered the M. E. Church and was licensed to preach. He was among the first to join the African M. E. Church after the war, and was admitted into the South Carolina Conference in 1867 at Macon, Georgia. This pioneer fell at his post in Selma.

Henry J. Johnson, like many in his day, was born a slave in Maryland. When a boy, he left the state, and on his way through Delaware, was arrested, and put in the New Castle jail as a runaway slave. When he entered the prison he had the presence of mind to get a fellow-prisoner to cut off his hair. In a few days after the advertisement appeared in the papers, he was represented as a "boy having very full and long hair." The authorities soon became convinced, from his appearance, that he did not answer the description given in the papers, and therefore discharged him. He then made his way to Philadelphia, and from there to New York, where he joined the Church, was admitted into the Conference, and for many years filled many important charges.

We have mentioned only a few of the loyal, self-sacrificing souls who through the years rallied to the standard set up by Richard Allen. There are others whose names are written in the Lamb's Book on high. In out-of-the-way places they labored, and went home, unobserved and unnoticed. They worked in missions and circuits. The great multitude were not Presiding Elders or metropolitan Pastors. With their consecrated wives they went, left all and followed Him. Ellen Coburn, whose husband, the Reverend Daniel Coburn, died in 1853, was the mother of many children. During her last illness she invited her friends to come and see a Christian die. She sang and clasped her hands, until the wheels of life stood still, and with a sweet smile upon her face she bade children and friends adieu; then her spirit went home to her Maker.

Theophilus Gould Steward was born at Gouldtown, New Jersey. He joined the Philadelphia Conference in 1864. The following year he was transferred to the South Carolina Conference. From there he went to the state of Georgia; served as Pastor, and Presiding Elder. He organized, and built the beautiful Steward Chapel at "Five Points" on Cotton Street, Macon, Georgia. Dr. Steward went as a missionary to Haiti, and was once Cashier of the Freedman's Bank. During the Spanish-American War, Dr. Steward served as a Chaplain with the famous Tenth U.S. Cavalry at San Juan Hill. *Fifty Years in the Gospel Ministry* is an interesting and valuable autobiographical account of a worthy servant of the Church.

"Uncle" Henry Jones of Conway, S.C., a "slaverytime preacher" was a blood relative of mine. He lived to be very old, and claimed that in the early days he walked from his home to Wilmington, North Carolina to preach, a distance upwards of fifty miles. His tall, rugged frame bespoke his Zulu ancestry. His dark bronze skin was smooth and satiny. His voice was strong and carried far. "Uncle Henry" always wore a long-tailed, dark-blue Prince Albert coat. Once he preached at Bethel, the home-town church, from the text: "I am the true vine, my Father is the husbandman." His method of preaching was to repeat the words over and over in a rising crescendo. As his Voice rose he got happy, and started shouting; jumping straight up and down: "Oh, yes, glory to God." Once after church he came home to Sunday dinner. Upon entering the passage through the house he found a large family Bible on a large center table, which my father had made with his own hands. "Uncle" Henry Jones would wet his finger, turn the pages, and get happy. He would hold the Bible to his breast and say with unction: "Glory to God, THEE BOOK, THEE BOOK, *THEE* Book!" Tears would stream down his sable cheeks. This old veteran was one of the unknown, unsung heroes who helped establish the Church in the Carolinas after "the war."

Jones was a spiritual descendant of Harry Hoosier and Richard Allen. All honor to those choice spirits of African descent who planted the Church in the North, East, and West, but the early pioneers in the South underwent hardships just as rigorous, dangerous, and exacting. They often faced the fury, whip, and lash of the Ku Klux Klan and Night Riders. Long before I knew the meaning of the words I often heard my mother say at nighttime: "Be good or the Klux'll get you."

There is an unwritten chapter in the history of the Church as it relates to the early work in Texas. Patton, Haywood, and Hammett endured hardness as good soldiers as they went forth to lay lasting foundations in the "Lone Star State." Other names which stand out upon the pages of the immortals are Leake, Love, Wilhite, Goins, Carson, Rudy, and Gilliard. Their trail of Gospel grace was blazed across the prairies from Houston and

Galveston to San Antonio, Austin, Waco, and Dallas. In those days the life of the preacher had little value. Often they were harrassed by "two-gun men" and desperadoes, and at the point of a revolver were shot at and told to dance to the music. They walked lonely trails and frequently saw the body of a recently lynched man swinging from the limb of a tree.

When Father Love went to Dallas for the first time, he spent the night sleeping on a tree stump. As a result of his visit Bethel, a large metropolitan church at 1908 Leonard Street, has a membership of over four thousand. The larger churches in the city are St. Paul on Metropolitan, and St. James at 620 Good Street. Reedy Chapel in Galveston is the mother of African Methodism in the state, but Bethel in Dallas, and Wesley Chapel in Houston are the largest churches. A gruesome incident was the cold-blooded murder of the Reverend Gilliard by outlaws, while he was Pastor at Austin. The only reason was that he was educated and cultured. He had come from Baltimore, and was in those days "a wonder" both to whites and colored.

Thomas W. Long was one of the early pioneers in the state of Florida. His ancestors came directly from Africa in the days of slavery. He planted churches in several parts of the state, and suffered greatly in the work. His son, the illustrious Dr. Charles Sumner Long, is still in the flesh, and full of years. He is still very active, and is Pastor of a large society at West Palm Beach, Florida, a church which he founded. For decades Dr. Long has been a most eloquent and able preacher. His speech is chaste, his language elegant, and his voice rings like a silver bell at eventide. His inspiration was T. M. D. Ward, and the mighty evangelist, Abram Grant. During the administration of Bishop John Hurst in Florida, the Lee Theological Seminary building at Edward Waters College was dedicated. Both the Council of Bishops, and the Connectional Council assembled there. R. B. Smith, of Camden, N.J. was President of the Connectional body. At the evening service a reception was held. Dr. Long was called for the response to the addresses made by distinguished churchmen from afar. Words can not describe the power of his impassioned speech on this occasion. His peroration ran something like this:

You have heard a great deal about Bishop John Hurst

and the men of Florida, but we have not produced a single leader low enough to curse his mother. All that has been done in Florida, has been done by John Hurst.

Some day, some afternoon, when you are strolling through your garden amid the oleanders, the roses, and crepe myrtles grandeur-like, smiling in their incomparable beauty, you are attracted by a scene in the sky. And looking up you see a hearse drawn by ten thousand white horses, and accompanied by ten thousand times ten thousand pallbearers. An angel with crayon of fire writes on the wall of the sunset: God is dead, and we are going to bury Him! Then, and not until then shall we, the people of Florida forsake John Hurst.

The effect of this address was atomic. The vast assemblage burst into ecstasy, loud and sustained applause. The brief quotation cannot begin to portray the charming beauty, force, and power of this "unsung hero." His son in the ministry, L. G. Long, Pastor of St. John, Montgomery, Alabama is "a chip off the old block."

Many African Methodist ministers were members of the National Congress and State Legislatures during the Reconstruction period. Richard Harvey Cain served with honor, and was elected a Bishop in 1880. Bruce H. Williams of Charleston, S.C. was a member of his State Legislature. He was an aristocrat, tall, stately, dignified. He closed his life as a Presiding Elder in the South Carolina Conference. W. W. Beckett was in the legislature; served as Presiding Elder, President of Allen University, Secretary of Missions, and in 1916 was elected to the Episcopacy. One of the most distinguished members of the Georgia House of Representatives was Henry McNeal Turner. His farewell address to the body, after the Negro's political sun had set in Georgia, is a classic down to this day.

These unheralded workers in the Master's vineyard were preceded by a grand army of Christian soldiers. Many sleep in unmarked graves. Some were women, at whose head stood the "Mother of the Church," Sarah Allen, wife of the founder. After 1816 when the Connection was organized, the first Annual Conference was held. The preachers came. Some of them were so indigent, and poorly clad that she ministered unto their needs with patches, needle and thread. Their elbows were visible through their coat sleeves. There were holes in their pants. She made them presentable. She helped her husband entertain his friends. Some of the old silver plate which was used is in the Museum Room of Mother Bethel at Sixth and Lombard Streets, Philadelphia. The names of those who foregathered and discussed their problems and contemporary events and were determined to go along with Richard Allen, are lost. Reuben Cuff, one of the Sixteen who founded the Church, was a prominent figure in establishing the Church in New Jersey, particularly at Salem in 1800. One of his daughters was the wife of Theodore Gould, who became a Pastor of Mother Bethel, Manager of the Book Concern, and founder of Allen, 17th and Bainbridge, Philadelphia. The nearest the writer has come to finding a picture of Cuff is a photograph of his grandsons, the Reverends Thomas Cuff and Burgoyne F. Cuff, prominent ministers in the New Jersey Conference in their day. Numerous descendants of Cuff reside in New Jersey, and are members of the Church. Stephen Hill, a layman, was one of the founders of the Church. He was a member of the Baltimore delegation in 1816. He was a man of some mental power, and rendered great service. He lived and died in the Church. One of the early pioneers was a Mr. Stephen Smith, a wealthy Local Elder, who was born at Columbia, Penna. The gentleman who reared him set him up in the lumber business. He was converted under the preaching of the Reverend David Smith, a contemporary of Richard Allen, who laid out the circuit. Shortly after his conversion he received license to exhort. Later he became an Elder. He was a member of the General Conference from 1836 to 1864, and acted as teller. He removed to Philadelphia in 1840, and purchased a house on Lombard Street where he lived and died in September 1873. Stephen Smith organized several churches, including the Zion Mission at Seventh and Dickerson Streets, Philadelphia, now Zion A. M. E. Church, and Murphy in Chester. He gave the ground for, and built, the Old Folks' Home at 41st and Girard. The institution still receives a handsome sum each year from a legacy bequeathed by him. Bishop Wayman delivered the dedication address. For a long time the Church regarded the Home as its project.

David Smith looms across the years as a hero. Had it not been for his *Autobiography*, much valuable material and information would have been forever lost. He was born a slave March 10, 1784, nine miles from Baltimore. A kind lady, Mrs. Matilda White, purchased him and set him free. He was converted and began his ministry in the African M. E. Church. He joined with Daniel Coker in founding the Church in Baltimore. With them were John C. Hall, Nathan Peck, Levin Lee, Charles Hackett, Alexander Murray, Charles Pierce, James Truston, Henry Harden, N. T. Hammond, Faton Blake, and Richard Williams. The names of Coker, Harden, and Williams appear among the Sixteen who were in the Convention of 1816. Smith claimed that he was present.

Daniel Coker was a great spirit. He was almost white. When a boy he ran away to New York, and received a liberal education. The liberal whites in Baltimore decided that the people of color might have a school. Coker was sent for. He came, but his friends had to raise money to pay for his "running away." He was a fluent speaker. As a religious leader he exchanged letters with Richard Allen. They discussed the lots of their people in both centers, for conditions in both cities were similar. Coker's popularity enabled him to be elected to the Bishopric, but he was rejected, "being nearly white."

Coker laid out preaching places in the vicinity of Baltimore, Little York, Penna., Wrightsville on the Susquehanna River, Columbia, Lancaster, Harrisburg, Carlisle, Shippensburg, Chambersburg, Greencastle, Hagerstown, Functown, and Fredericktown. Shadrack and David Smith kept up the circuit, and traveled it afoot. In those days the people — white and colored — came from miles around to the meetings. They walked, came in Conestoga wagons, on horseback, and used any means of conveyance. Their Annual Conference deliberations lasted about a week. During my boyhood the Bishops always read their appointments late Sunday nights. The preachers would leave for home on Monday. It was an impressive sight to observe them wearing somber black Prince Albert coats and stiff-bosom shirts that were fastened behind. Commencement at Allen University was a grand occasion. The ministers, trustees, and people came by the hundreds. Horses, mules, buggies, wagons lined the campus. The Harden Street side looked like an army picket line or corral. Often while the candidates for graduation were "saying their speeches," the horses and mules on the outside attracted by the sound of loud applause, would contribute vociferous neighs and brays between munching their noon-day meals of fodder.

These men and women were not highly or technically trained. It was not to be expected, but the miracle is how they appreciated training and desired it for their children. They set the pattern of giving, and it has been followed unto this day. That is one of the most thrilling chapters in the history of the Church and the race. They are gone but their influence still lives. In hundreds of instances the little wooden headpieces which marked their final resting-places have long since rotted away, and the flowers planted by loving hands choked with weeds. But the dust is hallowed.

> . . . I go to prove my soul.
> I see my way as birds their trackless way,
> I shall arrive, — what time, what circuit first,
> I ask not: but unless God send His hail
> Of blinding fireballs, sleet, or stifling snow,
> In some time, His good time, I shall arrive;
> He guides me and the bird. In His good time.

CHAPTER XI

Following the Trail of the Fathers

Every place which the sole of your foot treads have I
given you. — JOSHUA 1:3

It is easy to foot the trodden path
Where thousands walked before.
It is simple to push my fragile bark
Past reefs of a charted shore.
I find it good to ride the road
Where others laid the trail.
It is well to test the ocean's strength
Where others also sail.
But when a dream enslaves a man,
A dream of the vast untrod.
A dream that says, 'Strike out with me,
Strike out, or part with God';
A dream that leads to an untried path
Where unknown tempests blow,
And the only chart a man can boast
Is his will that bids him go;
Ah, then, my soul, bethink yourself,
For God has spread this scroll
To test the stuff of your rough-hewn faith
And the fiber of your soul.
— P. R. HAYWARD

During the last three or four decades the Church had within
its Communion "the big four" who were elected Bishops in 1888:
Abraham Grant, Benjamin W. Arnett, Benjamin Tucker Tanner
and Wesley J. Gaines. Each of these men was possessed of
marked ability. Bishop Grant was a wonderful preacher. Some
who heard him are still alive and speak of his great pulpit ability.
He was an evangelist. Bishop Arnett was a prodigious worker,

and had large capacity for sustained intellectual industry. He was methodical and exact. His passion was for facts and figures. Several volumes of valuable historical data have come from his prolific pen. Bishop Arnett was a statesman and a lawmaker. Bishop Gaines was an aristocrat and one of God's noblemen. He left to posterity a glorious record of achievement in the Church, and a valuable history of *African Methodism in the South, or Twenty-five Years of Freedom.*

The scholarly Bishop Tanner stands out like a mighty oak in a forest of giants. Before his election he was Editor of the *Christian Recorder.* He will be remembered as the founder of the *A. M. E. Review,* and its first Editor. Several books came from his pen: *Outlines of African M. E. Church History,* and *Tanner's Apology.*

Benjamin Franklin Lee, James Anderson Handy, and Moses Buckingham Salter were elevated to the Episcopacy in 1892 at Philadelphia. They were outstanding men. "Ben" Lee, as his friends called him, was from New Jersey, the great state which produced the Cuffs, Goulds, Stewards, and Pierces. He worked his way through Wilberforce, and became its President. Then he was elected Editor of the *Christian Recorder.* The Bishop was noted for his flawless Christian character. He was honest and upheld the sanctity of the law of the Church. In fact, Bishop Lee was a saint. He was no lover of money, and led a simple life. He is canonized in the heart of the Church. On May 6, 1924, he made the following farewell to the General Conference at Louisville:

> (1)   Although not weary in well-doing, and not beyond service, but still amenable to the wishes and orders of the Church to the extent of my powers and God's grace, I know that my days are gliding swiftly by. I am enjoying fair health and mental vigor, but having completed fourscore years in life, fifty-six years in the Christian ministry, and thirty-two in the Episcopacy, and having entered upon the fifth score in life, I am impressed that my days of active ministry are comparatively few. I would employ the remaining days of my life in assembling the facts and arranging the materials for the service of the Church and ministry.

(2)   I would extend my gratitude and thanks to the Episcopal Council, and the ministry and laity, for filling my place during absences, and all other courtesies.

Allow me to thank the Church for responsibilities imposed and honors bestowed as a representative at home and abroad. You may find me and Mrs. Lee at home with the family. Praying that God, who is with me, will be with me to the end, and with His Church. Amen.

[*Signed*] B. F. Lee

At the close of Bishop Lee's address, Bishop L. J. Coppin, who was in the chair, requested the Conference to sing: "Children of the Heavenly King." The scene was very touching. The adjournment was even more so, when Bishop Lee bade the Conference farewell on May 21. The gavel was handed to him, and upon the suggestion of Bishop Coppin the body stood and sang, "Try us, O God, and search the ground," while the Bishops and delegates shook hands — many for the last time on this side of the river. Those who were present will ever remember the occasion. Bishop Lee was dressed in a gray, single-breasted business suit. He was on the left of the platform as the delegates faced the front. Bishops Smith, Coppin, Parks, Heard, Flipper, John Albert Johnson, Ross, Beckett, Vernon, Carey, Brooks, W. D. Johnson, Conner, Jones, and Tyree were present that day. They have all vanished from the earth. Bishop William A. Fountain is the only one still with the Church who shook hands with Bishop Lee in this closing service. Bishops Ransom, Gaines, and Gregg had just been elected. The Fathers of the Church are passing.

James A. Handy was one of the early missionary pioneers. When he was three years old, a Conference was held in Baltimore by Richard Allen. He placed his hand upon the head of young Handy, and said to his mother: "Maria, take good care of this boy; he will be one of my successors." It was a true word of prophecy, for in the very city where he himself had been elected and set apart as a Bishop, Handy was made one of his "successors." As a Pastor he served in Baltimore, St. James in New Orleans, and did missionary work in Virginia, and South Carolina. Allen saw in Handy what Payne did not discover.

Bishop M. B. Salter was from Charleston, South Carolina. He was a saintly, dignified Christian gentleman, beloved and highly respected. When just a lad I saw the good Bishop. His long beard was impressive. The late Dr. A. E. Peets carried me to see him, and asked the Bishop to bless me. At his knees with bowed head and eyes closed, I reverently awaited the touch of his outstretched hands as he prayed ". . . that this young man may become a minister of Jesus Christ."

The city of Wilmington, N.C. was the seat of the General Conference of 1896. Bishops John Mifflin Brown, Ward, and Payne had laid aside their episcopal robes for garments of white in the city four-square. They were men of might and power. Such a galaxy of stars! Who was worthy of carrying on, and following in their train?

> Pass on the torch, pass on the flame;
> Remember whence the Glory came;
> And eyes are on you as you run,
> Beyond the shining of the sun.
>
> O Lord of life, to Thee we kneel;
> Maker of men, our purpose seal!
> We will, for honor of Thy Name,
> Pass on the Torch, pass on the Flame.

To fill the places of these Fathers the Church selected W. B. Derrick of Antigua, J. H. Armstrong, and James Crawford Embry. The first was a famous orator and platform speaker. Bishop Embry will be remembered as one-time Manager of the Book Concern, and author of *A Digest of Theology*. This General Conference also elected as Secretary of Education, the able Professor John Russell Hawkins of North Carolina. He climaxed his career in the Church as the honored Secretary of Finance. Very few who were in the General Conference abide in the flesh.

When the Twenty-fifth General Conference was convened at Columbus, Ohio in 1900, it was found necessary to elevate five Elders to the Episcopacy. The Class was composed of Evan Tyree of Tennessee, a sweet Gospel preacher, M. M. Moore of Florida, Charles Spencer Smith, Cornelius T. Shaffer, and Levi

Jenkins Coppin. Bishop Moore did not live long. The unique
thing about this group of Bishops is that three of them were
Doctors of Medicine: Tyree, Smith, and Shaffer. Smith was eloquent, and a great debater. Few opponents could stand before
him. Under his leadership and by his guiding influence the Sunday School Union was organized at Bloomington, Illinois. It was
later removed to Nashville. Upon the enduring foundation laid
by him the present institution has been built. Bishop Smith stands
out as one of the ablest members of the Episcopate. When he
laid down his pen he had just completed his excellent history of
the Church. Whereas Bishop Tyree was very dark of complexion,
C. T. Shaffer was very fair. He could have easily crossed the
color line had he desired. It has been reliably reported that when
traveling in Jim Crow territory he was always accorded first-
class passage, without any questions being asked.

Levi Jenkins Coppin was tall, robust, and full-bodied. He was
a preacher of exegetical ability. He was quite adept at discovering
and developing different shades of meaning in Greek words. At
the Louisville General Conference, he preached: "He that is born
of God cannot sin." He brought out of the text: "Is not *able* to
sin. . . ." He had a peculiar mannerism while preaching. He would
clap his hands, slap his left thigh, and again put his left hand to
the right side of his mouth with open palm to the right, and
whisper for emphasis. There was much unction in his words. He
was once Editor of the *Review*. His literary remains include a
treatise on Africa, *Sermon Syllabi*, and *Unwritten History*. He
served the Church in South Africa. Shortly after the General
Conference of 1924 at Louisville, Bishop Coppin passed into the
great beyond.

The General Conference of 1904 at Chicago elected no
Bishops. E. W. Lampton of Mississippi was Financial Secretary,
and Grand Master of Masons in his state. A large sum of money
was borrowed for the Department, and he was successful and
powerful enough to keep "the door closed" for four years until
the loan could be repaid. Then at Norfolk, Virginia, in 1908, he
was elected at the head of a class of five Bishops: Wm. H. Heard,
H. B. Parks J. S. Flipper, and John Albert Johnson. Lampton
died shortly after the adjournment of the General Conference.
Of the group John Albert Johnson was the polished shaft for

God in the pulpit. Flipper was the legalist, and Sunday school scholar. He was methodical and did not believe in wasting time. Everything must be done decently and in order. Heard was the Methodist. For a long time Parks was the Senior Bishop. Bishop Ward inspired him to enter the ministry and go to New Orleans during the yellow fever plague in 1879. He used to relate a touching story of how he bade his weeping mother good-bye. Bishop Ward had preached at a Conference in Madison, Ga. He went to New Orleans, was made Secretary of Missions, and finally a Bishop in the Church. His last appointment was placed in my hands, a transfer from the Fourth to the Thirteenth District, at Sparta, Ill. in the fall of 1935. These Fathers have all gone. Bishop Flipper was the last to depart from his beloved Atlanta residence at 488 Houston Street.

Wm. D. Chappelle, John Hurst, Joshua H. Jones, and J. M. Conner attended the General Conference at Kansas City in 1912, and came away Bishops. Chappelle had been a foremost leader in South Carolina, President of Allen University, and Secretary of the Sunday School Union. His ideal was Bishop Turner. He was an educator, and built the fine Chappelle Administration Building at Allen University. Chappelle was fearless and courageous. He would stand by his convictions, regardless. John Hurst came to the episcopal bench from the Secretaryship of Finance. The Church has not produced a more constructive personality. He remarked in the presence of the writer once: "Men talk, talk, talk; I work!" And he *did* work. Edward Waters College and Allen University are his monuments of improvement. Joshua H. Jones had been President of Wilberforce University. He was a magnetic leader, skillful in argument and disputation. The crowning work of his Episcopacy was the erection of the new Shorter Hall upon the campus of Wilberforce. Bishop Conner was a tower of strength in his day. The Conner Hall at Shorter College was erected while he was Bishop of Arkansas.

Bishops Isaac Nelson Ross and William Wesley Beckett have gone the way of the redeemed. The former was a sweet singer and preacher. He was a mighty power on his knees. He always prefaced his prayers with a song: "Fierce and wild the storm is raging." He fell in the Little Rock Union Station. His funeral was preached by Reverdy Cassius Ransom in Allen Temple,

Cincinnati. Text: "He was a burning and a shining light." President S. L. Greene represented Arkansas. He is now a Bishop. Bishop Beckett was a typical South Carolinian, and dearly loved Edisto Island. He was an alumnus of Gammon Seminary. He served the Church as Pastor, Presiding Elder, and Secretary of Missions; then as President of Allen University before his election to the Bishopric in 1916.

Of the Fathers who came into the Episcopacy at St. Louis in 1920, William Sampson Brooks, William T. Vernon, William Decker Johnson, and Archibald J. Carey have crossed the flood, and Bishop William Alfred Fountain, Sr. remains. Bishop Fountain is an educator, upon whose shoulders has fallen the mantle of Daniel Alexander Payne. Bishop Brooks was a financier, and a great soul, a missionary, and lover of men. Bishop Carey was a statesman, and fighter for social justice, and Johnson was happy to regard himself "a Commoner." He was a kindhearted man. The men loved him dearly.

Abraham Lincoln Gaines, '24; R. A. Grant and G. B. Young, '28, H. Y. Tookes, '32, and Edward James Howard, '36 have left the Church militant and joined the ranks of the Church triumphant. They followed the trail until God called them home. Bishops Reverdy C. Ransom, Wm. A. Fountain, John A. Gregg, S. L. Greene, M. H. Davis, Noah W. William, R. R. Wright, D. Ward Nichols, Frank Madison Reid, A. J. Allen, George W. Baber, J. H. Clayborne, L. H. Hemmingway, D. Ormonde Walker, Joseph Gomez, I. H. Bonner, W. R. Wilkes, and Carey A. Gibbs are following the trail of Gospel grace blazed by their illustrious predecessors.

And there were other "Fathers" who were not Bishops — Elders in the Church, who loved the cause, and made full proof of their ministry. Many of them aspired to be Bishops, but God saw fit to use them otherwise to His glory. They stand in the succession coming down from Daniel Coker, Richard Robinson, A. R. Green, and M. M. Clark to H. T. Johnson, H. N. Newsome, the late J. L. Butler, and a mighty host. But Bishops, and Elders, all follow the trail of the Fathers in trying to build a better Church as a means of bringing in the Kingdom of God, and His Christ.

CHAPTER XII

The General Conference of 1936

Upon this rock I will build my church, and the gates of hell shall not prevail against it. — St. Matthew 16:8

I love Thy church, O God,
Her walls before me stand;
Dear as the apple of mine eye,
And graven on my hand.
— Timothy Dwight

On the morning of May 6 the Thirtieth General Conference met in the Palace Casino, 154th Street and Eighth Avenue, New York City. The Reverend D. Ward Nichols, Pastor of Emanuel Church, was the host. Promptly at 9:30 Bishop Joseph Simeon Flipper of the Eleventh Episcopal District called the meeting to order. He was the Senior Bishop because Bishop Henry Blanton Parks, who was so honored for several years, had gone to his reward in the month of February.

Bishop Parks was a gigantesque personality. His ancestry must have stemmed from African kings. His voice was resonant. His speech was punctuated with staccato pauses. When he was making an oratorical flight, words rushed from his lips in veritable torrents. Congregations were thrilled. He was noted for rugged honesty, meticulous observance of the law, and love for the church. Once he remarked: "I swallow the African Methodist system whole, and it does not give me spiritual indigestion." The venerable Bishop came to the end of the Gospel trail while presiding over the Fourth Episcopal District, and died at his Oakland home "out on the coast," which he loved so well. The remains were brought to Kansas City, Kansas, and funeralized in Allen Temple, a church which he once served as Pastor. He always took pride in "the Fifth District." Bishop Flipper presided. A very touching prayer was offered by Bishop H. Y. Tookes of the

144

Thirteenth Episcopal District. The sermon was delivered by
Bishop W. H. Heard. Both Bishops Flipper and Heard were class-
mates of the deceased, having been elected at Norfolk in 1908.
Dr. E. E. Wittenburg of Louisiana sang: "We will walk through
the valley in peace."

The church was crowded to overflowing. The writer, scholarship beneficiary of the Class of Bishops of 1908, delivered a tribute on behalf of himself and Dr. E. E. Tyler, who was absent.
The funeral cortege moved by train to Atlanta. A fitting service
was held in "Big Bethel" on Auburn Avenue. Bishop William A.
Fountain presided, and Bishop Flipper gave the sermon. His text
was: "Know ye not that a prince has fallen this day in Israel"
(II Samuel 3:38). Tributes were paid by President W. A. Fountain, Jr. of Morris Brown College, Drs. L. L. Berry, Secretary of
Missions, New York, W. R. Wilkes, Pastor of Allen Temple,
Atlanta, and the writer. The family lot in which the remains of
the Bishop were interred is in the heart of the city of Atlanta,
and was purchased many years ago when the city was young, and
the lines of racial prejudice not so tightly drawn. A large crowd
of sorrowing friends witnessed the last sad rites.

The Kansas service had been witnessed by the members of
the Bishops, and Connectional Councils, which met at the same
time. The Church Fathers were represented by Bishops J. A.
Gregg, R. A. Grant, H. Y. Tookes, J. S. Flipper, and W. A.
Fountain. Bishop Tookes was absent. What Bishop Parks had
said about the passing of Bishop W. D. Chappelle of South Carolina might be said of himself. When the Bishops' Council was held
in St. Stephens Church, Fifth and Red Cross Streets, Wilmington,
N.C., in 1926, the noble South Carolinian was fatally ill at his
Columbia home. He never did recover from a throat condition
which developed as he went through the long period of electing
Bishops and General Officers in the Louisville General Conference
of 1924. In those days a Bishop under whose presidency the
election began held the chair until the work was completed.
Bishop Chappelle sent a telegram to the Council stating his in-
ability to be present. Bishop Parks, then the Senior, remarked:
"If he dies, there'll be a great man gone!"

Hence when the General Conference was opened in New
York, on all sides could be heard: "How we miss Bishop Parks!"

That majestic stride, stately form, correct clerical dress, the grunt in his lovely, guttural voice. Parks had vanished from the earthly scene. After devotions the Quadrennial Sermon was delivered by the very popular Bishop Reverdy Cassius Ransom. His very tall, Indian-like form, stringy, gaunt, and lean, filled the pulpit. Immediately there was close attention to his shrill, musical voice:

QUADRENNIAL SERMON

TO THE

THIRTIETH SESSION OF THE GENERAL CONFERENCE

May 6, 1936　A. M. E. Church, New York City

TEXT: Exodus 14:15. "And the Lord said unto Moses, Wherefore criest thou unto me? Speak unto the children of Israel, that they go forward."

THEME: "The Church That Shall Survive"

Delivered by Bishop Reverdy C. Ransom

The Quadrennial Sermon to a General Conference is no ordinary occasion. The speaker is called upon to address the elected delegates of our constituency, representing more than three-fourths of a million souls, scattered throughout all parts of America, the Islands, South America, West and South Africa. In approaching the task, I was immediately confronted with the question, "What should be the scope and character of a sermon to meet the requirements of the occasion?" Our program says a "sermon," not a lecture, not a formal address, but a "sermon." Now, a sermon should always deal not only with the subject of religion, but its emphasis should always be placed upon the revelation of God through Jesus Christ, His Son. The occasion asks not only for a sermon, but for a quadrennial Sermon (that is, one which should look both backward and forward). It should look backward at least to the things through which we have come for the past four years, and these things have naturally derived from the things in the past which make the history of our Church up to this hour. But more than this, it should look forward, facing the future as it relates to our opportunities, our duties, and our tasks. No institution, whether Church or State, can stand still without beating a retreat or moldering to decay. It must go forward. I do not mean that activity is synonymous with progress. There is much activity which is engaged in threshing old straw, or simply beating the air. We should be active by forever enlarging our vision to met the changed moral, social, and spiritual conditions of the succeeding generations in which our lot is cast. We must always have in mind that widening our activities through engaging in work on behalf of schools, hospitals, Y. M. C. A., Temperance, World Peace, and in forms of work for help and mercy, do not constitute a Church. They may and should, grow out of its life and spirit; but the Church is now, as of old, a body of believers however large or small, who are united through saving faith to Jesus Christ as Redeemer, Lord, and Master of their souls.

If the A. M. E. Church as a body is to be simply nothing more than just one of the religious bodies, holding the same standards, choosing the same aims and objectives, and attempting to do the same things as are being done by others, many of whom have far better equipment and resources than have we, there is really nothing unique or distinctive about it; there is no rallying point that stirs our zeal, kindles our enthusiasm, or causes us to be willing to lie upon the altar of self-denial, of suffering, and of pain.

Richard Allen and his followers achieved a place in the high company of men like Martin Luther and John Wesley because they met a turning point in religious history with intelligence, courage, and faith. They were the first to strike a blow for independence, freedom and equality in the church for Negroes in the United States. There was no thought of prestige, power, honor, or reward. They were engaged in the task of achieving for themselves that freedom which belongs to all persons who have been born of God through faith in Jesus Christ. Negro organization, Negro self-confidence, self-respect, self-support, management and control date from that very day.

"The Church that shall survive" is the theme for today, and my text may be found in the fifteenth verse of the fourteenth chapter of the Book of Exodus, the words of which are: "Speak unto the children of Israel that they go forward." While I may not, in what I shall say, directly refer to the text at all, it constitutes the main thread around which all I shall say today shall be woven.

The A.M.E. Church was born ten years after the Liberty Bell on Independence Hall in Philadelphia split its throat in ringing out the tidings of American Independence, which was the same year (1787) that our Federal Constitution was signed. At that time, the spirit of Freedom and Independence filled the very air.

Richard Allen's ears doubtless heard Liberty Bell ring out its defiant challenge. His eyes doubtless saw Washington, Jefferson, Franklin, and Adams passing through the streets of Philadelphia while engaged in the work of building a new nation. Richard Allen was a resident of Philadelphia when the spirit of the times gave prompting, inspiration, and courage for the momentous step he took. The stage for his appearance as an historic figure was perfectly set. The A.M.E. Church was born in due time. God set the stage and chose the actors to play the leading roles in producing its opening scenes.

It created nothing new in the religious doctrine or Church policy but took over bodily what it found in the Methodist Episcopal Church from which it withdrew. What was new about it and the thing that made it distinctive and unique, is the fact that it is the first organized movement by Negroes in the United States of America for Freedom, Independence, and Equality. How Negroes of every rank throughout the nation rallied to its standard through the power it made to manhood, how its different departments were organized, its schools and colleges established, is now a matter of history.

No race since Israel came out of Egypt, has traveled so far or gone as fast within such a brief period of time. Slavery with its degrading influence lies behind us; ignorance and degrading poverty are being overcome by leaps and bounds; self-confidence and self-respect are being achieved under our own leadership, management and control.

As we stand here today, we can judge the vitality, the spirit and the morale of our Church by the manner in which its leadership and following have met and faced the depression during the past four years. We have splendidly stood the test. We are alive and functioning. But this by no means assures our future as we face the dawn of a new age where the social end of our civilization itself is confronted by the most revolutionary changes in history.

Where past and present meet the future begins. We have arrived here today largely through the impact of the inertia of the past that has come from our fathers, rather than any power or foresight we have achieved for ourselves. He who clings to the past without at the same time going forth in the light of the present to meet the future, is bound to a body of death. This is why we now call upon God to meet us in this place as we now stand at the conflux of the past and future, to give us vision, courage and faith to meet the new age — a challenge that cannot be evaded or ignored. God changeth not but the methods by which his servants meet the changing conditions of a changing society must keep pace, change with God's unfolding plans to bring men near to Himself through the procession of ages. We cannot go back to Paul, to Luther and Wesley, to Allen and Turner, to Payne, or even so late a comer as Booker T. Washington. A changed atmosphere envelops us, changed conditions surround us, new problems confront us. In our bewilderment, we cannot call some Witch of Endor to summon our dead Samuels from the grave. We must furnish our own redeemers and prophets to lead us to go forth and walk with the timeless and ageless God. We must fight not only foes without, but the forces of reaction and the obstacles to progress within the borders of our own household of faith.

No institution or custom should be held sacred simply because it is old and comes to us as an inheritance from the past when it can no longer fit into or compete with the life of today. They should be superseded by forms of action and service that will reach our objectives. One steam shovel can accomplish as much in one day as the labor of a hundred men. An automobile can cover more distance in an hour than a horse and buggy can make in one day. Why the backwardness of Africa and China today? They are shackled and bound to the traditions and customs of the past. Why the power and mastery of Japan? The Japanese have overtaken and caught steps with the development and methods of modern civilization and progress.

No man, however respected or revered, however large the contribution of his service in the past, should be permitted to turn back the hands of the clock or to control improved machin-

ery of which he has little knowledge and in the operation of
which he has no skill. We need not overturn our idols or banish
our Gods. We should better put them upon pedestals of honor
that men of a new day may look up to them and be inspired to
meet their problems with equal wisdom, courage, and fortitude.

Doubtless, before many days have passed, within the walls of
this building where we now sit, will be raised the cry: "They
are trying to wreck, or destroy, the Church. Let everything remain as it is. Let us pass minor legislation, elect the necessary officers and adjourn." Certainly, this will be the case if we seriously
attempt the things that cry for attention.

Most of our schools and colleges were established when they
served a real need and furnished almost the only door of opportunity. But today, the state is increasingly serving that need. To
meet present-day standards and requirements in education, we
are not able to support more than two or three colleges and one
theological seminary. I boldly make the statement and defy a
challenge, by declaring that in the work of Religious Education
we occupy almost the lowest rung of the ladder.

We are trying to operate the work of our foreign Missionary
enterprises by methods used forty years ago, but which are un-
suited to present day conditions. The Christian nations of Europe
have torn Africa apart; and today, like ravening wolves, they
snap and snarl, ready to fly at each other's throats over the division of the spoils.

Italy, under the passionate urge of Mussolini, has wantonly
invaded the ancient kingdom of Ethiopia with the avowed purpose of taking it by force to become a colony of Italy. Africa
knows now that the white nations who send her missionaries are
really there to subjugate her people and to exploit the land. Since
we are a kindred people, the problem is not simple as to how our
Church can best heed the cry and answer the call of Africa. Is
our present missionary equal to the task?

Eight years ago, there was much talk on all sides of the union
of the three great bodies of Negro Methodists. It has now become
almost a dead issue. Will this General Conference revive it and
pursue it until it becomes an accomplished fact? Where we are
weak, all of us together might be strong. It is more, then, than
an ecclesiastical and/or religious question. It lies at the very roots
of the economic, political, and social welfare of the millions of

our people. If we cannot achieve denominational union, the day of united action along business, commercial, civic, and political lines seems far distant.

The representatives of the Methodist Episcopal Church, Methodist Episcopal Church South, and the Methodist Protestant Church have finally agreed upon a basis of union of these great Methodist bodies which, when ratified, will make them the largest body of Protestant Christians in the world. The name they have agreed upon is simply the "Methodist Church." Shall we still remain separate and divided over questions of official title and minor details, while the strength of our people continues to be weakened under the weight of burdens too heavy to be borne because of our separation? The A.M.E. Church in this General Conference should lead the way to unite all Negro Methodism so that the Church and race which support it should have the full benefit of the combined strength and influence of its leadership.

As a denomination, we have behind us a hundred and twenty years of organized life. In the beginning, we were simply seeking to achieve freedom and independence. What are our aims and objectives today? Have we a program that appeals to youth? Are our objectives such as will arouse and stir them to volunteer to enlist under our banner? Does anyone court or fear the weight of our influence?

Shall the exploiters and oppressors of our people be challenged here by our united voice? We want work, we want bread, we desire to occupy our proper place in the body of politics. Shall we dedicate ourselves to fight on every front where the battle lines are drawn for freedom and opportunity, and against industrial exploitation? Are we ready to fight for social justice and to throw the influence of our Church against civic, economic, and political exploitation and discrimination? Shall we in the Presidential campaign this year, display enough intelligent political sagacity to take advantage of the main issue on which the two great parties are divided; namely, on the one hand that the policies of the New Deal violate the Constitution which should be upheld as handed down to us, and on the other that the Constitution should be liberalized by judicial interpretation, or otherwise in the interest of the present economic and social condition of the people of this country as a whole?

Let those who would defend the sacredness of the Constitution be faced with the fact that the Fifteenth Amendment is being flagrantly nullified and flouted. Let them be challenged to put a plank in their platform to come to the rescue of our voteless people in this country of American democracy.

Some who hear me speak have, doubtless, already said within themselves, "What has all this to do with religion and the Church?" Amaziah, the priest of Bethel, felt the same way about the prophet Amos, when he told Jeroboam that "Amos hath conspired against thee in the midst of the house of Israel. . . ." All of this because Amos had denounced "the kine of Bashan which oppress the poor, which crush the needy!" "Ye who turn to wormwood and leave off righteousness in the earth. . . ." "Hear this, O ye that swell up the needy, even to make the poor of the land to fall, and that we may buy the poor for silver and needy for a pair of shoes. . . ." "Woe to them that are at ease in Zion . . ." thus saith the Lord God; "take away from me the noise of the songs, but let judgment run down as waters and righteousness as a mighty stream. . . ."

"Seek him that maketh the seven stars and Orion, and turneth the Shadow of Death into morning. The Lord is his Name." While Heaven is our final goal, our chief present concern is with life on this planet and human relations in our present society, to the end that the Kingdom of God may be established among men. I see little hope for the survival of the A.M.E. Church, or any other distinctly religious Negro denomination, if we do not so apply the Gospel of Christ as to make it a vital force in the life of society. While the National Association for the Advancement of Colored People and the Urban League may argue, petition, protest, and appeal, we are clothed with authority to declare, "Thus saith the Lord."

The world has little interest in us or concern about us as to what we do and what we say here. To them, we are just a group of Negroes here legislating and voting on matters that concern our Church. But once let us take up, in the name of a just and righteous God, the conditions that confront our people in this country; and the newspapers and every other public influence will immediately spring to attention. The sharecroppers of the South whose present conditions are but little removed from slavery are among the members of our Church who pay a large part of our Dollar Money from which our denomination derives its support. What have we done, what will we do, to help them to secure industrial and economic justice?

The most flourishing domain of lynchers and mobs is found in communities that are the greatest devotees of religion and the Church. We should turn the searchlight of the Gospel of Jesus Christ upon them and keep it centered there. If he thought about it at all, Senator Borah knew he was running little risk of repudiation at the ballot box by the great bulk of Negro voters when he frankly stated that, if elected President, he would veto a Federal law against lynching. No political party would nominate him or any other man out of sympathy with our people if it knew that every Negro pulpit in the country would thunder against him as from Heaven until its blast resounded throughout the nation.

While the weapons of our welfare are not carnal, we should make them mighty through God to the tearing down of the strongholds of the wicked. The Church, as organized by St. Paul, would not be able to recognize the Church of the Middle Ages. The Church in the days of Martin Luther, of John Calvin, and even the Church of Jonathan Edwards and Lyman Beecher, would not be able to recognize the Church as it stands today. The Church is constantly changing from age to age so far as the expression of its spiritual and outward activities is concerned. What, then, is "the Church that shall survive?" It is evident that in Paul's phrase, it should "become all things to all men," in the sense of being flexible enough to minister to the actual conditions that confront it at a given time. Few things in the Church's history are more pathetic and distressing than the manner in which the Church functioned during the World War, unless it is the manner in which it is behaving in the face of the social, political, economic and spiritual crisis that menaces the civilized world today.

Through accommodating it to the philosophy and organization of our materialistic and commercial age, we look almost in vain for the life and manifestation of the spirit radiating from the altars of religion. While none of the white races either in Europe or America have ever given to the world a religion, they have taken the simple story of the Cross of Christ and so twisted, distorted and submerged it to accommodate their political and economic practices, that most of the beauty and power of God's dear Son has been crushed out of it. The only religion left among the white races today that has vitality is communism, practiced in Russia. Communism, with all its cruelties, actually tries to practice what it preaches. We say this without either approving it or condemning it. We simply state a fact. Let English Christianity in India and South Africa, or American Christianity in the United States, practice what it preaches but for a single day, and its cruel features would be wreathed in smiles, its ruthless spirit would be so transformed as to envelop the world in the folds of a mantle of good will.

How may the Negro Church survive as a thing apart? It is already a thing apart in management and control. But there is small hope for its survival if it continues to copy and follow the programs and practices of fellow Christians.

The Church that shall survive must know neither race, color, nor nationality nor recognize distinctions of wealth, class or station, but only the dignity and sacredness of our common humanity. The Church that shall survive cannot rest secure upon the foundation of wealth or learning or temporal prosperity and power. Like Abraham, it must forever "look for a city which hath foundations . . . whose builder and maker is God." It must "follow peace with all men and holiness without which no man shall see the Lord," and have the abiding witness that God hath delivered it from the power of darkness and translated it into the Kingdom of His dear Son, who is the head of the Church and first born from the dead. We, having been reconciled to God in the body of His flesh through death, shall find that time is only the gate to eternity where our life shall be hid with Christ in God.

The Bishops and ministers that lead this Church must have their call and commission from God, and the genuineness of their credentials and the divine authority with which they are clothed must be witnessed by their power and faith to proclaim and uphold the Gospel message in an evil time. It must be a prophetic Church, not only beholding the Lord and lifting up, while the cherubin cry "Holy, Holy, Holy," round His throne; but while the Church is marching through the wilderness, they must point to the realm of hope and promise that lies just beyond. They must proclaim liberty to the captives — those that are socially, economically, and politically disinherited — with authority of a Divine justice that will not rest until every fetter of injustice and oppression is broken. The Church that shall survive has power to call down consuming fire from heaven upon all the altars of Baal. It is supported by the angels and all the host of heaven led on by the Son of God.

I salute you as both pilgrims and pioneers of the Negro race, in self-confidence, administration and control. I admit we are still marching through the wilderness; we still make our tents among the mountains or in valleys dark and bare where violent men assail us. Only a few have lacked faith and confidence and deserted from our fold while others bade us carry on while they changed their armor for robes of white as they ascended into the skies.

We have been out for four years, some tending the flock of Christ, others following their shepherds. We come from lonely missions and circuits out in far-flung islands, the heat of Africa's burning sun, the snows of Canada and of our Northern Lakes, as well as from more favored paths in towns and cities where we were daily put to the test amid the clash and struggle of the forces of sin against the cause of moral and spiritual salvation.

For just a few days, we shall tarry here in labor and fellowship to return again to the tasks that await us. Some of us have already heard faint strains of celestial music occasionally wafted down to us from paradise. These tell us we are drawing near to the City of God and may not return to behold the Joshuas and Calebs that are preparing in our midst to arise and come to lead our people forth, out of the wilderness, over the mountains and across the Jordan to slay the giants that confront us and to level the Jerichos that are walled up against us. But those of us who have joined the cloud of witnesses on the thrones of light where stand Allen, Quinn, Payne and Turner, Arnett and Grant, with Coppin and Johnson, Brooks and Parks, will give an answering shout from heaven to your triumphant song of victory for the survival of a Church, that through faith in Christ has moved mountains, "subdued Kingdoms, obtained promises and wrought righteousness" — Wherefore God shall not be ashamed to be called our God.

The veteran, Dr. R. S. Jenkins of Texas, was again chosen Secretary, with his assistants. Bishop William Alfred Fountain read the Episcopal Address. A little excitement was caused by an effort on the part of Profesor Ira T. Bryant to sit as a member of the powerful Episcopal Committee, which has the function of assigning Bishops to the various Districts. He had been elected to membership by the Thirteenth Episcopal District delegation of which he was a part. In the meantime he was a General Officer by right of his status as Secretary-Treasurer of the Sunday School Union, a Connectional publishing house. Mr. Bryant did not succeed in his contention. Soon the General Conference entered upon its general routine of business: hearing Departmental reports, fraternal messages, and legislation. Bishop Reverdy C. Ransom, who stood high in the councils of the Democratic party, had sent an invitation to Franklin Delano Roosevelt, President of the United States. He could not be present, but sent his personal representative, Daniel Roper, a member of the Cabinet, who interspersed his address by reading a letter from the distinguished Chief Magistrate:

> *The White House*
> *Washington, D.C.*
> *May 13, 1936*

MY DEAR BISHOP RANSOM:

Please assure the members of the General Conference of the African Methodist Episcopal Church of my sincere appreciation of their invitation to attend one of the sessions of this important gathering. I greatly regret that the pressure of public business here in Washington prevents that. Through you, however, I wish to extend my greeting to the Conference and to the Churches which its delegates represent.

I have read the story of the progress of the African Methodist Episcopal Church from its humble begin-

ning in 1816 to its present position. Moreover, the story
of your progress parallels, in many particulars, the long
strides forward which, in so many lines of endeavor, are
being made by the American Negro community. That,
I think, is as it should be: spiritual progress going forward with an undergirding progress in other fields.

I have been particularly interested in the democracy
of your Church and in its devotion to education. It is significant and in keeping with the Methodist tradition that
one of the first undertakings of your founders was the
establishment of a book concern for the publication of
literature for your membership; and that your schools,
both at home and abroad, have grown to such importance.

With 945 accredited delegates your General Conference is, I believe, the largest delegated Negro assembly
in the world. To judge from the fact that nearly eleven
million dollars have been raised in the last twenty-four
years by dollar contributions, I should say that your financial support is on a sound basis. That too, is a sign of
health.

May I again congratulate you and the members of
your Church both in the United States and on the mission field, upon these accomplishments and express the
confident hope that this General Conference will advance the best interests of your Organization.

                         Very sincerely yours,
                         FRANKLIN D. ROOSEVELT

At the conclusion of the above address Dr. John R. Hawkins,
Financial Secretary, responded on behalf of the General Confer-
ence. Much interest was manifested in the election of Bishops and
General Officers. When the hour arrived, prayer was offered by
Bishop R. A. Grant. It was almost a foregone conclusion that
Drs. R. R. Wright, Jr., Editor of the *Christian Recorder*, and
Edward James Howard, Pastor of Wesley Chapel, Houston, Tex-
as would be elevated. It so happened. Editor Wright was the first
Bishop ever elected in the history of the Church who had an

earned Ph. D. degree. It was in the field of sociology from the University of Pennsylvania. Wright had edited the *Recorder* twenty-eight years. Once he had the additional duties of Manager of the Book Concern. He played an important part in the founding of Jones Tabernacle, which is now a metropolitan church in Philadelphia. When a crisis developed at Wilberforce, he shouldered the responsibility in addition to his editorial duties and succeeded admirably. After his elevation to the Episcopacy, having received 524 votes out of 865 on the third ballot, Howard was added to the bench of Bishops with 619 votes out of 808. He was saddened, however, because his wife, Dallas, was dying in their parsonage home in Houston, Texas.

Howard was a man of unusual spiritual force and power. He was a saintly character. Years ago we had become fast friends. Once he said: "Suppose you and I should be elected by the same General Conference — I to the Bishopric, and you to the Editorship of the Mother *Recorder*." It happened, as we shall later see. Dr. Daniel M. Baxter, who had come to the Management of the Book Concern from the pastorate of Mt. Zion at Jacksonville, Florida, and was a physical wreck from his Herculean task of erecting the Allen Building, 746 South Nineteenth Street, Philadelphia, was re-elected. Shortly thereafter he retired. R. R. Wright, III, was made Deputy Business Manager. The Allen Building was lost. The Publication Board elected G. E. Curry of Florida as Manager. Within a few months he had "saved the Allen Building," and the business moved back to the former site from 1900 So. College. This had been purchased by Bishop Joshua H. Jones when the Allen Building was lost.

In his aspiration to the Episcopacy, Editor Wright made a report to the Publication Board that he would not stand for re-election. The news was brought to the writer by Drs. H. H. Cooper and R. O. Napper of Philadelphia. The former was a member of the Board. When the balloting began, the writer lacked only 33 votes of victory, 229 votes ahead of his nearest rival. On the second ballot it was a landslide. A motion was made by David Norris of Georgia, and seconded by M. D. Potter of Florida, aspirants, that the vote be made unanimous. So Howard's prophecy made in Texas several years before came to pass.

Dr. John Russell Hawkins was re-elected Financial Secretary,

L. L. Berry Secretary of Missions, J. H. Clayborne Editor of the *Southern Christian Recorder*. J. G. Robinson had a serious contender for the *A. M. E. Review* editorship in Dr. Thomas Jefferson Clement of Texas. P. W. Rogers of New Orleans, Louisiana polled over three hundred votes for the Church Extension Department, but the incumbent, Dr. A. J. Wilson, many years the Chairman of the Episcopal Committee, was re-elected. The hand of affliction was upon him. He had suffered a paralytic stroke. His spirit passed at the Church Extension Department, Washington, D. C. April 20, 1937.

The vote for Secretary of the Sunday School Union was E. A. Selby 436, Ira T. Bryant 363, and 10 ballots thrown out. It was almost unbelievable that Bryant, "the stormy petrel," was defeated. When the General Conference Committee on the Sunday School Union reported, a "minority report" by Dr. Womack of Texas was substituted and adopted. This indicated the trend of thinking. For the first time, laymen sat on the Episcopal Committee. The business of the august assembly neared completion. Sunday was a bright, beautiful day. The Consecration sermon was delivered by Bishop David Henry Sims, who had recently returned from four years service in South Africa. The spacious auditorium was packed for the service. His text was St. John 19:5. Theme: "The Man, Christ Jesus." It was an impressive message. I was sitting next to Dr. A. S. Jackson, and E. A. Selby remarked to the former: "That was a superb effort and thought-provoking message." He rejoined: "He can do it!" The General Conference adjourned sine die with the following assignments of Bishops:

Second District	Bishop M. H. Davis
Third District	Bishop Reverdy C. Ransom
Fourth District	Bishop John A. Gregg, who filled the unexpired term of Bishop H. B. Parks
Fifth District	Bishop Noah W. Williams
Sixth District	Bishop W. A. Fountain, Sr.
Seventh District	Bishop W. D. Johnson
Eighth District	Bishop S. L. Greene
Ninth District	Bishop D. H. Sims
Tenth District	Bishop G. B. Young

Eleventh District	Bishop R. A. Grant
Twelfth District	Bishop H. Y. Tookes
Thirteenth District	Bishop J. S. Flipper
Fourteenth District	Bishop E. J. Howard
Fifteenth District	Bishop R. R. Wright, Jr.

Shortly after the adjournment of the General Conference the Church was shocked to learn of the demise of Bishop W. D. Johnson, Plains, Georgia, Secretary of the Council of Bishops. He was known as "the commoner." He lived the simple life, and died among his people at home. All the Bishops and General Officers were at his funeral. The death of Bishop Johnson necessitated a change in the episcopal assignments to the extent that Bishop Flipper went to the Seventh District. The Kentucky and West Kentucky Conferences of the Thirteenth District were given to Bishop Reverdy C. Ransom. The East Tennessee, Tennessee, and West Tennessee Conferences of the Thirteenth District were given to Bishop E. J. Howard.

Among the stalwart leaders of the Church who have passed to their eternal reward since the rise of the General Conference are Drs. J. H. Hughes, chairman of the Texas Delegation, M. A. Hollins of South Carolina, "Jeff" Williams, Pastor of Bethel at Eighth and Towne Streets, Los Angeles, and James S. Hatcher, preacher-musician, and author of *I cannot drift.*

Two things occurred in the General Conference which have had repercussions. According to the Journal: "The report of the Committee on Revision changed the composition of the General Conference, giving to each Annual Conference three ministerial and three lay members. After much caviling pro and con upon the report, Bishop Flipper announced that the part of the report of the Committee on the composition of the General Conference was out of order and unconstitutional as it carried no repealing act to the now established constitutional law. The report was adopted by motion of the Reverends W. T. Johnson, and G. T. Sims."[1]

The law was designed to reduce the size of the General Conference and make it more wieldly. There was doubt in the minds

1. *General Conference Minutes, 1936,* 14; *Book of Discipline, 1936-1940,* 206.

of the Compilation Committee, when it met at the Book Concern, Philadelphia, whether the law was actually passed. Unfortunately the Journal of the General Conference never was printed.

The delegates faced homeward, many never to meet again. The closing brought a note of sadness. Well did they know that before another such gathering many of their comrades in the cause would answer their final roll call. But they remembered Him who had said: "Lo, I am with you always, even unto the end of the world." I went immediately to Philadelphia, and began my duties as Editor of the *Christian Recorder*.

CHAPTER XIII

Radicalism and Reform

I have come to bring fire down to the earth, and how I
wish it were already kindled. — LUKE 12:49

An idea is irresistible. — VICTOR HUGO

A full decade had passed since World War I, when the General Conference of 1928 met in the 8th Illinois Armory, Thirty-
fifth and Vernon Streets, Chicago. The writer was a student in the
University of Chicago on a La Verne Noyes Scholarship, and a
beneficiary of the Class of Bishops of 1908. He was a member of
the General Conference, and had been since the Louisville meeting.

The war, the greatest in the history of the world up to that
time, had as its popular slogan: "Fighting to make the world safe
for democracy." It was coined by the late war President, Woodrow Wilson. In reality it was a colossal struggle to make the
world safe for the investments of international bankers, cartels,
and foreign trade. Germany, under the leadership of Kaiser Wil-
helm, sought to realize the ancient Bismarckian dream of a *Mittel
Europa*, a Berlin-to-Bagdad railway, cut the British lifeline in the
Mediterranean, exploit the raw materials of Africa, and gain access
to India through the Suez Canal. Millions of men and treasure
were sacrificed, and a tremendous war debt piled up which will
never be paid. In the meantime the popular imagination of the
common people and oppressed minority groups was fired. The
Church felt the surging tide of resentment against autarchic rule.

During the Quadrennium of 1924-28 there was a mounting crescendo of criticism against the use of "the episcopal big stick,"
and "burdensome assessments." There was a corresponding belief
that certain Bishops had served too long on their respective Districts, and should be removed. One had been on a District twenty
years, and another sixteen. "Little episcopal principalities" had
been built up, and the common expression was "My District." The

spirit of freedom in the ministerial ranks was crushed. In some instances a brother minister was not permitted to make a motion unless he first told the Presiding Bishop in private what it was. There was the tragic picture of a minister who had for some reason gotten on the wrong side of a Bishop, rose to ask pardon. The Bishop requested him to apologize upon his knees. "Get down on yours knees, my brother. Get down on your knees!" Another said to an Annual Conference with reference to appointments: "If you can't plow that mule, bring me the bridle." Again: "I've got the biscuits!" "There is nothing beyond the Episcopacy." "You can't do anything to a Bishop. Once a Bishop, always a Bishop." "You needn't think you're too big to be removed!" The Episcopacy had reached untenable heights. A challenging pamphlet came out of Tennessee under the caption: "Reformation or Revolution." It bore the signatures of the Reverends Elmer Reid, G. L. Jackson, and M. E. Jackson.

This was leading up to the General Conference of 1928. In February, the Council of Bishops met at St. John Church, 712 No. 15th St., Birmingham, Ala., Dr. H. N. Newsome, Pastor. Dr. H. D. Canady of Atlanta delivered the sermon to the Connectional Council, but Bishop Reverdy C. Ransom stirred the Church with his message representing his colleagues. Text: 1 Timothy 3:15, "The Church of the living God, pillar and ground of the truth." He dealt specifically with problems of the Church, with particular emphasis upon "burdensome assessments" for education. "The clock is wound up so tight, that if you give it just one more turn, something will snap." It was electrical and joyfully received by the rank and file, but he was censured roundly by his peers. Bishop Hurst of South Carolina was incensed and indignant. But the seeds of reformation had been sown. The irresistible idea was destined to bear an abundant harvest.

After the service a few serious-minded men went across the street in front of the church, and sat together in a house. There they planned definite action for the forthcoming General Conference, to remove the Bishops and get relief for the pastors and people. Now for the first time their names are mentioned for posterity: The Reverends D. Ormonde Walker, E. A. Adams, George A. Singleton, John Harmon, A. D. Avery, W. T. Pope, S. H. V. Gumbs, and J. W. McDade. The last four have closed their ministerial labors and gone to receive their reward. They went up from Georgia, North Carolina, Arkansas, New York, and Texas. Dr. Walker is a Bishop, Adams, Secretary of Education, and the writer is striving to be a "good minister of Jesus Christ."

The group was in agreement that the solution to the pressing problem lay largely in removing the Bishops and "breaking their strangle hold upon the Districts." The question was how it could be done. Great strategy was required. This was finally worked out by Dr. C. P. Cole, a veteran Pastor in the New York Conference. It was done in the parsonage of St. James, Cleveland, Dr. D. O. Walker, Pastor. It was then on 85th Street, near Cedar. A resolution was proposed which would be read in the General Conference. The trick was to obtain a secret vote by ballot. In that way the men would be emancipated from the watchful eyes of the Bishops upon the platform. The next problem was to make the move on a day when a Presiding Officer favorable to the resolution was in the chair. It was agreed that Bishop John Albert Johnson would be the proper President. He was beloved and respected by all. He was an excellent parliamentarian, and could handle the General Conference without a gavel. When the delegates had assembled in Chicago, Walker and I went around to 5131 South Michigan Boulevard to the residence of Dr. H. Y. Tookes, the Pastor of Bethel, to confer with Bishop Johnson. He and Bishop A. L Gaines were domiciled there. We went into a closed session with him and talked until the wee hours of the morning when he was to preside trying to convince him that the measure could be put through. He repeatedly said that it could not be done. Finally near break of day he came down to the front door with us, and while standing in the doorway, hands behind his back, said: "Gentlemen, I will do it!" We shook hands and left. It was a great night. With a wildly beating heart I walked back along the streets and finally made my way back to the Armory. There was little rest that night.

The General Conference was opened by Bishop Flipper of Georgia, and after the usual devotions and the reading of the Journal of the previous day's session, Bishop Johnson took the chair. In the meantime Walker found me, and had a sheet of white paper in his hands. He said: "George, have this typed, and do not let it get out of your sight or possession." I found Mrs. Marie Spencer-Bard, Secretary to Dr. S. S. Morris of the A. C. E. League Department, and she willingly typed it. I did not permit her to touch it, but read to her while she typed the resolution. When she had finished, I took the document from the machine with my hands, found D. O. Walker, and gave it to him. He in turn gave it to Dr. Gomez of Detroit, the author.

We knew exactly what was going to happen. It had been agreed that the resolution was to be read by Dr. Gomez. The motion to adopt was to be seconded by Dr. J. W. Walker of North Carolina. Dr. Tookes would make an unreadiness point, and a motion that the resolution be tabled "by secret ballot." This would confuse the opposition, and in the meantime cause the voting to be by ballot. Shortly after the regular opening, several men were on the floor trying to get the attention of the Chair. Bishop Johnson in a clear voice said: "The Chair recognizes Dr. Joseph Gomez of Detroit." He came to the stand with the resolution in his hands. Only a few men knew what was in the offing. He began to read in a strong, clear voice. There was silence, and after a while consternation on the platform among the Bishops; he read on:

The Methodist Church, born of the great Evangelical Revival in England, has affected the development of the world in a most definite and salutary way. With utter self-effacement, and with glad abandon have its ministers walked the hot and parched soil of distant Africa, climbed the steeps of far-off India, and chanted ancient dirges set to new words, so that the message of the Christ may be carried to the remotest corner of the globe.

Through the zeal for the salvation of men, worthy pioneers brought the glad tidings to America, and Methodism became at once the star of hope, and the city of refuge to all oppressed. Richard Allen was among those who felt the impact of this new message of life, and so imbued was he with its spirit, that when those responsible for its preservation would put unholy members on this altar of ancient faith, conceived in, and dedicated to Liberty, he at once snatched the falling standard from enfeebled hands, and became the real defender of the Faith. This, then, is the genius of African Methodism. Out of the travail of days of bitter warfare for Liberty's sake she has come. The African Methodist Episcopal Church is the result of the most vigorous and manly protest against injustice, intolerance, and tyranny. And, anything said to the contrary notwithstanding, the pages of our history show that along this path as a Church we have come through the years; that we have accepted every challenge unafraid; and that the leaders have had the courage and vision to face every crisis and to stamp out any practice inimical to the growth and perpetuity of our Bethel.

Today we face as of old, a great challenge. The time has come for us as a Church to decentralize the Districts, and connectionalize the Church. This will, in a large measure, be done by a change in our present form of episcopal supervision. Be it Therefore

Resolved: That this General Conference here assembled, do hereby instruct the Episcopal Committee to change all Bishops who have served for two or more Quadrenniums on a District. Be it further

Resolved: That this resolution be adopted by a secret ballot.

By THE REVEREND JOSEPH GOMEZ
Fifteenth Episcopal District

The effect was electrical. The scene cannot be described. Hundreds of delegates were on their feet at once. The platform was astir. The status quo Bishops were caught completely off guard. Bishop Johnson: "The Chair recognizes Dr. J. W. Walker of North Carolina." He was a portly man, slightly round-shouldered, dark-brown-skinned, clean shaven, with a shrill, keen voice. It rang out: "Mr. Chairman, I second the motion." Then pandemonium did break loose for fair. There was a lot of moving about, talking in little groups and gesticulating. An attempt was made to intimidate the Presiding Officer from the platform, but he stood like Athanasius at Nicea — "a rock amidst a stormy sea." The Chairman called for unreadiness. Several persons were on the floor with hands directed toward him. He said: "The Chair recognizes Dr. H. Y. Tookes of Chicago." He came forward to the stand and said: "Mr. Chairman, I move that the resolution be tabled by a secret ballot." There was so much noise that many did not hear the "by ballot." The platform contended that he did not say by ballot. Bishop Johnson said: "Mr. Tookes is of age, let him come forward and repeat what he said." Tookes returned to the stand. Bishop Johnson said: "Mr. Tookes, did you not say, 'by secret ballot'?" He replied: "Yes." More noise, and milling about. Someone on the platform attempted to intimidate the Presiding Officer. He said: "You can't scare me. There is nothing before the house but to vote on tabling the resolution. If you want it, vote 'No'; if you do not want it, then vote 'Yes.' Prepare your ballots." The vote was taken; 569 "No," and 263 "Yes." The resolution was then before the house for disposition. At this point Bishop Flipper unconsciously helped the passage when he remarked: "We have submitted the assignment of the Bishops to the Episcopal Committee as a matter of convenience, and the Conference has no right to instruct the Episcopal Committee, in reference to the assignment of a Bishop. If you do, I tell you, the Bishops will assign themselves at this General Conference." The original motion was put and was carried 641 to remove, against 263.

Reverend V. C. Monk, militant Editor of the *New Era,* a Philadelphia tabloid, and others suddenly appeared with large placards and banners which read: "Emancipation Day has Come," "Move them all." For a brief moment the sign painters did a lucrative business. The hour was exciting. Such a move had never been made in the history of the Church. Bishop Johnson was the hero.

Most of the participants in the moving drama have passed from the earthly scene: Bishops John Albert Johnson, Vernon, Carey, Brooks, W. D. Johnson, Flipper, Parks, Heard, Hurst, Jones, Gaines. Bishops Fountain, Ransom, and Gregg survive. Of the planning group, Drs. Sims, Tookes, Walker, and Gomez were elected Bishops. Adams is Secretary of Education. Singleton served as Dean of Theology at Morris Brown, Editor of the *Christian Recorder* for two terms of four years each, Dean of Theology at Shorter College, teacher in Allen University, and President of Paul Quinn College.

Bishop Johnson was "punished" by being sent to Kentucky, and Bishop Ransom by being sent to Louisiana. After the close of the General Conference, I went over to tell Bishop Johnson good-bye. The scene was in the same doorway where he, Walker, and I had our early morning conversation the day when the Bishops were removed. I sought to console him and said that we would see that ultimate justice was done him. He said: "Singleton, I have learned to go wherever the Church sends me." It was the last sight I had of the distinguished Bishop. Shortly afterwards I read of his death. I thought of his favorite lines from "Crossing the Bar":

> I hope to meet my Pilot face to face,
> When I have crossed the bar.

Good Bishop Hurst was sent to South Carolina, and when I was ready to return to my teaching position, I had none. An offer to work in another institution did not materialize because of his influence. But that is the price one has to pay for sponsoring progressive programs. The General Conference enacted legislation which granted layman equal representation. It was advocated and offered by Bishop Flipper and Professor Ira T. Bryant.

The wave of radicalism and reform moved steadily forward, and Bryant was re-elected in spite of a strong episcopal coalition against him. Bryant was the embodiment of "radicalism" to the old conservatives. He was the idol of the youthful progressives, many of the ministers and most of the laymen. An effort to defeat him four years previously was abortive, and Bishop Chappelle literally sacrificed his life in guaranteeing his re-election. He remained in the chair several days through the entire election of Bishops and General Officers. The rule was then that the Chairman who began the election must see it through to the conclusion.

Reforms never move backwards. No one could have foreseen in that General Conference that four years hence the General Conference of 1932 at Cleveland would try three Bishops, find two of them guilty, and suspend two. But it did. Bishop W. T. Vernon was set aside for eight years, and Bishop Joshua Jones for four. The former served out his period of suspension, but the General Conference at Detroit did not restore him, for some reason. A few years after, he died one day, and his wife the next.

She was the daughter of Bishop J. C. Embry. Time has proven that Bishop Jones was not guilty. He was a great inspirational leader, but careless with his accounts. Shorter Hall at Wilberforce will ever remain as a monument to his sacrificial labors. Bishop Wm. D. Johnson made an appeal to the house, and was exonerated.

CHAPTER XIV

Years of Trial

To him that overcometh will I give to eat of the tree of
life, which is in the midst of the paradise of God.
—THE APOCALYPSE 2:7

Heaven is not reached at a single bound;
But we build the ladder by which we rise
From the lowly earth to the vaulted skies,
And we mount to the summit, round by round.
— HOLLAND

The General Conference took high ground when it voted to
merge the two Connectional Missionary Societies. The Women's
Mite Missionary was organized in 1844, and Dr. John M. Brown,
a product of Oberlin, was the first Secretary. The Women's Home
and Foreign Missionary was organized in 1892 at Selma, Alabama,
by Bishop H. M. Turner. The General Conference was motivated
by a desire to economize, and break down sectionalism, which was
a grave threat to the unity of the Church. The *Christian Recorder*
was a strong proponent of the movement. Many were the stand-
patters led by Bishop Parks, and Christine S. Smith, President of
the Mites. Lucy Medorah Hughes of Cameron, Texas was President of the Home and Foreign group. She was in favor of the
merger. The Mites had as their field, West Africa and the Islands.
The Home and Foreign helped to support the work in South
Africa. The Bishops elected were Noah Williams, Pastor of St.
Paul, St. Louis; H. Y. Tookes, a Presiding Elder in Florida, who
had caught the eye of the Church while serving as Pastor of
Bethel, Chicago, and D. H. Sims, President of Allen University,
Columbia, S.C.

The reform movement was destined to sweep through the next
General Conference of 1936. From 1908 the Church had been
dominated by three strong laymen: John Hawkins, Ira Bryant,

170

and A. S. Jackson. By 1936 they had broken, and Bryant was left standing alone. For a long time he had been a stormy petrel. He edited and published from the Sunday School Union *The Young Allenite*. He was a caustic writer, a relentless foe whose pen was dipped in vitriol. His chief objects of attack were the Bishops. His powerful episcopal friend, Bishop W. D. Chappelle, had long since passed. His friends among the Bishops were J. S. Flipper, R. C. Ransom, and H. Y. Tookes. Bryant in the meantime advocated better care for retired ministers, their widows, and orphans. He championed the cause of the laymen. His following was large. Whenever he obtained the floor, there was instantaneous silence and attention. On the outside there was always a small group around him. He committed a fatal blunder when he published an attack in the Sunday School Quarterlies. This caused some of his most ardent supporters to leave him. Such leaders as Drs. J. E. Beard of South Carolina, J. H. Smith, and C. W. Abington of Texas wrote telling articles against him. So when Bryant came up for re-election the tide was definitely turned. A remark attributed to him reflected upon the southern delegates. It was resented in a resolution read by Dr. W. R. Wilkes, Pastor of Allen Temple, Atlanta. A minority report was read by P. E. Womack of Texas. It was adopted, and had lethal effect. At the same time Professor E. A. Selby of the State Normal School at Huntsville, Alabama, was the rallying point for Bryant's opponents. The defeat of Bryant was almost unbelievable. George A. Singleton was elected Editor of the *Christian Recorder*, from the pastorate of St. Paul, Lexington, Kentucky. A lasting friendship was born with Selby, Thomas Jefferson Clement of Texas, and George Wilbur Baber of Detroit.

The night before the election Bishop Tookes held a meeting which lasted from about ten o'clock until daybreak next morning. Hundreds of delegates were present and he would not permit a single one to leave. It turned out to be a continuous Prayer Meeting and Love Feast. Spiritual fervor ran high. Just before daybreak Bishop Tookes made an impassioned speech and remarked: "Everybody who is going to be elected to anything in this General Conference is in this room now." When we adjourned, J. G. Robinson and I walked together down Seventh Avenue to our hotel, the Woodside. The sun was rising. When the General Conference was convened and the election begun, Drs. Wright and Howard were chosen Bishops. They had been in the all-night meeting. I ran to the platform, put my hand upon Bishop Tookes' shoulder, and said: "Bishop, do you see what is happening? It is the fulfillment of your prophecy." He said, as he patted my hand: "Just wait; just wait." Then came the elections of Singleton, Robinson, Morris, Selby. Bishop Tookes frequently remarked thereafter that his good friend, Ira T. Bryant, was absent that night of prophecy. I went to the platform and spoke to Bishop W. D. Johnson, my good friend. He said: "Now you have got what you want. Go on, and give us a good paper."

Bryant was so popular at the time that it was the consensus of many, he would have been more powerful in defeat had he acknowledged it and promised to return. Perhaps the unusual thing might have happened — an attempt to have the election reconsidered. Instead he girded himself for battle, which solidified the opposition. The Church was sharply divided and lines closely drawn. The office, property and equipment were not turned over to Mr. Selby. Friends through the years parted company. There was much bitterness. The newly created Department of Christian Education was forced to take quarters in the Allen Building, Philadelphia. There the Sunday school literature was published. Selby was the Manager, Morris headed the Young People's work, and Abington was Editor of Religious Literature and of the *Journal of Religion*. But several Sunday school Superintendents and Sunday schools continued to purchase supplies from Bryant. Selby resorted to the courts. A Legal Redress Committee was appointed to direct the suit brought by Drs. Harvey E. Walden and David Eugene Rice, and Mr. James Dorsey of Baltimore. They sued as members of the Corporation of the African M. E. Church.

The Legal Redress Committee was composed of Bishops W. A. Fountain, M. H. Davis, D. H. Sims, and E. J. Howard; Dr. Vince M. Townsend; Prof. John R. Hawkins, and E. A. Selby. Upon the death of Hawkins, Dr. A. S. Jackson was placed on the committee. The unofficial headquarters while attending trials at Nashville was the residence of Dr. Morris at 1400 Hawkins Street. In his home and on his front lawn plans were made for future advances whenever the Church received a setback in the courts.

"The Morris House" was the place of retreat. Once Judge Elmer Davies made it plain that he was not ruling on the matter of an accounting "at this time." Church counsel had definitely shown that there had been a collusion and admixture of the Sunday School Union accounts, and those of a private nature. Later a Master was named by the Court. In the meantime an appeal was taken to the Federal Court in Cincinnati, where three judges heard the appeal. A decision was handed down in favor of the Church. A suit was then entered in the State Court of Tennessee in an effort to break the old Sunday School Union charter. This required considerable time. A suit was begun to prevent the defendant from using the name of the A. M. E. Church on his building and literature. The building was across the street, corner Eighth and Lea Avenue, from the property owned by the Church.

The man who had charge of the accounting was called to service in World War II. He was away several years and the case was held up. When hostilities ceased, he returned to Nashville, completed his work, and submitted his report to the Court. The defendant was required to pay the connection $97,085.11 plus interest. Several pieces of property were awarded to the Church in addition.[1] Thus after thirteen years, from 1936 to 1949, the Church finally won. The Sunday School Union returned to the Financial Department $20,000 which had been posted as a bond.

In connection with this litigation the names of Bishop E. J. Howard, John R. Hawkins, and Dr. W. A. Lewis should never be forgotten. They died before the victory. A. L. Pinkston, C. W. Abington, S. S. Morris, and F. D. Coleman, Sr. are yet in the flesh. The home of Mrs. Rethea Beck was ever open. Hers was next door to that of "The Morris House." She and her brilliant physician husband are members of the Baptist Church, and came of African Methodist stock in Arkansas. Selby has fully justified the confidence reposed in him by the Church. The Sunday School Union is a flourishing business. Selby is a master printer, an alumnus of Hampton in Virginia.

The 1936 General Conference exonerated Bishop D. H. Sims, and four years later he came to Detroit as Bishop of the Ninth

---

1. U. S. Circuit Court of Appeals for the Sixth District, Vols. I, II, No. 8841, Judgment 739, Eg. *vs.* Ira Bryant; *The Christian Recorder,* June 16, 1949.

Episcopal District, and in charge of the First. His leadership was unquestioned and incomparable. It was unique in the long history of the Church. His will was supreme, his personality magnetic. By a peculiar turn of fate, by the time he reached the Philadelphia General Conference four years later a new power had appeared. It was a coalition of Bishops D. Ward Nichols and G. E. Curry, whose elections he had engineered at Detroit. Sims sat upon the platform shorn of his power, and weak. The high points in this General Conference were the addresses by Mrs. Eleanor Roosevelt, wife of President Franklin Delano Roosevelt, Dr. E. Stanley Jones, world-famous missionary to India and China, and the able response by Attorney Sadie Alexander, delegate from Philadelphia. The reform spirit was in evidence when the General Conference set up the Pension Department, and elected Dr. D. L. Witherspoon as the Secretary-Treasurer. He had advocated it in the face of opposition, even from the bench. He was ably assisted by Bishop Nichols. The Department is now a blessing to the Church. Witherspoon did not live to meet the ensuing General Conference. When Dr. Baber was elected a Bishop, and Witherspoon to the Pension Department, they were domiciled at 5828 Race Street, Philadelphia, in the home of the writer. The Secretary of Finance, Dr. A. S. Jackson, was also there.

In Europe, Adolf Hitler was on the warpath. He was leading Germany again in an effort to realize the dream of Bismarck to dominate the world. World War II had broken in fury beyond any power of description. The civilization of the globe was threatened. The earth was converted into a battlefield. The ideal of democracy was intensified. Kings lost their thrones. The sun of empire was set. Proud England was humbled. The doctrine of white supremacy received a severe jolt, and a mortal wound. The Church was confronted with serious disaffection within the episcopal ranks. Bishop G. E. Curry was experiencing difficulties in the Twelfth District, over which he was presiding. Charges were preferred against him. He was tried in Vernon Chapel, Tulsa, March 29, 1946, and found guilty. The trial judge was Bishop Reverdy C. Ransom. Fred A. Hughes, Editor of the *Western Christian Recorder* was the Bailiff. The Chairman of the Jury was Bishop Noah W. Williams. During the suspension, Bishop J. H. Clayborne was given the supervision of Oklahoma, and Bishop

G. W. Baber was to supervise Arkansas. Bishop Sims was having his problems in the First District, particularly in New York. The Council of Bishops met in Kansas City, Kansas, and heard the case. It was agreed that he would have R. R. Wright as Associate Bishop over New York. Later Sims repudiated this action, and a long, bitter series of lawsuits ensued. There was much acrimony. The members of the District, ministerial and lay, were divided. A line of cleavage ran throughout the Connection. Sims' popularity and brilliance brought many to his side. When he refused to abide by the decision of his colleagues the resort was civil action.

There was a meeting at the Missionary Department in New York, but to no avail. The first Church Court was set for Bridge Street Church, at Jefferson and Stuyvesant, Brooklyn. A crowd assembled. With Sims were Bishops Fountain, Davis, and Curry. There was confusion. Pandemonium broke loose. Law officers were called but refused to interfere. The trial was adjourned to meet at Bethel Tabernacle, on Schenectady Avenue. There a restraining order was read by Attorney W. A. Gay. The Church was also restrained at Allen Temple, Cincinnati. The Bishops then made a grave decision, since the machinery of the Church was stalled. They would call an Extra Session of the General Conference, according to law. Two-thirds of the Annual Conferences would have to vote their approval. The time and place would be designated. The committee was composed of Bishops S. L. Greene, R. R. Wright, G. W. Baber, and J. H. Clayborne. They met in the Wright School of Religion Building, Memphis, second floor upstairs front, Beale Street. There was anxiety all over the Church. Many feared for the future of the denomination. There was also a determination to set the "Ecclesiastical House in order."

In response to the call, over a thousand delegates assembled at Little Rock on November 22, 1946 in the Robinson Auditorium. Bethel at 9th and Broadway was the entertaining church, and Dr. G. Wayman Blakely the host Pastor. An attempt was made by Sims' attorneys to get another restraining order to prevent the meeting of the General Conference. The case was heard by Federal Judge T. C. Trimble. The Church was represented by Attorneys Fred A. Isgrig, J. A. Hibler, J. R. Booker, and the Reverend John Adams. V. M. Townsend was an expert in Church

Law. The defendant was represented by Attorneys Austin Norris and W. A. Gay of Philadelphia. The Court suggested that both sides agree to go forward in peace and hold the General Conference. It was agreed to.

The next day the first Extra Session of a General Conference in the long history of Methodism was convened in the John T. Robinson Memorial Auditorium, Markham and Broadway. The delegates were solemn and serious. The first contest came over the election of a Secretary. Dr. G. T. Sims, Secretary of the General Conference, was defeated by Russell Brown, Pastor of St. Paul, St. Louis. The opening address was delivered by Bishop Reverdy C. Ransom. He did not think that he would have lived to see such a day. The Church had come to "Judgment." Not a single point of order was raised. Everything was orderly. No word of complaint was heard about the entertainment or anything. Dr. O. Sherman, Chairman of the Judiciary Committee called for Bishop Sims over the public address system, but he failed to appear. The committee then proceeded according to law and recommended his expulsion from the Episcopacy. A strange thing happened. Bishop G. E. Curry had served out his suspension, but had become involved in the interim of his trial in Oklahoma and the Extra Session in the worsening affairs of the First Episcopal District. He was recommended for expulsion. Bishop M. H. Davis was suspended, and Bishop W. A. Fountain was required to make an apology. He complied. The Episcopal Committee, chairmaned by Dr. H. T. Primm, Pastor of Union Bethel, New Orleans, Louisiana, Mrs. Alma Polk, of Pittsburgh, Secretary, assigned Bishop Baber to supervise the Baltimore Annual Conference, and Bishop Clayborne to take charge of the Virginia, North Carolina, and Western North Carolina Annual Conferences. The law was revised, and *provided for the election of a President of the Council of Bishops, and the removal of a Bishop from a District by a majority vote of the Bishops instead of two-thirds.*

One of the high points of the Extra Session was the visit and address of Judge Fred A. Isgrig, chief counsel for the Church. The response on behalf of the General Conference was made by the eloquent Bishop Reverdy Cassius Ransom of Wilberforce, Ohio. The address was stenographically reported by the Reverend Dr. S. E. Churchstone Lord, Official General Conference Amenuensis:

Speaking of conditions of appreciation as responding to life, there are two things I want to say. First, I want to say that ever since I have been in this building, I have thought of the late Senator Joseph T. Robinson many times because this building is a memorial to him. In the National Democratic Campaign Committee of 1932, the handful of colored men who had left the Republican party to join the Democrats, wanted to have some assurance of consideration in the matter of Federal appointments. We wanted to be assured that the Democratic party leader in the Senate would not be opposed to the confirmation of Negroes. A remark was made by a certain gentleman that even if we got to the Senate, some of the Democrats would try to prevent our taking seats. It was then that Robinson said: "I will be the one to take you by the arm and march down the aisle. You escort the Negro down the aisle of the Senate for confirmation." We salute the preceding speaker in like manner.

The second thing I want to say is that we appreciate our relation to our nation's formation and growth. I mean the parallel history of the African Methodist Episcopal Church, and the United States of America. In 1787, when the Constitution was being framed in Philadelphia, we were five or six blocks away on Sixth and Lombard, organizing the African Methodist Episcopal Church. As the first lines of the bill proclaiming independence for the United Colonies from Great Britain were struck off, we too, floated our flag six blocks away for manhood, and independence to the establishment of a Church to the glory of God.

However, our great nation split, North against South, killing millions of our citizens . . . but we have continued one Church for more than one hundred and fifty years. Yes, the other denominations have divided — the Methodist Episcopal Church split wide open into the Methodist Church North, and the Methodist Church South. The Presbyterian Church split; also the Baptist Convention. But during all that period of one hundred and fifty years we have remained solid while other leaders in Church, and State, and armed forces have fought and divided, and responded to the great General, and Commander of the universe.

The popular call is a long way from the humble beginning of this great Church, but it is a call that has been answered by solidarity of purpose of more than one hundred and fifty years; providing a way to minister to Negro congregations, and all people as well for heaven-born opportunity for achievement. And although we are the oldest organization in this country, owned and controlled by Negroes, we too, like others, have been assailed by foes from within and without, but they could not hit upon the things that would actually be able to split us. Going down the lines of the ministry of the past up to the present, we call out people together who own the Church, who keep it up, control it, pray for it — and then together, under God, we adjust our differences as best we can in kindness and brotherly love, remembering as always that God is keeping watch over His own. But in the past two years the forces of evil seemed to have actually been able to hit upon an idea that would be able to split us. That idea was *division* in the head of the Church. "A house divided against itself cannot stand."

I always thought that I would never go to judgment until Gabriel blows his horn, but THIS IS JUDGMENT DAY! (*Loud applause.*) And the decrees of the past day, and today's session of this august body, which may be the greatest in history, prove that the foes within and without can't budge our Church from its platform of right and righteousness. (*More applause.*)

These Americans of African descent are so much like the Children of Israel. Both went through the wilderness, and desert land, guided by the Heavenly Father, and kept by His grace through the ages. God makes no mistakes. HE KNOWS WHY WE ARE HERE. We do not have to act like white folks. They are doing their job, and we are doing ours! (*Loud applause.*) They have industrialized the world as of the present; gone into various parts of the sea, and of the air, achieving wonders everywhere.

Let them go down the river, or go up — that is not our job. We Americans of African descent are the Gulf Stream of this American nation. Were it not for the warmth of the Gulf Stream flowing near our land we would be frozen more or less. So we are the spiritual Gulf Stream, and should we shirk our task because the storms of the world are fraught with death and destruction? We flow along and warm the hearts of this country, and of Great Britain, and Africa, and all great powers through the centuries; just as the Gulf Stream has warmed the continents for more than three million years, coming from the burning sands of the desert, coming from the warmest rays of the sun — we too, came from the jungles of Africa across the seas, reached out in the dense darkness, and touched the right hand of God, and through that guidance, walked with God amidst the American people down to this very hour — over a split nation of race hatred, world wars; perhaps more to come. But it is for us to be the spiritual Gulf Stream in every wilderness, grasping the opportunity to spread the productive blood of the Divine in the humble stations of life: house servants, factory workers, porters on the trains — all spread it like the Gulf Stream floats. In every life, let it flow. "Swing low, sweet chariot," "Steal away to Jesus," "Study war no more," . . . until the dusty, thirsty land is satisfied . . . warming the heart and soul of the life of America . . . until black hands and white hands are clasped in brotherhood under the cross of our blest Redeemer, under the flag of brotherly love.

The applause was loud and sustained. The effect was electrical.

A serious-minded group met each night before, and planned their work for the following day. D. Ormonde Walker was agreed upon as "Floor leader." He was superb, and was in the eye of the Church for episcopal honors. On the floor he was supported by the "key men" all over the house. Finally there came adjournment, and the delegates went to their several homes in distant parts of the country. They had made history.

But Sims continued litigation in the civil courts of Pennsylvania and New York. An attempt was made to show that the Extra Session of the General Conference was illegally called and constituted. Bishop S. L. Greene had been sent to preside over the Philadelphia and Delaware Conferences. Bishop Wright already had the New York and Bermuda Conferences. Both he and Bishop Greene were compelled to seek legal help for freedom to function, backed by the authority of the Church. In Philadelphia the Church was represented by the law firm of Raymond Pace Alexander and Sadie Alexander, Montgomery McCracken, Walker and Rhoades, and C. Russell Phillips. The defendant was represented by Walter A. Gay, Austin Norris, and others — all brilliant lawyers.

The litigation was long-drawn-out. The Church was inspired and encouraged by a favorable decision in New York, spearheaded by Bishop Wright, whose attorney was Mr. Lieberman.[2] The Philadelphia case was heard by Federal Judge George A. Welsh. From the outset it was apparent that the current was against the Church. Finally Attorney Raymond Alexander made a plea of prejudice, but the Judge refused to disqualify himself. From that point Alexander did not take an active part in the pleading. Mr. Phillips came forward in his stead. The lines were so taut that supporters of the Church sat on one side of the courtroom, and the defense group on another. With Bishop Greene were Bishops Ransom, Wright, Gregg, Williams, Nichols, Baber, and Clayborne. The Church watched, waited, and prayed. The final decision was handed down in its favor. The validity of the General Conference was thus sustained by the civil power and federal authority.

The regular session of the Thirty-third General Conference was in the offing. Bishop Sherman Lawrence Greene held that it would be of supreme importance because it would ratify the Extra Session. It met at Kansas City, Kansas, with the First Church, the Reverend S. H. Lewis, Pastor; Noah W. Williams, Bishop. An attempt was made to hold the opening Communion Service at the church, but it was too small for the excessively large delegation of almost two thousand delegates. Immediately

---

2. J. S. Brookens, *Victory of Bishop R. R. Wright, Jr.* (reprinted from Court Decisions, New York Supreme Court).

thereafter delegates repaired to the Soldiers and Sailors Hall, a few blocks away.

The Quadrennium had been hectic, yet not a single church left the connection. Since the Little Rock Extra Session there had been a shifting of episcopal alignments. Dr. John A. Alexander, Pastor of Bethel, Indianapolis, was elected Chairman of the powerful Episcopal Committee. He was sponsored by Bishop G. W. Baber. Relatives of Bishops were not permitted to have membership on the Committee. They were removed upon the adoption of a resolution read by Bishop D. Ward Nichols of New York City, and presiding over the state of Alabama. Dr. D. Ormonde Walker, very prominent in the Extra Session, introduced a resolution which instructed the Committee on Episcopacy to remove all Bishops who had served Districts for eight years or more. When he obtained the floor, the Reverend Dr. S. H. V. Gumbs was attempting to get the floor to read a similar resolution which the writer, George A. Singleton, had written over two years previously. The chair recognized Dr. Walker. The General Conference enacted legislation calling for a Judicial Court, but for some reason it was not set up. Many held that it also enacted a time limit of eight years for pastors to remain at a charge. It proved to be very controversial. Some claimed that the law never was enacted. The delegation was too large and unwieldy. Mrs. Fannie Kerbo Smith of St. Paul, West Palm Beach, Fla. died at the General Conference of a heart attack. She was Clerk in her local church and a fine churchwoman. She was one of the General Conference Clerks.

The election of Bishops was exciting. Dr. L. H. Hemmingway, Secretary-Treasurer of the Church Extension Department, and a native of Conway, S.C., was the first to be elevated. For years there had been a "whispering campaign against aspirants who were born in the Islands." The particular reference was to Drs. D. O. Walker, and Joseph Gomez. The Church showed its growing spirit of progressive liberalism by electing both of these fine clergymen on the same ballot. Dr. W. R. Wilkes, Pastor of Allen Temple, Atlanta, was another to be given a seat among the Episcopal Fathers. Because of the lateness of the hour the General Conference went to the First Church to finish the work of electing Bishops. There was a close race between Drs. Fred D. Jordan of the First Church, Los Angeles, and Carey A. Gibbs, Pastor of Mt. Zion, Jacksonville. The latter was successful.

Bishop Reverdy C. Ransom was made Historiographer of the Church. Bishops Noah W. Williams and G. B. Young were retired from active work. Bishop H. Y. Tookes of Florida delivered his last sermon before the vast throng on Sunday morning. In 1928 he was Pastor of Bethel, Chicago. His heart was thrilled when the Gospel Choir of his old charge appeared and sang, "I Have a Saviour With Me All the Way." He was a preacher of great power and eloquence. The General Conference was literally stirred. With the close of the General Conference he was assigned to Texas, and got as far as Dallas. His spirit passed into the great beyond. This General Conference was epochal. "District projects" without the authority of the General Conference were prohibited. "Burdensome assessments" were not allowed, following the adoption of a resolution introduced by Bishop D. Ward Nichols. The salaries of Bishops and General Officers were increased, and Bishops were not to receive any outside monies, or to permit any "testimonials and receptions."

The Church had traveled a long distance since the sermon delivered by Bishop Reverdy C. Ransom at Birmingham, Ala. in 1928, and the challenging address delivered by Dean Charles Leander Hill of the Turner Theological Seminary of Morris Brown College, Atlanta in the same church fifteen years later. The forces of Radicalism and Reform move steadily forward.

CHAPTER XV

The Department and System of Finance

Not slothful in business, fervent in spirit;
serving the Lord. — ROMANS 12:11

The Dollar Money is the Lifeblood of the Church. — PARKS

The Church was fully a half-century old before a really sound system of finance was instituted. The present Financial Department was set up by the General Conference of 1868. At Nashville, the 1872 General Conference originated the Dollar Money system, which made it obligatory upon each pastor to report to his Annual Conference "one dollar for or from every member."[1] This money was turned over to a Finance Committee of the Annual Conference, which made the proper legal division, and forwarded the respective amounts by drafts to the Financial Secretary and the various other Departments of the Church.

The Dollar Money is the unitive bond of the Connectional organization. With the funds received, the Financial Secretary pays the salaries of the Bishops, their traveling expenses while attending Council meetings, and General Conference sessions, and other expenses incidental to their supervision of the Church. The Financial Secretary pays the salaries of certain designated General Officers, and in some cases their house rent — those which do not have "parsonages" in their Department quarters. He is the custodian of the General Conference Delegates Fund, which is collected at the various Annual Conferences, and forwarded to him.

The percentage division of the Dollar Money varies from Quadrennium to Quadrennium, according to General Conference legislation. For example the distribution, 1920-1924 was as follows:

1. A. W. Wayman, *My Recollections*, 186-87; *General Conference Minutes, 1872*, 94; *General Conference, Minutes, 1880*, 152 f.

40% to Financial Department for general purposes.
20% to Financial Department for Pension Fund.
 8% to Church Extension Department.
 8% to Missionary Department.
 8% to Educational Department.
16% to Annual Conference Finance Committee.

1932

38% to Financial Department.
25% to Financial Department for Pension Fund.
 5% to Missionary Department.
 4% to Church Extension Department
 8% to Educational Department.
20% to Annual Conference Finance Committee.

1940

38% to Financial Department
25% to Financial Department for Pension Fund
 4% to Church Extension Department
 5% to Missionary Department
 8% to Educational Department
20% to Annual Conference Finance Committee

1944

38% to Finance Department
       20% of net profits of the Book Concern
       20% of the net profits of the Department of Christian Education.
       These two incomes shall constitute a chartered fund, the interest of which shall be used for the support of superannuated Bishops and preachers, widows and orphans of Bishops, and itinerant preachers.
 8% to Educational Department
 5% to Missionary Department
30% to Pension Department
 4% to Church Extension Department
15% to Annual Conference Finance Committee

1948

48%   to Finance Department

31½% to Pension Department
5%   to Annual Conference Finance Committee
5%   to Education Department
4%   to Church Extension Department
1½% to Christian Education Department
5%   to Department of Missions

RECAPITULATION OF DOLLAR MONEY

Financial Secretary

1872-1879	J. H. Burley	$ 95,553.93
1879-1880	J. C. Embry	99,999.42
1880-1884	B. W. Arnett	175,252.45
1884-1888	B. W. Arnett	229,013.85
1888-1892	J. A. Handy	225,930.47
1892-1896	J. H. Armstrong	357,942.00
1896-1900	M. M. Moore	406,074.26
1900-1902	P. A. Hubbard	118,750.97
(May-January 14)		
1902-1902	E. W. Lampton	120,627.23
1902-1904	E. W. Lampton	139,990.35
1904-1908	E. W. Lampton	665,494.20
1908-1912	John Hurst	790,088.50
1912-1916	John R. Hawkins	850,214.04
1916-1920	John R. Hawkins	1,053,679.01
1920-1924	John R. Hawkins	1,371,098.25
1924-1928	John R. Hawkins	1,522,628.76
1928-1932	John R. Hawkins	1,404,393.71
1932-1936	John R. Hawkins	1,033,332.47
1936-1940	John R. Hawkins ⎰ Arthur S. Jackson ⎱	1,168,254.37
1940-1944	Arthur S. Jackson	1,357,735.87
1944-1948	Arthur S. Jackson	1,784,605.58
1948-1951		1,092,234.98
1872-1951	Grand total	$16,263,549.46[2]

2. *A. M. E. Discipline, 1932,* 388; *1940,* 412; *1944,* 291 ff; *1948,* 257. Figures furnished by Dr. Arthus S. Jackson, Financial Secretary of the A. M. E. Church, 1541 Fourteenth Street, N. W., Washington, D. C.

The chief departmental beneficiaries of the Dollar Money[3] are the Departments of Missions, Church Extension, Education, and Finance. The Department of Pensions was established in 1944 at Philadelphia, under the leadership of Dr. Daniel Lee Witherspoon. He had the influential support of Bishop D. Ward Nichols, who dominated the General Conference. Through the Quadrennium the cause of pensions was championed by the *Christian Recorder*, edited by George A. Singleton. He collaborated with Dr. Witherspoon in securing material, information, and publicity.

The new Department superseded the old Hawkins Plan, and relieved the Department of Finance from the responsibility of handling the Fund, and paying the Conference Claimants 30%[4] of the Dollar Money to be sent to the Secretary-Treasurer of Pensions. This would be augmented by ten cents per capita, which each pastor would report to his Annual Conference. The sum total would be increased by donations and bequests, gifts, and special collections by churches and Annual Conferences.

Since the organization of the Department of Finance, eleven persons have served as Secretaries. Seven of them were elected to the Bishopric. The Church wisely decided to fill the office with a layman. Consequently the last two have been laymen — Drs. John R. Hawkins and Arthur S. Jackson. The former died in office while serving his seventh Quadrennium consecutively, and the incumbent is in his third. This precludes the office of Financial Secretary being used as a "stepping-stone into the Episcopacy." The Fathers of the Church were wise.

The power of the Financial Secretary reached great heights under Dr. Hawkins. He was refined, cultured, eloquent. In his heyday his will was almost supreme from the top to the bottom. He dominated the temporal economy in the General Conference, the Committee on Revision of the Discipline, and the General Conference Commission. At the same time he was respected, revered, beloved. He lived to a ripe age. After a delicate operation he carried on until the end came at the Departmental Headquarters, 1541 Fourteenth Street, N. W., Washington, D. C., August

---

3. The Pension Department now receives 31½ per cent of the Dollar Money directly from the ninety-six Annual Conferences.
4. B. W. Arnett, *The Budget*, 1900, 142 f.; *A. M. E. Discipline*, 1944, 203.

24, 1939. A true, warm personal friend had passed. I was one of the active pallbearers along with Drs. V. M. Townsend of Arkansas, G. T. Stinson of Louisiana, and J. O. Haithcox of Ohio, members of the Financial Board. The funeral was held in Metropolitan Church. He was buried in a beautiful cemetery in Anacostia.

The Financial Board complied with the wishes of the deceased Dr. Hawkins and elected as his successor, his lifelong friend, Dr. Arthur Smith Jackson, who followed him as Secretary of Education in 1912 at Kansas City, Missouri. He has rendered faithful service to the Church over a period of forty years as a General Officer. To his credit he has been re-elected each Quadrennium by acclamation, and without opposition. Dr. Jackson brought modern methods into the office of Financial Secretary. On the evening of February 23, 1951, while the Council of Bishops, and the Connectional Council met with Ward African M. E. Church, 25th and Magnolia Streets, Los Angeles, a brilliant reception and testimonial were tendered the capable Secretary in recognition of sixty years of service in the Church, and forty years as a General Officer. The Bishops, General Officers, ministers, and laymen from all over the Connection participated. The service was impressive. Secretary Jackson is a fine orator, and a master in the art of word-witchery. His response was of a high order. Dr. E. A. Selby, Secretary of the Sunday School Union, was Master of Ceremonies, and the presentation was made by Editor E. C. Hatcher of the *Southern Christian Recorder*. The delegation from Texas was much in evidence as it represented Dr. Jackson's native state. It was led by Bishop and Mrs. Joseph Gomez. The present President of the Financial Board is Bishop G. W. Baber of the Fourth Episcopal District. A different Bishop serves for a period of four years. The governing Board is composed of a member from each District.

Dr. Hawkins used to say in his brilliant addresses at Annual Conferences that the dollar which African Methodists pay is the most serviceable and useful of any spent by any people. This was demonstrated by a mathematical division, showing how the dollar was expended: Missions, Education, Church Extension, Pensions, Church operation. It is impossible to calculate the amount of good which the Dollar Money has accomplished through the years since the system was set up back in 1872. It has been the economic foundation of the Church, a Connectional program in which all co-operate. Its effects are felt in the United States, Africa, South America, the Islands, and Canada. In collecting the Dollar Money the saturation point has not been reached. Each year there are notable increases. The reason more is not being collected is that some of the Episcopal Districts have the responsibility of financing schools, and they collect more funds to run them than they do for Dollar Money.

CHAPTER XVI

The Forward Look

I press toward the mark for the prize of the high calling
of God in Christ Jesus. — PHILIPPIANS 3:14

> *Make Beauty and make Rest give place,*
> *Mock Prudence loud — and she is gone,*
> *Smite Satisfaction on the face,*
> *And tread the ghost of Ease upon.*
> *Light-lipped and surging press we hard,*
> *Over old earth which now is worn,*
> *Triumphant, buffeted, and scarred,*
> *By Billows howled at, tempest torn*
> *Toward blue horizons far away.*
> — CHARLES HAMILTON SORLEY

The task is finished. A feeling of imperfection possesses me.
Others better qualified will make improvements down the years.
But it has been a veritable, thrilling romance, living in the distant
past with those heroic spirits, who in the days of American slavery, founded the Church and sent it down the centuries. To com-
mune with them was a rare privilege, and compensatory beyond
the mere power of words to express. Long and tedious has been
the journey from the labors of Allen in the last quarter of the
eighteenth century to the middle of the twentieth century. The
Church which he founded was, in a unique sense, the Church in
the wilderness.

The bicentennial of African Methodism approaches. Only the
youthful scholars in Cradle Roll Classes of Sunday Schools may
live to see and fittingly observe it. Fortunate shall they be. We
pray that their eyes may behold a more glorious Church, made
stronger by victory in trials and tribulations. By faith we press
on, but is an inexorable law of nature that man's knowledge must

189

be based upon experience, and experience is always in the past.
The look is forward, and we build upon the durable foundation
laid by worthy ancestors when the day was dark.

Richard Allen started out with nothing but a sublime faith in
God. Today, according to Bishop Monroe H. Davis, "If all the
members of the African Methodist Episcopal Church were reported there would be not less than one and a quarter million."[1]
If all of the pastors the Connection over, home and abroad, should
report one Monday morning the number of conversions, new
members received, and baptisms for the previous Sunday, the
figures would be startling. In like manner, if it were possible to
get a report of all monies received in all of the churches a first
Sunday in any month, the grand total would be astounding. Large
and strong is the African Methodist Episcopal Church.

The institutions of learning are making outstanding contributions toward the enlightenment of the people and the perpetuity of the Church. Allen University at Columbia, S.C., and Morris Brown College, Atlanta, are in the vanguard, accredited and
recognized by standardizing agencies. For years Wilberforce
University has been our premier university. "There will always
be a Wilberforce!" Its spirit cannot die. Edward Waters, Payne,
Quinn, Campbell, and Shorter are coming to the fore. But for
them to develop, their Presidents must be qualified in mind and
heart. Their fidelity and loyalty to the ideals of African Methodism must be unquestioned. Then they must be permitted to function as heads of institutions, free from outside interference —
heads, and not mere "figureheads."

One of the greatest needs of the Church is more adequate
preparation of ministers to take charge of our pulpits to lead
and serve the people, long after the present generation shall have
passed away. Bishop Fountain saw the need at Morris Brown,
and made a real ambitious attempt to build a theological seminary.
The most commendable program for training in Divinity is being
made at Payne Seminary, Wilberforce, Ohio. A commodious
building is being erected to house the institution, and the faculty
is being strengthened. Payne has a separate charter from the university, and its own Board of Trustees. The need is for a Connectional School of Religion.

---

1.   M. H. Davis, *Dogmas and Precepts of the Fathers,* 10.

As we face the future with the hope of building a stronger African Methodism, it is evident that the Department of Education, as it functions, has about outlived its usefulness. It is ineffective in its operations, and uneconomic. Because of the Episcopal District setup it is not in position to supervise. Under the present system, thousands of dollars which the schools could use, do not reach them. The Department of Church Extension does not receive enough funds to justify its present method of operating. It may well be merged with the Department of Missions, and thereby reduce the overhead. The Publication Department in Philadelphia could easily be merged with the Sunday School Union Publishing Plant at Nashville. The assets in Philadelphia are few, the Allen Building is not owned by the Church, but the institution at Nashville is a going concern.

The Pension Department must not rest upon its oars, but press steadily forward for increased benefits to Conference Claimants. There is enough insurance ability in the Church, if used, to make possible the writing of life and health insurance for ministers, their families and church members. A forward step has been made with the setting up of the Department and the future outlook is bright.

The emphasis needs to be placed increasingly upon a program for the rural Church. The majority, a large majority, of our Churches are in the rural regions, which constitute the basis of support. Thus far the Church has not ventured upon a program to meet this imperative need. Incidentally, the problem is not "more funds," but a more advantageous use of what we have. In the same way, there is a need for housing our people who come into the cities. In most instances they come from churches "at home" and upon their arrival in the large metropolitan areas they are "lost" to the Church. In many old centers where our Church has been established for scores of years no new societies are being organized, or additional church houses built or acquired. Again, the city Church, especially, must move along the path pointed out by Union Bethel in New Orleans. Religion concerns the whole of man, and the modern Church, where practicable, should minister to his every need.

Looking forward to a more effective Church press, it is agreed in many quarters that it needs reorganization. We have a multiplicity of papers where one strong paper would serve the needs of the denomination. Under the present system, when either paper is read one gets all of the news; for articles are prepared, usually in triplicate, and a copy sent to each of the editors. The expense is multiplied by three, and the value received by the Church is doubtful. One Connectional Paper under an Editorial Board would be self-supporting. One paper with all of the Church supporting it would justify the experiment within less than one Quadrennium. Somebody must place the good of the Church of Allen above personal preference for place. The sun is too high for the Church to continue to neglect its strongest asset and means of guiding public opinion. This is vital, if the Connectional spirit is to be fostered.

A concentrated effort must needs be made to produce a devotional literature. When members join us, we have nothing to give them that is informative, religious, or denominational. Some department should prepare and make available inexpensive tracts, and booklets, which the pastors may use in their local societies. Instead, our people are reading literature which does not make for the production of strong and loyal African Methodists. A man's thinking is conditioned largely by what he reads. "As a man thinketh in his heart, so is he." A few thousand dollars spent in the production of religious booklets and pamphlets would bring large returns in the development of church fidelity, pride, and appreciation for the deeper things of the spirit. The profound heart-hunger of the people has not been met in this way. And the need is great.

Following World War II, the Church experienced a period of unparalleled prosperity. In the labor world work was plentiful and wages reached an all-time high. This was reflected in the improved "financial ability of the people." Large sums of money were raised all over the Connection, and today there are few church properties with mortgages and large indebtedness. The value of African Methodist real estate runs into astonomical figures. There are church buildings, parsonages, lots, apartment houses, Homes for the Aged, religious education centers, colleges, publishing plants, seminaries, and Departmental Headquarters.

From the beginning with "Mother Bethel" in Philadelphia,

named by the Reverend John Dickins of the Methodist Episcopal Church, Bethels are now scattered over the continental United States, Africa, and the isles of the sea. A few of the most prominent "Bethels" are in New York City, Wilmington, Del., Baltimore, Pittsburgh, Columbia, S. C., Atlanta, Miami, Little Rock, Dallas, San Antonio, St. Louis, Chicago, New Orleans, and Detroit.

"Great churches" are Charles Street in Boston, Bridge Street in Brooklyn, and St. Luke in New York City; St. Matthew and Mt. Pisgah, Philadelphia; St. John and St. James in Cleveland; Allen Temple, Cincinnati; Mt. Zion in Jacksonville, Emanuel, Morris Brown, and St. Luke in Charleston, S. C.; St. Stephen in Wilmington, St. Joseph, in Durham, and St. James in Raleigh, N. C. Metropolitan stands out in the nation's capitol, Shorter in Denver, and Eighth and Towne in Los Angeles. Upon these as a sure foundation we look forward. And they are only a scattered few. To be sure the Quadrennium of 1948-1952 will be rightly regarded as one of expansion. More new churches were built, and church properties purchased than in any one period of African Methodism. Some of the most signal purchases were the Nichols Memorial, the new home of Mt. Olive, Ward, and Union in Philadelphia, D. Ward Nichols, Bishop. In Washington, D. C. a new home was purchased for Turner Memorial, L. H. Hemmingway, Bishop. Ebenezer in Charleston, S. C. erected a new edifice. Bethel in Georgetown, and Allen Temple in Greenville, S. C. erected Religious Education centers, Frank M. Reid, Bishop.

Perhaps the most outstanding expansion program was in the Fourth Episcopal District, G. W. Baber, Bishop. Before his election to the Episcopacy he had given the Connection several churches. His work as a Pastor was climaxed with the large, and modern-equipped Ebenezer in Detroit. His spirit was contagious, and Dr. J. Arminius Charleston built a new home for St. Paul, Dr. Chas. S. Spivey completed beautiful St. Stephens. These are all in Detroit. C. Baker Pearle restored the pristine glory of Bethel, Chicago, by completing the building which had been started under the pastorate of A. Wayman Ward. A new church was purchased on the densely populated West Side, and Dr. J. L. Roberts completely remodeled Coppin on Michigan Boulevard. Grant Memorial (Dr. Harvey E. Walden, Pastor) moved into a large, new home on Drexel Boulevard. It rivals Ebenezer in Detroit, and will seat thousands. St. Paul, Springfield, Ill. is being finished. The fine, huge Clayborne Temple in Memphis stands as a monument to the genius and indefatigable toil of Bishop John Henry Clayborne. The newly acquired Ward, Los Angeles, was seen by thousands the third week in February when they visited the coast when the Council of Bishops, and the Connection Council convened in their Winter Sessions. The society had recently moved into the new home under the pastoral leadership of Dr. Frederick D. Jordan; D. Ormonde Walker, Bishop. There are scores of other newly acquired and built churches along the frontier of expansion and advance. The beachhead gained and established by Richard Allen and his compeers has been widened, and extended in depth until today African Methodism is a stronghold impregnable for making definite the program of the Kingdom of God.

The Church will forever exist so long as it meets the needs of the people. Within it lies the germ of perpetuity, but it must adjust itself to the ever-changing demands of the succeeding generations. The Church cannot hope to unlock the future with the past's rusty old key. The level of intelligence is being gradually lifted. This calls for an enlightened ministry, trained in newer theological disciplines. These must accept the findings of the new science, and ultimately express themselves upon the level of brotherhood. The motto of the Church will be maximized: "God our Father, Christ our Redeemer, Man our Brother." In this lies the hope not only of the African M. E. Church, but of all the Churches, nations, and the human race.

The days which lie ahead are pregnant with evil forebodings. The common people the globe around are stirring as never before. In the Far East the Chinese hordes are on the move under the Red Star. An undeclared war is being waged in Korea. In the background are the teeming millions in Russia. Other millions are in India, and Africa, the long-exploited continent, the giant of the centuries, is slowly opening her eyes in wonder. The dark-skinned peoples of earth want some of the good things of life. In America they want freedom with liberty. They desire and seek full, unqualified citizenship rights under the Constitution. They look to the church for spiritual leadership and guidance. The African M. E. Church has never failed the people. It will not fail them now. It will prove to the world that the founders of Richard Allen's day did not live, labor, and die in vain.

While the Cross and the Sickle are upon the verge of mortal combat, the Church of Allen clings to its ancient loyalty to the government. Her sons and daughters have gone forth under "Old Glory," the flag that set their forefathers free; the flag of hope, and opportunity; the flag which represents the highest and best outworking of the ideals of Jesus Christ upon the earth. But in the meantime we shall continue to fight uncompromisingly for complete integration within our American social life, within the framework of the Constitution, holding aloft. ". . . the torch of freedom and equality lighted by Richard Allen and his followers, when, in 1787, they walked out of the door of St. George M. E. Church, in Philadelphia."[2]

---

2. Reverdy C. Ransom, *Preface to the History of the A. M. E. Church*, 207.

APPENDIXES

and

BIBLIOGRAPHY

Appendix A

A copy of this letter from Dr. Benjamin Rush to his wife Julia was obtained from Dr. L. H. Butterfield of the Princeton University Library. Dr. Butterfield is the assistant editor of the *Papers of Thomas Jefferson* and editor of *The Letters of Benjamin Rush*.

Philadelphia, 22nd Aug., 1793

MY DEAR JULIA,

This day agreeably to invitation I dined a mile from town under the shade of several large trees with about an hundred carpenters and others, who met to celebrate the raising of the roof of the African Church. They forced me to take the head of the table much against my inclinations. The dinner was plentiful, the liquors were of the first quality, and the dessert which consisted only of melons was very good. We were waited upon by nearly an equal number of black people. I gave them the two following toasts. "Peace on earth, and good will to men" and "may African churches every where soon succeed to African bondage." After which we rose, and the black people (men and women) took our seats. Six of the most respectable of the white company waited upon them, while Mr. Nicholson, myself and two others were requested to sit down with them which we did much to the satisfaction of the poor blacks. Never did I witness such a scene of innocent, nay more, such virtuous and philanthropic joy. Billy Grey in attempting to express his feelings to us, was checked by a flood of tears. After they had dined, they all came up to Mr. Nicholson and took him by the hand, and thanked him for his loan of money to them. One of them, an old man whom I did not know, addressed him in the following striking language: "May you live long, Sir, and when you die, may you not die eternally." The company broke up and came to town about 6 o Clock in good order, few or perhaps none of them having drunken more than 3 or four glasses of wine. To me it will be a day to be remembered with pleasure as long as I live.

In order that my other class of friends the criminals in the jail who overheard or witnessed the raising of the roof of the church might sympathize a little in the joy of the day, I sent them about one o Clock a large wheel barrow full of melons with the following note. "Dr. Rush sends herewith a few melons for the persons who are suffering in the jail for their offenses against society. He begs that while they are partaking of this agreeable fruit, they will remember that that Being who created it, still cares for them, and that by this, and other acts of kindness conveyed to them by his creatures, He means to lead them to repentance and happiness."

Adieu. In consequence of my absence only two hours from town, my business encreased so much as to keep me employed till after 10 o Clock. The malignant fever is stationary, and the influenza as violent as was mentioned in my letter of yesterday. The family through divine goodness continue well and none of them now more so than

Yours sincerely

BENJ^N RUSH

P.S. Love as usual. Read this letter to your mama. She belongs to *our* African church.

Aug. 23rd. We continue *all* well.

(*Addressed*: Mrs. Julia Rush, at Richard Stockton Esq., near Princeton, New Jersey.

MS.: Lloyd W. Smith, Madison, New Jersey.)

Appendix B

Author's Note to the
Speech on the Eligibility of Colored Members
To Seats in the Georgia Legislature

By Hon. H. M. Turner

This speech by the Hon. Henry McNeal Turner is a rare document and comes out of the Reconstruction Period immediately following the Rebellion, when the former slave-holding states were holding Conventions to revise their laws and oust the Freedmen from political power. Turner was a member of the Georgia Legislature and was active in attempting to organize the Negro for economic security. In spite of his and others' efforts, zeal, and indefatigable labors, his people were betrayed in the Hayes-Tilden debacle when the Republicans sold them down the river.

The original printing of the speech was given the author by the late Bishop Joseph Simeon Flipper of Atlanta, Georgia, who knew Turner well. This copy may be the only one in existence. DuBois regards Turner as one of the most capable men in the Convention. He was also one of the most able and outstanding members of the Georgia Legislature. He was feared and disliked by the whites, and several attempts were made to ensnare and inveigle him with plots and false charges, but each time he escaped. He believed firmly in social justice, political equality, and education for all. He would not dispossess the aristocracy and stood for the pardoning of Jefferson Davis.

The following sixteen pages are a photographic facsimile of the original printing of the *Speech*.

SPEECH

ON THE

ELIGIBILITY OF COLORED MEMBERS
To Seats
In the Georgia Legislature.

By Hon. H. M. TURNER,

(*Colored.*)

Delivered before that Body September 3d, 1868.

Mr. Speaker:

Before proceeding to argue this question upon its intrinsic merits, I wish the Members of this House to understand the position that I take. I hold that I am a member of this body. Therefore, sir, I shall neither fawn nor cringe before any party, nor stoop to *beg* them for my rights. Some of my colored fellow-members, in the course of their remarks, took occasion to appeal to the *sympathies* of Members on the opposite side, and to eulogize their character for magnanimity. It reminds me very much, sir, of slaves begging under the lash. I am here to demand my rights, and to hurl thunderbolts at the men who would dare to cross the threshold of my manhood. There is an old aphorism which says, "Fight the Devil with fire," and if I should observe the rule in this instance, I wish gentlemen to understand that it is but fighting them with their own weapon.

The scene presented in this House, to-day, is one unparalleled in the history of the world. From this day, back to the day when God breathed the breath of life into Adam, no analogy for it can be found. Never, in the history of the world, has a man been arraigned before a body clothed with legislative, judicial or executive functions, charged with the offence of being of a darker hue than his fellow-men. I know that questions have been before the Courts of this country, and of other countries, involving topics not altogether dissimilar to that which is being discussed here to-day. But, sir, never, in all the history of the great nations of this world—never before—has a man been arraigned, charged with an offence committed by the God of Heaven himself. Cases may be found where men have been deprived of their rights for crimes and misdemeanors; but it has remained for the State of Georgia, in the very heart of the nineteenth century, to call a man before the bar, and there charge him with an act for which he is no more responsible than for the head which he carries upon his shoulders. The Anglo-Saxon race, sir, is a most surprising one. No man has ever been more deceived in that race than I have been for the last three weeks. I was not aware that there was in the character of that race so much cowardice, or so much pusillanimity. The treachery which has been exhibited by gentlemen belonging to that race has shaken my confidence in it more than anything that has come under my observation from the day of my birth.

What is the question at issue? Why, sir, this Assembly, to-day, is discussing and deliberating on a matter upon which Angels would tremble to sit in judgment; there is not a Cherubim that sits around God's Eternal Throne, to-day, that would not tremble—even were an order issued by the Supreme God himself—to come down here and sit in judgment on my manhood. Gentlemen may look at this question in whatever light they choose, and with just as much indifference as they may think proper to assume, but I tell you, sir, that this is a question which will not die to-day. This event shall be remembered by posterity for ages yet to come, and while the sun shall continue to climb the hills of heaven.

Whose Legislature is this? Is it a white man's Legislature, or is it a black man's Legislature? Who voted for a Constitutional Convention, in obedience to the mandate of the Congress of the United States? Who first rallied around the standard of Reconstruction? Who set the ball of loyalty rolling in the State of Georgia? And whose voice was heard on the hills and in the valleys of this State? It was the voice of the brawny-armed negro, with the few humanitarian-hearted white men who came to our assistance. I claim the honor, sir, of having been the instrument of convincing hundreds—yea, thousands—of white men, that to reconstruct under the measures of the United States Congress was the safest and the best course for the interest of the State.

Let us look at some facts in connection with this matter. Did half the white men of Georgia vote for this Legislature? Did not the great bulk of them fight, with all their strength, the Constitution under which we are acting? And did they not fight against the organization of this Legislature? And further, sir, did they not *vote* against it? Yes, sir! And there are persons in this Legislature, to day, who are ready to spit their poison in my face, while they themselves opposed, with all their power; the ratification of this Constitution. They question my right to a seat in this body, to represent the people whose legal votes elected me. This objection, sir, is an unheard of monopoly of power. No analogy can be found for it, except it be the case of a man who should go into my house, take possession of my wife and children, and then tell me to walk out. I stand very much in the position of a criminal before your bar, because I dare to be the exponent of the views of those who sent me here. Or, in other words, we are told that if black men want to speak, they must speak through white trumpets; if black men want their sentiments expressed, they must be adulterated and sent through white messengers, who will quibble, and equivocate, and evade, as rapidly as the pendulum of a clock. If this be not done, then the black men have committed an outrage, and their Representatives must be denied the right to represent their constituents.

The great question, sir, is this: Am I a man? If I am such, I claim the rights of a man. Am I not a man, because I happen to be of a darker hue than honorable gentlemen around me? Let me see whether I am or not. I want to convince the House, to-day, that I am entitled to my seat here. A certain gentleman has argued that the negro was a mere development similar to the ourang-outang or chimpanzee, but it so happens that, when a negro is examined, physiologically, phrenologically and anatomically, and, I may say, physiognomically, he is found to be the same as persons of different color. I would like to ask any gentleman on this floor, where is the analogy? Do you find me a quadruped, or do you find me a man? Do you find three bones less in my back than in that of the white man? Do you find less organs in the brain? If you know nothing of this, I do; for I have helped to dissect fifty men, black and white, and I assert that by the time you take off the mucous pigment—the color of the skin—you cannot, to save your life, distinguish between the black man and the white. Am I a man? Have I a soul to save, as you have? Am I susceptible of eternal development, as you are? Can I learn all the arts and sciences that you can—has it ever been demonstrated in the history of the world? Have black men ever exhibited bravery, as white men have done? Have they ever been in the professions! Have they not as good articulative organs as you? Some people argue that there is a very close similarity between the larynx of the negro and that of the ourang-outang. Why, sir, there is not so much similarity between them as there is between the larynx of the man and that of the dog, and this fact I dare any Member of this House to dispute. God saw fit to vary everything in Nature. There are no two men alike—no two voices alike—no two trees alike. God has weaved and tissued variety and versatility throughout the boundless space of His creation.— Because God saw fit to make some red, and some white, and some black, and some brown, are we to sit here in judgment upon what God has seen fit to do? As well might one play with the thunderbolts of heaven as with that creature that bears God's image—God's photograph.

The question is asked: "What is it that the negro race has done?" Well, Mr. Speaker, all I have to say upon the subject is this: that if we are the class of people that we are generally represented to be, I hold that we are a very great people. It is generally considered that we are the Children of Canaan, and that the curse of a father rests upon our heads, and has rested, all through history. Sir, I deny that the curse of Noah has anything to do with the negro. We are not the Children of Canaan; and if we were, sir, where should we stand? Let us look a little into history. Melchisedeck was a Canaanite; all the Phœnicians—all those inventors of the arts and sciences—were the posterity of Canaan; but, sir, the negro is not. We are the children of Cush, and Canaan's curse has nothing whatever to do with the negro. If we belong to that race, Ham belonged to it, under whose instructions Napoleon Bonaparte studied military tactics. If we belong to that race, St. Augustine belonged to it. Who was it that laid the foundation of the great Reformation? Martin Luther, who lit the light of Gospel Truth—a light that will never go out until the sun shall rise to set no more; and, long ere then, Democratic principles will have found their level in the regions of Pluto and of Proserpine.

The negro is here charged with holding office. Why, sir, the negro never wanted office. I recollect that when we wanted candidates for the Constitutional Convention, we went from door to door in the "negro belt," and begged white men to run. Some promised to do so; and yet, on the very day of election, many of them first made known their determination not to comply with their promises. They told black men, everywhere, that they would rather see *them* run; and it was this encouragement of the white men that induced the colored man to place his name upon the ticket as a candidate for the Convention. In many instances, these white men voted for us. We did not want them, nor ask them, to do it. All we wanted them to do was, to stand still and allow us to walk up to the polls and deposit our ballots. They would not come here themselves, but would insist upon sending us. Ben. Hill told them it was a nigger affair, and advised them to stay away from the polls—a piece of advice which they took very liberal advantage of. If the "niggers" had "office on the brain," it was the white man that put it there—not carpet-baggers, either, nor Yankees, nor scalawags, but the high-bred and dignified

Democracy of the South. And if any one is to blame for having negroes in these Legislative Halls—if blame attaches to it at all—it is the Democratic party. Now, however, a change has come over the spirit of their dream. They want to turn the "nigger" out; and, to support their argument, they say that the black man is debarred from holding office by the Reconstruction measures of Congress. Let me tell them one thing for their information. Black men have held office, and are now holding office, under the United States Government. Andrew Johnson, President of the United States, in 1865, commissioned me as United States Chaplain, and I would have been Chaplain to-day, had I not resigned—not desiring to hold office any longer. Let the Democratic party, then, go to Mr. Johnson, and ask him why he commissioned a negro to that position? And if they inquire further, they will ascertain that black men have been commissioned as Lieutenants, Captains, Majors, Brevet Colonels, Surgeons, and other offices of trust and responsibility, under the United States Government. Black men, to-day, in Washington City, hold positions as Clerks, and the only reason why Mr. Langston is not at this time a Consul Diplomat or Minister Plenipotentiary in some foreign country, is, because he would not be corrupted by President Johnson and made to subscribe to his wicked designs. Is not that an office, an I is it not a great deal better office than any seat held in this body?

The honorable gentleman from Whitfield (Mr. Shumate), when arguing this question, a day or two ago, put forth the proposition that to be a Representative was not to be an officer—"it was a privilege that citizens had a right to enjoy." These are his words. It was not an office; it was a "privilege." Every gentleman here knows that he denied that to be a Representative was to be an officer. Now, he is recognized as a leader of the Democratic party in this House, and generally cooks victuals for them to eat; makes that remarkable declaration, and how are you, gentlemen on the other side of the House, to ignore that declaration? Are you going to expel me from this House, because I am an officer, when one of your great lights says that I am *not* an officer? If you deny my right—the right of my constituents to have representation here—because it is a "privilege," then, sir, I will show you that I have as many privileges as the whitest man on this floor. If I am not permitted to occupy a seat here, for the purpose of representing my constituents, I want to know how white men can be permitted to do so? How can a white man represent a colored constituency, if a colored man cannot do it? The great argument is: "Oh, we have inherited" this, that and the other. Now, I want gentlemen to come down to cool, common sense. Is the created greater than the Creator? Is man greater than God? It is very strange, if a white man can occupy on this floor *a seat created by colored votes,* and a black man cannot do it. Why, gentlemen, it is the most short-sighted reasoning in the world. A man can see better than that with half an eye; and even if he had no eye at all, he could forge one, as the Cyclops did, or punch one with his finger, which would enable him to see through that.

It is said that Congress never gave us the right to hold office. I want to know, sir, if the Reconstruction measures did not base their action on the ground that no distinction should be made on account of race, color, or previous condition! Was not that the grand fulcrum on which they rested? And did not every reconstructed State have to reconstruct on the idea that no discrimination, in any sense of the term, should be made? There is not a man here who will dare say, "No." If Congress has simply given me merely sufficient civil and political rights to make me a mere political slave for Democrats, or anybody else—giving them the opportunity of jumping on my back, in order to leap into political power—I do not thank Congress for it. Never, so help me, God, shall I be a political slave. I am not now speaking for those colored men who sit with me in this House, nor do I say that they endorse my sentiments [cries from the colored Members, "We do!"], but I am speaking simply and solely for myself. Congress, after assisting Mr. Lincoln to take me out of servile slavery, did not intend to put me and my race into *political* slavery. If they did, let them take away my ballot—I do not want it, and shall not have it. [Several colored Members: "Nor we!"] I don't want to be a mere tool of that sort. I have been a slave long enough already.

I tell you what I would be willing to do: I am willing that the question should be submitted to Congress for an explanation as to what was meant in the passage of these Reconstruction measures, and of the Constitutional Amendment. Let the Democratic party in this House pass a Resolution giving this subject that direction, and I shall be content. I dare you, gentlemen, to do it. Come up to the question openly, whether it meant that the negro might hold office, or whether it meant that he should merely have the right to vote. If you are honest men, you will do it. If, however, you will not do that, I would make another proposition: Call together, again, the Convention that framed the Constitution under which we are acting; let them take a vote upon the subject, and I am willing to abide their decision.

In the course of this discussion, a good deal of reference has been made to the Constitution of the United States. I hold, sir, that, under that Constitution, I am as much a man as anybody else. I hold that that document is neither proscripted, or has it ever, in the first instance, sanctioned slavery. The Constitution says that any person escaping from service in one State, and going to another, shall, on demand, be given up. That has been the clause under which the Democratic fire-eaters have maintained that that document sanctioned slavery in man. I shall show you that it meant no such thing. It was placed there, according to Mr. Madison, altogether for a different purpose. In the Convention that drafted the Constitution,

Mr. Madison declared, he "thought it wrong to admit in the Constitution the idea that there could be property in man." On motion of Mr. Randolph, the word "SERVITUDE" was struck out, and "service" unanimously inserted—the former being thought to express the condition of SLAVES, and the latter the obligation of free persons.—3D MAD. PAP., 1429 and 1569.

Now, if you can, make anything out of that that you find in it. It comes from one of the fathers of the Constitution. Sir, I want the gentleman to know that the Constitution, as Mr. Alexander H. Stephens said, I think, in 1854, so far as slavery is concerned, is neutral. He said, that if slavery existed in Georgia, it existed under the Constitution and by the authority of the Constitution; that if slavery did not exist in Pennsylvania, or in New York, *it was equally under the Constitution.*

That is a distinct avowal that the Constitution was neutral, and it is the opinion of a man who is acknowledged to be a man of great mind and large acquaintance with political affairs. Again: the Constitution of the United States has the following clause:

" This Constitution, and *and all laws made in pursuance thereof,* shall be the supreme law of the land."

Every law, therefore, which is passed under the Constitution of the United States, is a portion of the supreme law of the land, and you are bound to obey it.

But gentlemen say that the Democrats did not pass the Reconstruction measures. I know they did not. Such Democrats as we are having in this State come pretty well under the description given of the Bourbons by Napoleon Bonaparte, who said that they never originated a new idea, nor ever forgot an old one. They certainly never would pass such measures. Did the Revolutionary Fathers intend to perpetuate slavery? Many say they did; I say they did not. What was meant by the clause which states that no bill of attainder or *ex-post facto* law shall be passed? I will tell you what I believe the Revolutionary Fathers meant: I believe it was intended to put a clause there which should eventually work out the emancipation of the slaves. It was not intended that because the father had served in slavery the curse should descend.

One of the strongest objections to the negro holding office is based upon the fact that he has been a slave, and had no rights; but the Fathers of this country framed a Constitution and Laws, whose spirit and letter condemn this everlasting proscription of the negro.

Let us take, for example, an extract from a memorial sent to Congress in 1794. It was written by a Committee of which Dr. Rush was Chairman, and is signed by such men as Samuel Adams, John Adams, Isaac Law, Stephen Hopkins, and a host of other prominent gentlemen. This memorial says:

"Many reasons concur in persuading us to abolish slavery in our country. It is inconsistent with the safety of the liberties of the United States. Freedom and slavery cannot long exist together."

Let it be remembered that some of the gentlemen who signed this memorial had been Presidents of the United States. It is also well known that General Washington, in his will, earnestly expresses a desire that all his slaves should receive their freedom upon the death of his wife. He says:

"Upon the decease of my wife, it is my will and desire that all the slaves held by me in my own right should receive their freedom. And I do moss pointedly and solemnly enjoin on my Executors to see that the clause regarding my slaves, and every part thereof, be religiously fulfilled."

Did *he* intend to perpetuate slavery or negro proscription? What says he, when writing to General Lafayette?—

"There is not a man living who wishes more sincerely than I do, to see a plan adopted for the abolition of slavery, but there is only one plan by which it can be accomplished. That is by legislative authority, and this, so far as my suffrage will go, shall not be wanting."

General Lafayette once said:

"I never thought, when I was fighting for America, that I was fighting to perpetuate slavery. I never should have drawn my sword in her defence, if I suspected such a thing."

Jefferson says:

"And can the liberties of the nation be thought secure, when we have removed the only firm basis—the conviction of the minds of the people that liberty is the gift of God? Indeed, I tremble for my country, when I reflect that God is just, and that injustice cannot last forever."

I could quote from such men for days and weeks together, to show the spirit that was in them upon this subject, if I thought it necessary to my cause.

We are told that we have no right to hold office, because it was never conferred upon us by "specific enactment." *Were we ever made slaves by specific enactment?* I hold, sir, that there never was a law passed in this country, from its foundation to the Emancipation, which enacted us slaves. Even the great Mr. Calhoun said: "I doubt whether there is a single State in the South that *ever enacted them slaves.*" If, then, you have no laws enacting me a slave, how can you question my right to my freedom? Judge Lumpkin, one of the ablest jurists that Georgia ever had, said that there never was any positive law in the State of Georgia that forbade negroes from testifying in Courts; "and they are," said he, "only debarred by their ignorance and ignoble status." Neither did Queen Elizabeth, when she gave to Sir John Hawkins a charter to bring negroes to this country, give him that right with any other understanding than that no violence or force should be used therefor; and she never intended that they should be anything more than apprentices. Mr. Madison, in speaking upon the subject of jury-trials for negroes, says: "Proof would have to be brought forward that slavery was established by preexisting laws;" "and," said he, "it will be impossible to comply with such a request, *for no such law could be produced.*" Why, then, do gentlemen clamor for proof of our being free "by virtue of specific enactment?" Show me any specific law of Georgia, or of the United States, that enacted black men to be slaves, and I will then tell you that, before we can enjoy our rights as free men, such law must be repealed.

I stand here to-day, sir, pleading for ninety thousand black men—voters—of Georgia; and I shall stand and plead the cause of my race until God, in His providence, shall see proper to take me hence. I trust that He will give me strength to stand, and power to accomplish the simple justice that I seek for them.

Why did your forefathers come to this country? Did they not flee from oppression? They came to free themselves from the chains of tyranny, and to escape from under the heel of the Autocrat. Why, sir, in England, for centuries together, men—and *white* men at that—wore metal collars around their necks, bearing, in graven characters, the names by which they were known. Your great and noble race were sold in the slave-marts of Rome. The Irish, also, held many white slaves, until 1172; and even Queen Elizabeth, in her day, had to send a deputation to inquire into the condition of such white slaves as had been born in England. King Alfred the Great, in his time, provided that for seven years' work the slave should be set free. And, going back to more ancient and more valuable authority, did not God himself, when he had brought the Children of Israel out of Egypt, say unto them: "Remember that you were slaves in Egypt?" I say to you, white men, to-day, that the great deliverance of the recent past is not altogether dissimilar to the great deliverance of ancient times. Your Democratic party may be aptly said to represent Pharaoh; the North to represent one of the walls, and the South the other. Between these two great walls the black man passes out to freedom, while your Democratic party—the Pharaoh of to-day—follows us with hasty strides and lowering visage.

The gentleman from Floyd (Mr. Scott) went down amid the chambers of the dead, and waked up the musty decision of Judge Taney in the Dred Scott case. Why, the very right on which he denied citizenship to Dred Scott, was, that if he were a citizen, he would be a free man, and invested with all rights of citizenship. The Constitution says that

"All persons born or naturalized in the United States, and resident in this State, are hereby declared citizens of this State; and no law shall be made or enforced that shall abridge the privileges or immunities of citizens of the United States, or of this State, or deny to any person within its jurisdiction the equal protection of its laws."

2

For what purpose was this clause inserted in that Constitution? It was placed there, sir, to protect the rights of every man—the Heaven-granted, inalienable, unrestricted rights of mine, and of my race. Great God, if I had the voice of seven thunders, to-day, I would make the ends of the earth to hear me. The Code of Laws known as Irwin's Code of Georgia, clearly states the rights of citizens. Section 1648 is as follows:

"Among the rights of citizens are the enjoyment of personal security, of personal liberty, private property and the disposition thereof, the elective franchise, the right to hold office, to appeal to the Courts, to testify as a witness, to perform any civil function, and to keep and bear arms."

Section 1649 of the same Code says:

"All citizens are entitled to the exercise of their right as such, unless specially prohibited by law."

I would like to ascertain, Mr. Speaker, what prohibition has been put upon me, or upon my race, and what can be put upon it, under the provision of the Constitution, which would deprive us of holding office. The Constitution of Georgia, Article 2, Section 2, says that

"Every male person who has been born or naturalized, or who has legally declared his intention to become a citizen of the United States, twenty years old or upward, who shall have resided in this State six months next preceding the election, and shall have resided thirty days in the county in which he offers to vote, and shall have paid all taxes which may have been required of him, and which he may have had an opportunity of paying, agreeably to law, for the year next preceding the election (except as hereinafter provided), shall be declared an elector; and every male citizen of the United States, of the age aforesaid (except as hereinafter provided), who may be a resident of the State at the time of the adoption of this Constitution, shall be deemed an elector, and shall have all the rights of an elector as aforesaid."

Now let me read to you the meaning of the word "citizen," as given by Mr. Bouvier in his Law Dictionary:

"In American law, one who, under the Constitution and Laws of the United States, has a right to vote for Representatives in Congress and other public officers, and who is qualified to fill offices in the gift of the people. Any white person born in the United States, or naturalized person born out of the same, who has not lost his right as such."

Now, sir, I claim to be a citizen, I claim to be an elector, and I claim to be entitled to hold office.

We have heard a good deal said about Greece and Rome, and the great nations of antiquity, and of such great men as Socrates, Seneca, Aristotle, Plato, Herodotus, Horace, and Homer. Well, I make a reference or two to these times and nations. A freedman among the Romans was nothing more than, in the time of slavery in this country, a free negro would be. He could not come in contact with the citizen upon an equal footing, but when the Empire came under the sway of Constantine, he provided that all slaves who were made free upon account of meritorious conduct should be enfranchised. Go back, then, Georgians, to the days of Constantine, and learn from him a lesson of wisdom. In the days of Justinian, too, provision was made that every slave who was made free should be enfranchised and made a full citizen of Rome. The celebrated Roman writer, Horace, boasted that he was the son of a freedman; and I would remind you, also, that one of the Emperors and rulers of Rome had a slave mother. Another provision of those times was, that a slave could become free and a citizen by the consent of six thousand other citizens. Now, sir, even following the example of Rome, am I not a citizen? Have not more than six thousand white citizens voted me my rights as such? And have not forty thousand white citizens voted for the Constitution which grants me my rights as such?

We learn some peculiar points in regard to slavery from many of the writers of ancient times. Tacitus, for instance, tells us that, amongst the ancient Germans, if, in gaming, the slave should win, the master became his property and slave, while he became master. Mohammed gave political rights to all slaves who defended his religion; and so, indeed, in general, did the Crusaders; and the Popes of Rome used to teach their flocks that all men were the Lord's freemen. St. Jerome once remarked that a man's right to enfranchisement exi ted in his knowledge of the truth. I might quote for hours from such authorities as these upon the rights which rested in, and were acquired by, the slaves of old, but I deem it unnecessary to do so at this time.

These colored men, who are unable to express themselves with all the clearness, and dignity, and force of rhetorical eloquence, are laughed at in derision by the Democracy of the country. It reminds me very much of the man who looked at himself in a mirror, and, imagining that he was addressing another person, exclaimed: "My God, how ugly you are!" [Laughter.] These gentlemen do not consider for a moment the dreadful hardships which these people have endured, and especially those who in any way endeavored to acquire an education. For myself, sir, I was raised in the cotton field of South Carolina, and, in order to prepare myself for usefulness, as well to myself as to my race, I determined to devote my spare hours to study. When the overseer retired at night to his comfortable couch, I sat and read, and thought, and studied, until I heard him blow his horn in the morning. He frequently told me, with an oath, that if he discovered me attempting to learn, he would whip me to death, and I have no doubt he would have done so, if he had found an opportunity. I prayed to Almighty God to assist me, and He did, and I thank Him with my whole heart and soul.

Personally, I have the highest regard for the gentleman from Floyd (Mr. Scott), but I need scarcely say that I heartily despise the political sentiments which he holds. I would pledge myself to do this, however: To take the Holy Bible and read it in as many different languages as he will. If *he* reads it in English, *I* will do it; if *he* reads it in Latin, *I* will do the same; if in Greek, *I* will read it in that language, too; and if in Hebrew, *I* will meet *him*, also, there. It can scarcely, then, be upon the plea of ignorance that he would debar me from the exercise of political rights.

I must now direct your attention to a point which shows the intention of the framers of the Constitution of Georgia, which you have sworn to support. In the "Proceedings of the Constitutional Convention," which framed this Constitution, I find, under date of March 3d, 1868, that, on motion of Mr. Akerman, the report of the Judiciary Committee on the subject of the qualifications of persons for membership to the first General Assembly, after the ratification and adoption of the Constitution, was taken up, and, without amendment, adopted. That report is as follows:

"*Be it ordained by the people of Georgia, in Convention assembled*, That the persons eligible as members of the General Assembly, at the first election held under the Constitution framed by this Convention, shall be citizens of the United States who shall have been inhabitants of this State for six months, and of the district or county for which they shall be elected for three months next preceding such election, and who, in the case of Senators, shall have attained the age of twenty-five years, and, in the case of Representatives, the age of twenty-one years, at the time of such election."

Gentlemen will observe the word "inhabitant" in that Ordinance; and it was put there especially, in order that no question could arise as to who were eligible to fill the positions of Senator and Representative.

So far as I am personally concerned, no man in Georgia has been more conservative than I. "Anything to please the white folks" has been my motto; and so closely have I adhered to that course, that many among my own party have classed me as a Democrat. One of the leaders of the Republican party in Georgia has not been at all favorable to me for some time back, because he believed that I was too "conservative" for a Republican. I can assure you, however, Mr. Speaker, that I have had quite enough, and to spare, of such "conservatism."

The "conservative" element has pursued a somewhat erratic course in the reconstruction of Georgia. In several instances— as, for instance, in Houston county—they placed negroes on their tickets for county offices, and *elected* them, too, and *they are holding office to-day*. And this policy is perfectly consistent with the doctrine taught, in public and in private, by the great lights of Democracy, all through the last canvass. They objected to the Constitution, "because," said they, "it confers upon the niggers the right to hold office." Even Mr. Alexander H. Stephens—one of the greatest men, if not *the greatest* man, in the South, to-day, and one for whom I have the utmost respect—in a conversation that I had with him before the Legislature convened (Governor Brown's Marietta speech being one of the topics under consideration very generally throughout the State at the time), said: "Governor

Brown says that the black man cannot hold office under that Constitution, but he *knows* that he can."

But, Mr. Speaker, I do not regard this movement as a thrust at me. It is a thrust at the Bible—a thrust at the God of the Universe, for making a man and not finishing him; it is simply calling the Great Jehovah a fool. Why, sir, though we are not white, we have accomplished much. We have pioneered civilization here; we have built up your country; we have worked in your fields, and garnered your harvests, for two hundred and fifty years! And what do we ask of you in return? Do we ask you for compensation for the sweat our fathers bore for you—for the tears you have caused, and the hearts you have broken, and the lives you have curtailed, and the blood you have spilled? Do we ask retaliation? We ask it not. We are willing to let the dead past bury its dead; but we ask you, now, for our RIGHTS. You have all the elements of superiority upon your side; you have our money and your own; you have our education and your own; and you have our land and your own, too. We, who number hundreds of thousands in Georgia, including our wives and families, with not a foot of land to call our own—strangers in the land of our birth; without money, without education, without aid, without a roof to cover us while we live, nor sufficient clay to cover us when we die! It is extraordinary that a race such as yours, professing gallantry, and chivalry, and education, and superiority, living in a land where ringing chimes call child and sire to the Church of God—a land where Bibles are read and Gospel truths are spoken, and where courts of justice are presumed to exist; it is extraordinary, I say, that, with all these advantages on your side, you can make war upon the poor defenceless black man. You know we have no money, no railroads, no telegraphs, no advantages of any sort, and yet all manner of injustice is placed upon us. You know that the black people of this country acknowledge you as their superiors, by virtue of your education and advantages.

There was a Resolution passed here at the early part of this session stating that all persons who were in their seats were eligible thereto. What are gentlemen going to do, with that Resolution staring them in the face? Your children and my children will read that Resolution, and they will be astonished that persons, claiming to be men, with souls and consciences, should, contrary to the express provision of that Resolution, turn the colored man out of his seat in this Hall. Another Resolution came before this House, a short time ago, praying Congress to remove all political disabilities from the white people of Georgia. I stood up in my place here, sir, and advocated that Resolution, and advised all colored Members to do the same; and almost every one of them voted for it. We were willing to give the white man every right which he ever rightfully possessed, and, were there forty negroes in this country to one white man, I would have precisely the same feeling, and act precisely the same way. The action of the House reminds me very much of a couple of lines of verse which we occasionally read:

> " When the Devil was sick, the Devil a saint would be;
> When the Devil was well, the Devil a saint was he."

When this House was "sick" with fear for the safety of the seats of ineligible Democrats, they were all very gracious and polite. But, when the Resolution was passed, declaring, in the face of facts, that all who were in their seats were eligible, then the foot was raised which was to trample on the poor negro, and that, too, by those who claim bravery and chivalry.

You may expel us, gentlemen, but I firmly believe that you will some day repent it. The black man cannot protect a country, if the country doesn't protect him; and if, to-morrow, a war should arise, I would not raise a musket to defend a country where my manhood is denied. The fashionable way in Georgia, when hard work is to be done, is, for the white man to sit at his ease, while the black man does the work; but, sir, I will say this much to the colored men of Georgia, as, if I should be killed in this campaign, I may have no opportunity of telling them at any other time: Never lift a finger nor raise a hand in defence of Georgia, unless Georgia acknowledges that you are men, and invests you with the rights pertaining to manhood. Pay your taxes, however, obey all orders from your employers, take good counsel from friends, work faithfully, earn an honest living, and show, by your conduct, that you can be good citizens.

I want to take your memories back to 1862. In that year, the Emperor of Russia, with one stroke of his pen, freed twenty-two millions of serfs. What did Russia do, then? Did she draw lines of distinction between those who had been serfs and her other citizens? No! That noble Prince, upon whose realm the sun never sets, after having freed these serfs, invested them with all the political rights enjoyed by his other subjects. America boasts of being the most enlightened, intelligent and enterprising nation in the world, and many people look upon Russia as not altogether perfectly civilized. But, look at what Russia has done for her slaves; there were twenty-two millions of them, while there are but four millions of us in the whole South, and only half a million in Georgia. If the action is taken in this House that is contemplated to-day' I will call a colored Convention, and I will say to my friends: Let us send North for carpet-baggers and Yankees, and let us send to Europe and all over the world for immigrants, and when they come here, we will give them every vote we have, and send them to the Legislature, in preference to sending a Georgian there.

Go on with your oppressions. Babylon fell. Where is Greece? Where is Nineveh? and where is Rome, the mistress Empire of the world? Why is it that she stands, to-day, in broken fragments throughout Europe? Because oppression killed her. Every act that we commit is like a bounding ball. If you curse a man, that curse rebounds upon you; and when you bless a man, the blessing returns to you; and when you oppress a man, the oppression, also, will rebound. Where have you ever heard of four millions of freemen being governed by laws, and yet have no hand in their making? Search the records of the world, and you will find no example. "Governments derive their just powers from the consent of the governed." How dare you to make laws by which to try me and my wife and children, and deny me a voice in the making of these laws? I know you can establish a monarchy, an autocracy, an oligarchy, or any other kind of an "ocracy" that you please; and that you can declare whom you please to be sovereign; but tell me, sir, how you can clothe me with more power than another, where all are sovereigns alike? How can you say you have a Republican form of Government, when you make such distinction and enact such proscriptive laws?

Gentlemen talk a good deal about the negroes "building no monuments." I can tell the gentlemen one thing; that is, that we could have built monuments of fire while the war was in progress. We could have fired your woods, your barns and fences, and called you home. Did we do it? No, sir! And God grant that the negro may never do it, or do anything else that would destroy the good opinion of his friends. No epithet is sufficiently opprobrious for us now. I say, sir, that we have built a monument of docility, of obedience, of respect, and of self-control, that will endure longer than the Pyramids of Egypt.

We are a persecuted people. Luther was persecuted; Galileo was persecuted; good men in all nations have been persecuted; but the persecutors have been handed down to posterity with shame and ignominy. If you pass this Bill, you will never get Congress to pardon or enfranchise another rebel in your lives. You are going to fix an everlasting disfranchisement upon Mr. Toombs and the other leading men of Georgia. You may think you are doing yourselves honor by expelling us from this House; but when we go, we will do as Wickliffe and as Latimer did. We will light a torch of truth that will never be extinguished—the impression that will run through the country, as people picture in their mind's eye these poor black men, in all parts of this Southern country, pleading for their rights. When you expel us, you make us forever your political foes, and you will never find a black man to vote a Democratic ticket again; for, so help me, God, I will go through all the length and breadth of the land, where a man of my race is to be found, and advise him to beware of the Democratic party. Justice is the great doctrine taught in the Bible. God's Eternal Justice is founded upon Truth, and the man who steps from Justice steps from Truth, and cannot make his principles to prevail.

I have now, Mr. Speaker, said all that my physical condition will allow me to say. Weak and ill, though I am, I could not sit passively here and see the sacred rights of my race destroyed at one blow. We are in a position somewhat similar to that of the famous "Light Brigade," of which Tennyson says, they had

> " Cannon to right of them,
> Cannon to left of them,
> Cannon in front of them,
> Volleyed and thundered."

I hope our poor, down-trodden race may act well and wisely through this period of trial, and that they will exercise patience and discretion under all circumstances.

You may expel us, gentlemen, by your votes, to-day; but, while you do it, remember that there is a just God in Heaven, whose All-Seeing Eye beholds alike the acts of the oppressor and the oppressed, and who, despite the machinations of the wicked, never fails to vindicate the cause of Justice, and the sanctity of His own handiwork.

E. H. PUGHE, Book and Job Printer, Augusta, Ga.

Appendix C

Opinion in the District Court of the United States
for the Eastern District of Pennsylvania,
the Honorable George A. Welsh, Chancellor,
Dismissing the Bill of Complaint in Civil Action No. 6657,
David H. Sims, Plaintiff, *vs.* S. L. Greene, Defendant
July 1, 1947

The plaintiff and defendant in this action are bishops of the African Methodist Episcopal Church, both of whom are highly respected and much-beloved men and leaders in their respective districts. Each seeks to enjoin the other from presiding over conferences of the First Episcopal District of said Church.

The question submitted to us presents problems that are not usually presented to a Chancellor in the Civil Courts. In a strictly legal sense the problem may not be unusual, yet a Chancellor cannot remain entirely oblivious of the far deeper questions that are raised by the pleadings and the evidence. Those deeper problems do not affect our judicial judgment, but they are consciously present and call for the greatest wisdom in making a decision. There is ever present before the Chancellor the thought that while this contest is one involving persons and personalities, the greater question is one that transcends personalities—we refer to the long established philosophies of our courts that must govern us in deciding a question in which the administration and interpretation of the supreme law of the Church is involved. That philosophy must be the polestar that guides us in mapping our course through such a troubled sea of internal church conflict as has been presented in this case. Therefore, in our reasoning and in our interpretation of facts and theories, and in our conclusions, we feel that we should frankly state our adherence to that philosophy.

The African Methodist Episcopal Church is a voluntary association claiming approximately one million communicants throughout the United States and foreign countries. It is divided into seventeen episcopal districts, each of which is presided over by a bishop. The episcopal districts are composed of several Annual Conferences. The First Episcopal District comprises the Philadelphia, New York, New Jersey, New England, Delaware, Bermuda and the Maritime Conferences. The government of the Church is established by its Book of Discipline, which contains all laws and bylaws relating thereto.

The supreme governing authority is the General Conference, which meets every four years. It is composed of bishops, clergymen, laymen, college officials and delegates elected from the episcopal districts. A Bishops' Council composed of the bishops presiding over the episcopal districts regulates the affairs of the Church and has full supervision during the interim between the General Conferences. The powers granted to the Bishops' Council include the hearing of complaints against any of the bishops, and the power to remove or transfer a bishop to or from a district by two-third vote if the good of the church demands it.

The plaintiff has served as bishop of the First Episcopal District since 1940, his last formal assignment being by the General Conference of 1944 and extending to 1948. In June, 1946, the Bishops' Council formally determined that a change should be made in the administration of the New York Conference and designated Bishop Wright as associate bishop with full authority to act in that Conference. Although Bishop Sims had subscribed to the resolution making such a change, he caused an action to be instituted in the Supreme Court of New York, to enjoin Bishop Wright from assuming full presiding authority in said Conference. Bishop Sims contended that because accusations had been made against him he could not be removed from the Conference except upon trial.

By reason of such controversy the Bishops' Council held a special meeting on August 15 at Washington, D.C., for the purpose of clarifying the earlier resolution by expressly describing the extent of Bishop Wright's authority. The meeting failed of its purpose and was adjourned because certain of the bishops sought to withdraw their approval of the resolution previously adopted, and challenged the power of the council to relieve Bishop Sims of jurisdiction in the New York Conference.

Thereafter charges were preferred against Bishop Sims ac-

cusing him of rebellion against the Bishops' Council, maladmin-
istration and other offenses. The charges were served upon him on
September 15 and a trial committee was appointed to hear the
charge on September 25. On that date the trial committee convened but was prevented from proceeding by the boisterous conduct of persons in attendance, whereupon the committee adjourned to another place. Before the trial committee could proceed, it was temporarily restrained by an order of court obtained
upon complaint of parties favoring Bishop Sims in the controversy. Ecclesiastical charges were also preferred by Bishop Sims'
group against nine of the bishops opposed to them.

The restraining order precluding the trial of Bishop Sims in
New York on September 25 was dissolved and the trial committee
sought to change its venue, fixing October 22 and Cincinnati as
the time and place for its hearing. Just prior to that date Bishop
Sims obtained a restraining order from the Federal District Court
of Ohio enjoining the trial committee from holding the trial.

On September 23 the Bishops' Council held a meeting attended by 15 bishops at which it was proposed that a special session of
the General Conference be called to deal with the controversies
between the contending factions. The meeting was broken up by
a violent disturbance before anything was accomplished, whereupon ten of the bishops adjourned to a hotel where they initiated
steps to call a special session of the General Conference.

An extra session of the General Conference was held at Little
Rock, Arkansas, November 20 to 23. The actions taken included
the trial and conviction of Bishop Sims and his dismissal from the
bishopric of the church. Thereafter the Bishops' Council replaced
him in conference of the First Episcopal District by appointing
Bishop Greene to such district.

The principal question raised by the pleadings and the evidence
is whether the plaintiff was legally unfrocked as a bishop and the
defendant assigned as his successor in the First Episcopal District.
The answer to that question is dependent upon a determination as
to the legal propriety of the extra session of the General Conference, whether the church judicatories were constituted and functioned in accordance with the rules of the Discipline, and whether
the plaintiff was provided with proper notice and an opportunity
to defend his position.

We are not concerned with the controversies and litigation be-

tween the contesting parties prior to the steps taken to call the
Extra Session of the General Conference, except to recognize them
as evidence of serious disputes within the church and of the necessity for some affirmative action by the church leaders. The open
differences then existing between the factions of the bishops'
group involved interpretations of the Discipline and of the powers
and functions of the Bishops' Council. The minority group opposed the construction of the church law and the proposed actions
of the majority group because they adversely affected the interests of the minority. None of the disputes concerned spiritual
or doctrinal matters.

One of the leading cases on this subject is that of Krecker v.
Shirey, 163 Pa. 534, 546, 555, wherein Mr. Justice Williams, after
declaring the principles that should govern the civil courts in a
church dispute, used the following language:

> The conduct of the parties and their sympathizers on both
> sides seems to have been hasty, uncharitable and ill tempered.
> It affords a travesty, rather than an illustration, of the pre-
> cepts of the religion of peace for the support and diffusion
> of which the church was organized and the parties on both
> sides profess to have devoted their energies and their lives.
> But our concern is with the legal aspects of the case presented
> to us, and to them we turn, leaving the moral side of the
> controversy to the consciences of the combatants.

Whether there is a parallelism between the facts as above outlined and whether the language of Mr. Justice Williams in that
case is applicable here, I leave to the Christian conscience of the
clerical and lay members of the great Church that is involved in
this unfortunate controversy.

We are concerned here with the controversies over the call of
the extra session of the General Conference and the propriety of
its procedure. But before analyzing the issues, it is important to
recognize that the differences between the factions of the bishops'
group and their followers had affected the affairs of the church in
certain sections and precluded the church authorities, the Bishops'
Council especially, from effectively performing their normal functions. Bitterness had arisen. The majority deemed the minority a

rebellious group and the minority believed that the majority sought autocratic power and the destruction of Bishop Sims' position and influence in the First Episcopal District. The majority was in the stronger position to apply the church law according to its interpretation and to accomplish its objectives by the weight of numbers; and the minority was thus impelled to resist and defend by challenging the legal propriety of the actions taken by the majority. Charges and countercharges intensified the conflict and, whether made in good faith or not, they were of strategic importance in the contest between the factions.

Both sides contributed appreciably to the struggle, and the actions of neither side were prompted entirely by an unselfish zeal for the welfare of the Church or the accomplishment of its Christian purposes. We are inclined to believe, however, that since the contest *had* developed and the issues *had* become complicated to the point where resort was had to the civil courts, the majority of the church leaders were justified in the opinion that nothing short of the action of the supreme church authority could effectively handle the problems. The steps taken by the majority with the view to calling an Extra Session of the General Conference, the call, the proceedings of the Conference, and the expulsion of Bishop Sims are challenged by the plaintiff and his group on the general grounds of legal inadequacy and impropriety. It therefore becomes necessary to examine the contentions of the respective parties with respect to the conference procedure and to determine the duty of this court.

It has been determined that the pleadings in this case present a justiciable controversy as to whether the plaintiff was legally installed and later expelled as a bishop, and the defendant legally appointed in his place, under the laws of Pennsylvania; and that this court has jurisdiction by reason of the diversity of citizenship of the parties (Sims *v.* Greene, CCA 3, Oct. 1946, No. 9342). The present inquiry is confined to the ascertainment of the pertinent church law and the determination of whether such law has been construed and complied with by proper church tribunals.

The A. M. E. Discipline, like other constitutions, codes and regulations, contains some uncertainties, ambiguities and inadequacies as to details, and it may be expected that church tribunals untrained in legal philosophy may arrive at conclusions at variance with those which a court of law might reach. But if the church law has been construed and applied reasonably by the Church itself, a different construction or application by the civil courts could not be justified upon any theory which recognizes the essential principle of the separation of church and state.

The first irregularity charged is that the majority of the bishops, assuming that the senior bishop was disqualified from presiding over the council by charges against him, chose the next in seniority, Bishop Ransom, to act in his stead in arranging for the Extra Session. Plaintiff contends that the pending charges only precluded the senior bishop from appointing or sitting on his own trial committee, and that he was therefore the presiding officer of the council; only a legally constituted Bishops' Council could propose an extra session of the General Conference, and since the moving bishops did not constitute a Bishops' Council, they were without authority to propose a special conference. In support of this contention the plaintiff cites Section 172 of the Discipline granting to the Bishops' Council full supervision over the entire Church during the interim of the General Conference.

The defendant's position is that by reason of the existing circumstances the Bishops' Council was unable to hold formal meetings or to function effectively because of the hopeless division between the factions, that necessity induced the majority group to initiate the required steps to call the conference, and that the general power of supervision given to the council did not preclude the majority of the bishops from proposing such a conference.

The Discipline authorizes extra sessions of the General Conference and presumably intended that they be proposed by the incumbent senior bishop or the Bishops' Council as the ruling church authorities. The circumstances, however, precluded them from taking such action, and of necessity the proposal as issued by ten of the bishops was a practical expedient. We do not find that their course of conduct is in conflict with either the provisions or the spirit of the Discipline, and we find no patent irregularity in the proposal and invitation issued. The collateral question as to whether the senior bishop was disqualified by the pending charges is therefore immaterial.

Plaintiff contends that since the Discipline requires the call for an extra session of the General Conference to be advised and approved by two-thirds of the annual conferences, such approval could only be given by the annual conferences in their regular annual sessions, and not by special sessions called for such purpose; and further that the special sessions held could not be deemed annual conferences in that they did not transact the business prescribed as the order of a business by the Discipline. He relies on the fact that the Discipline expressly provides for special annual conferences for the single purpose of electing delegates to an extra session of the General Conference, and deems mandatory the provision that the annual conferences transact certain business in order to constitute itself an annual conference. The defendant urges that special sessions of annual conferences are customary and traditional, that the authorization of special sessions for the single purpose designated by the Discipline implies authority for such sessions for all practical purposes, and that the Discipline does not prohibit special annual conferences at any time or place, nor render them invalid for failure to transact all of the business within their authorized scope.

The contention that special sessions of the annual conferences were illegal because they are not authorized by the Discipline and because they failed to transact all of the business prescribed would, if sustained, require a strained and unnatural interpretation of the law of the Church, and we decline to adopt it. The authorization of the special sessions of the annual conferences for a specified purpose neither expressly nor by inference precludes the holding of special sessions for other necessary purposes, and the custom of this and like organizations confirms the legal propriety of such special sessions. Nor do we believe that the Discipline by prescribing the order of business renders void those special sessions which fail to formally proceed according to the outline stated for the annual conferences.

The returns of approval by the annual conferences are challenged by the plaintiff on the grounds that they were made to an irregular and unconstituted authority, that they were informal and defective, and were so burdened with discrepancies as to create doubt as to their propriety and authenticity. He urges that the burden of proving the propriety of the action of two-thirds of the one hundred and eleven annual conferences is upon the defendant, and unless it is affirmatively shown that the eighty-six approving conferences actually and formally approved and made proper report thereof, the call and the subsequent conference were of no effect. The defendant differs from the plaintiff over the burden of proof and points out that the reports of approval of the annual conferences were verified by a committee of five of the majority group of bishops and by the Credentials Committee of the Conference, and that the Discipline is silent as to the method to be used in determining the fact of the two-thirds approval.

The approval of the call by two-thirds of the annual conferences is a question of fact. There is no provision in the Discipline as to how or to whom the returns of approval shall be made, nor is any special tribunal designated to determine their authenticity. These matters are obviously left to the judgment and integrity of the incumbent administrators of the church affairs, subject however to the approval of church judicatories acting within the scope of their authority. Having concluded that the ten bishops were justified in inviting approval of the annual conferences, it is not unreasonable to conclude that the returns of the annual conferences might, with equal propriety and in the absence of disciplinary direction, be made to the source of that invitation, subject of course to official count and verification. The evidence in support of approval, consisting of formal and informal resolutions, letters and telegrams, was sufficient to convince a committee of the bishops and later the Credentials Committee of the General Conference that two-thirds had in fact advised and approved the call for an extra session. No substantial evidence to the contrary was offered at the trial. We do not believe it is the duty of the court to examine into the place or procedure of the special sessions of the annual conferences or to undertake to count and verify the authenticity of the returns. Any doubt as to such matters by reason of discrepancies and informality must more properly be left to those bodies responsible for the enforcement of the church law.

Considerable emphasis is placed by the plaintiff on the contention that the call for the Extra Session was made by ten of the bishops acting without the authority of the Discipline, and that by reason thereof the call and the actions taken at the Conference were illegal and wholly void. The basis of this contention is that the language of Section 162 of the Discipline authorizing "The Bishops, with the advice of two-thirds of the Annual Conferences," to call an Extra Session must be construed to mean "all" of the bishops and not merely a majority or quorum. The defendant replies that there is nothing in the Discipline requiring the bishops to act unanimously or as a council in issuing such a call, that the functions of the Bishops' Council as outlined in the Discipline (Section 168-176) are silent as to the calling of extra sessions, and the issuance of the call by ten of the bishops was a mere ministerial act since two-thirds of the annual conferences had advised it.

Plaintiff argued that the implied purpose of the call was to penalize the minority and especially to remove Bishop Sims, that such action required two-thirds vote of the Bishops' Council, and that since such a majority had not issued the call it was fatally defective. He declared that the call was illegal, in that the agenda of the proposed conference was not published until after some of the annual conferences had authorized the extra session, that no necessity existed therefor, and also because of the inadequacy of the distribution of the call due to errors and omissions in the lists of delegates, especially with regard to the foreign territories and the districts supervised by the dissenting bishops. He maintains generally that in the absence of proof of accurate and universal notice, and because of the existence of discrepancies in the lists used, the inference must be that the conference was packed and therefore illegal.

Defendant believes that none of such arguments are supported by the Discipline or the evidence, and he points out that there was a full disclosure of the purposes in the communications and the call, an actual necessity existed, and that every effort had been made to effectively notify all parties, notwithstanding the absence of a central directory and the failure of dissenting bishops to disseminate the call.

The narrow construction placed by the plaintiff upon Section 162 authorizing "the bishops" to call the extra session is not justified by the language used or the practical purpose to be served. The term might possibly be construed to mean the Bishops' Council, a majority of the bishops as a group or as a council, or as urged by the plaintiff "all" of the bishops or at least two-thirds thereof with the assumption that the purpose was to remove the plaintiff from his district. In the absence of any specific provision or of any impelling inference to the contrary we are inclined to believe that the authorization to "the bishops with the advice of two-thirds of the annual conferences" was justifiably exercised by the ten bishops who issued the call, and especially so since the call was a ministerial act done in compliance with the advice of two-thirds of the annual conferences. Nor are we convinced that the call was illegal and void because the agenda was not publicized in a timely manner or because of errors and omissions in the lists of delegates and the distribution of notice to foreign territories and districts of dissenting bishops. The fact is that both the controversies and the call were given wide distribution throughout the Church. All reasonable efforts were exercised to make known to the proper parties the necessity for the extra session and the call thereof in compliance with the Discipline. There being no central registry, some of the burden of disseminating the call fell upon the bishops. The failure of those dissenting to do so and the existence of discrepancies did not preclude eleven hundred communicants of the church from assembling, and we are satisfied with the judgment of the conference that the call was adequate and universal.

As to the Conference itself, the plaintiff claims that it was illegally organized in that it elected a new chief secretary and designated committees, whereas it should have continued in office the committees and officers of the 1944 Conference. The defendant, the majority group, and the conference itself deemed the Extra Session to be a new General Conference and acted on the assumption that it was subject to the rules and should follow the usual procedure of General Conferences. The fact is that the Discipline is silent as to the procedure for an Extra Session and no precedent is available in as much as the Extra Session was the first in the one hundred and fifty years' life of the church.

The conduct of an extra session is not affirmatively prescribed by the Discipline, and whether the Little Rock Conference was justified in electing a new general secretary and forming new Credentials and Episcopal Committees was open for the dispute which developed. No precedent is available. We decline to hold with the plaintiff that the officers and committees of the 1944 Conference must continue in office in order to constitute the Conference a legal one and its actions valid. This appears to be a question exclusively for the church authorities.

Bishop Sims denies that he received notice of his trial at the Conference, the denial being in the sense that he did not receive the thirty days' formal notice prescribed by the Discipline. There can be no doubt however that he had *actual* notice, and there is evidence that notice and the charges were served upon him forty-three days in advance of the Conference, although not by the president or secretary of the Bishops' Council. Defendant denies the necessity of the formal notice prescribed by the Discipline for the trial of bishops, in as much as the expulsion of Bishop Sims was by the action of the Conference on the recommendation of the Episcopal Committee, and points to Bishop Sims' acknowledgment of notice of his impending trial and his efforts to preclude it as evidence of the opportunity to appear and defend and to appeal to the Conference.

The plaintiff concludes that he received no notice of his trial at the Extra Session notwithstanding evidence to the contrary and his own acknowledgment that the trial was to be had. While it is true that the Discipline requires thirty days' notice to be given by the president or secretary of the Bishops' Council when a trial is to be had before a trial committee in the interim between General Conferences, it is not clear that such formality is required where charges or complaints are considered by the Episcopal Committee at a General Conference. It is certain however that the actions of the trial committee would be limited to prescribing suspension and that final expulsion could in any event only be decreed by a General Conference. The question of whether the formal thirty days' notice was necessary and whether it was in fact given are technical ones involving an interpretation of the Discipline, and in the absence of any expressly controlling provision we are not in a position to declare the trial or the examination by the Episcopal Committee void for want of notice or an opportunity to the plaintiff to defend his legal position.

As to the action of the Episcopal and Judiciary Committees as reported by the minutes, and there is nothing in the record to the contrary, we find no serious violation of the Discipline. There can be no doubt of the opportunity of the plaintiff to appear and defend against the charges and to justify his conduct before the Episcopal Committee and the Conference itself. The Bishops' Council as constituted under the amendment to the Discipline adopted at the Conference formally assigned the defendant to the plaintiff's Episcopal District. Assuming that the Conference was a legal one and that the amendment was adopted as reported, such action of the council is not subject to question. Although the plaintiff vigorously contests the propriety of the procedure which resulted in his expulsion on technical grounds, it is obvious that the Conference and its promulgators sought to conform to the letter of the law and that they succeeded to the extent that the Conference itself approved of their actions.

It is apparent from this discussion that the points of difference between the parties rest upon conflicting interpretations of the Discipline and that both sides seek to have this court resolve those differences in their respective favors. The plaintiff would also have us examine into the propriety and accuracy of the actions of the eighty-six annual conferences and the qualifications of the delegates to the Conference, and to find as a fact that inaccuracies inevitably involved in so complex a project have rendered void all of the things purported to have been accomplished by the Conference.

We do not believe that it is the function of the civil courts to weigh and interpret the provisions of the laws established for the government of a church organization which has jurisdiction to do so for itself. Their duty extends no farther than the determination of the existence of the church law, whether it has been fairly interpreted and applied, and whether there are judicatories which have functioned in practical compliance with the law and within their jurisdiction.

The evidence does not disclose any plain or flagrant violation of the laws of the Church in the call or in the conduct of the Extra Session of the General Conference, nor do we find that it was unlawfully packed for the ruthless accomplishment of a preconceived purpose. There is evidence of the necessity for the Extra Session, of an attempt by the majority of bishops to comply with the letter of the law, adequate notice to all parties concerned, a large Conference of church representatives, and the exercise of the functions of government by the Conference within the scope of the law as interpreted by that authority. Our conclusion is a negative one. Sustaining the effectiveness of the Extra Session is not intended as an encouragement to the dominating element in a church organization to administer its laws for the service of its selfish will or to exercise its power over the minority regardless of justice or the virtue of its cause. Rather it is on the ground that the civil courts must wherever possible avoid interference with church affairs and leave to the church tribunals the determination and application of their own laws.

This conclusion is amply supported by the law of Pennsylvania. Upon questions arising under the Discipline, as upon those arising under the articles of faith, the decisions and the actions of the ecclesiastical tribunals are ordinarily final, and they will be respected by courts of law (German Reformed Church *v.* Seibert, 3 Pa. 282; Schlichter *v.* Kerter, 156 Pa. 119). But if the decisions plainly violate the law they profess to administer or are in conflict with the laws of the land they will not be followed.

The regularity and legal effect of the organization of a General Conference in the manner in which it was accomplished raises an ecclesiastical question. Its determination depends upon an interpretation of the provisions of the Discipline which it is the duty of the General Conference to make. If the decision actually made does not violate the laws of the state or the Church, and is conclusive upon the ecclesiastical body of which the General Conference is the chief tribunal, it should be followed by the civil courts. Whether the General Conference disposed of the questions in the wisest manner or with legalistic exactitude are not to be considered. Its decisions and interpretations settle the law and its applications and the civil courts must recognize its effectiveness (Krecker *v.* Shirley, 63 Pa. 534).

A majority of a church organization may direct and control church matters consistently with the laws of the Church but not in violation of them (Long *v.* Harvey, 177 Pa. 473). If the acts of the majority are justified and adopted by the supreme church tribunal, they may not be deemed unlawful even though they result in the removal of an official and the incidental loss of his emoluments (Furmanski *v.* Iwanowski, 265 Pa. 1). Civil courts do not review the merits of a decision rendered in an ecclesiastical matter by the appropriation church tribunal (Post *v.* Dougherty, 326 Pa. 97, 102).

We have tried to set out the legal principles that have been laid down by our courts in a controversy of this kind. We have refrained from going beyond the applicable legal principles involved. By refraining from doing so we are not unmindful of some very important questions that may perhaps require reference to if not commented upon by us. Nor are we unmindful of the fact that the legal principles upon which we rely have left untouched in this opinion the question of the security of the tenure of office of the bishops of the African Methodist Episcopal Church under the Discipline. We could not help but be impressed by the almost absolute control of the bishops with respect to the special conferences held in their jurisdictions. This was evidenced by the almost unanimous votes in many of the conferences; the speed with which some of these so-called trials were conducted cannot help but raise a question in the mind of the Chancellor. The question of the probability or possibility of a trial in the civil sense or meaning of the word at the Extra Session quite naturally was injected into the picture as was the question of the right of actual appeal on the part of those who were called upon to face trial. These questions if raised in a civil or political organization would be judged by the democratic theories governing such organizations and the procedure that should prevail. The plaintiff claimed that with respect to many of the above matters the defendant resorted to what the outside world calls "steamroller" tactics. However, this being entirely an ecclesiastical matter, set up and operated by ecclesiastical authorities, the civil courts are loath to impugn Christian leadership even though the court might feel that the actions savor somewhat of wordly weaknesses, if the reasonable letter of the governing law has been observed. In other words, we feel that it would be highly dangerous to substitute for the judgment and opinion of the ecclesiastical authorities the judgment of a civil court unless both letter and spirit of the governing law had been practically ignored. This is especially true today because we cannot close our eyes to the fact that all over the world, on all continents, there is great conflict raging along the economic and political front. History teaches us that when such conflicts rage in the breast of humanity, even the Church is drawn into the conflict. When the Church is so drawn into that conflict, it must act under its own laws and be responsible to its membership unless the supreme law of the land governing its actions has been trangressed. A breaking down of this principle of law will result in the civil courts ruling the Church rather than the Church being ruled by duly-constituted ecclesiastical bodies.

Whatever the cause of this schism, we can say that the effect has been tragic. Such bitterness is not often presented to us in a court of law. We do take pleasure, however, in saying that, lest this unfortunate affair be seized upon by the scoffer and be prejudicial and damaging to the whole Church and the entire group, there is nothing as far as we have been able to ascertain in any of these charges that reflects upon the personal honesty and morality of the persons involved. No moral stigma has attached to anyone, and it is a church dispute in which personal rivalries, ambitions and rival purposes have blended to make a warfare that if persisted in can only destroy the organization of the Church and its great spiritual influences on millions throughout the world.

From the evidence submitted, we make the following

FINDINGS OF FACT

1. The plaintiff David H. Sims is a citizen of the State of Pennsylvania; the defendant S. L. Greene is a citizen of the State of Arkansas; and the amount in controversy exceeds three thousand dollars ($3,000).

2. The plaintiff David H. Sims is a Bishop of the African Methodist Episcopal Church, and was assigned in 1944 by the General Conference of said Church to the First Episcopal District thereof for a tenure extending until May, 1948.

3. The First Episcopal District of the African Methodist Episcopal Church consists of the following conferences: Philadelphia, New Jersey, New York, New England, Delaware, Bermuda and Maritime Conferences.

4. The plaintiff receives from the African Methodist Episcopal Church as salary and other emoluments of office, a sum in excess of three thousand dollars ($3,000) annually, and by virtue of his office is the president of the Board of Managers of the property and business of the Book Concern of said Church located in Philadelphia.

5. By virtue of such assignment the plaintiff took charge of the affairs of the African Methodist Episcopal Church within the

First Episcopal District with authority to assign ministers and other officials and to supervise the annual conferences in said district. Such authority continued up to the time of the controversies upon which this suit is based.

6.   On or about December 4, 1946, the defendant, a bishop of the African Methodist Episcopal Church assigned as presiding bishop of the Philadelphia, Delaware and Maritime Conferences of the First Methodist Episcopal District, by virtue of an extra session of the General Conference of said Church held on November 20, 1946, sought to interfere with the administration of the affairs of the African Methodist Episcopal Church in said conferences and the supervision thereof by the plaintiff by giving general notice to the pastors and communicants thereof of his assignment and by giving notice of the calling of a special session of the Philadelphia Annual Conference. By reason of such actions the plaintiff instituted the present suit.

7.   The laws and regulations of the African Methodist Episcopal Church which govern and control the authority and functions of the General Conference, the Annual Conference and all other affairs of the Church consist of the A. M. E. Discipline.

8.   The Discipline provides:

> (1)   The bishops with the advice of two-thirds of the Annual Conferences, when necessary, shall call an extra session of the General Conference.
>
> (2)   The bishops . . . shall, in writing, notify the preachers in charge of circuits and stations to inform all delegates in good standing, as members of the last quadrennial session, to attend the extra session at the time and place appointed by the bishops. . . . After notice being thus duly given, if two-thirds of the delegates be present at the appointed time and place, they shall proceed to business and their proceedings shall be lawful.

9.   The Bishops' Council was on and prior to September 23 unable to properly administer the affairs of the Church by reason of the existence of controversies and litigation between opposing factions of the members of the Council. The faction of which Bishop Greene is a representative included the ten bishops who deemed it necessary to call an extra session of the General Confer-

ence to deal with the problems then pending. They were opposed by six bishops of whom Bishop Sims is a representative.

10. On October 5 ten of the bishops issued communication addressed to the ministers and members of the Church and the members of the various annual conferences reciting the existence of deplorable and unsavory conditions in the Church and the necessity for an extra session of the General Conference to deal therewith, and proclaiming that the annual conferences should be called to authorize a Special Session for the purpose of hearing, considering and acting upon a report of the bishops to the Episcopal Committee in reference to the matters recited in the communication. This was disseminated to the Church through the bishops and by publication in the official church press.

11. On October 22 an additional special communication was issued by the same ten bishops specifically charging Bishop Sims with openly and flagrantly ignoring the Discipline and with disrespect for and open rebellion against the laws, doctrines and government of the church; and suspending and referring to the special session the trial of Bishop Sims then pending. The communications were published in the official church press and a response thereto by Bishop Sims was published in the same issue.

12. The annual conferences of the episcopal districts acted upon the request made in the communication of October 5 and reported their actions to the bishops. Bishops Clayborne, Baber, Wright, Greene and Reid examined the returns of the annual conferences and determined that two-thirds thereof had approved and advised the call of the Extra Session.

13. On November 5 ten of the bishops issued a call for an extra session of the General Conference to be held at Little Rock, Arkansas, November 20-24, requiring all members and delegates of the 1944 Conference to attend, directing all pastors to notify the delegates, declaring that the purpose of the Session was, *inter alia*, to hear and act upon a report of the bishops on matters referred to in the special communications of October 5 and October 22 previously recited, and proclaiming that the Conference was called in compliance with the requirements of the Discipline.

14. Bishop Sims notified the elders of the First Episcopal District that said District was not participating in the Conference, that it had been called illegally and expressly for the purpose of

trying him upon charges on which he had been previously exonerated.

15.   Prior to the date fixed for the Conference, the ten bishops who had issued the call started suit in the United States District Court for the Eastern District of Arkansas to restrain the plaintiff and the minority group from interfering with the conduct of the Conference. The defendants therein answered the complaint alleging illegality in the call of the Conference, and asking that it be restrained from proceeding to a trial of Bishop Sims on charges on which he had been acquitted by an ecclesiastical court. After hearings on November 18 and 19, the suit was terminated by a stipulation of all parties that "all court action on both sides with reference to the holding of the General Conference will be dropped, and that we proceed with the Extra Session of the General Conference."

16.   Pursuant to the call, the Conference was attended by the bishops of the Church, and approximately 1,100 ministers, officials, delegates and other members of the Church. Plaintiff appeared at the first session but denied attendance in his official capacity.

17.   The proceedings at said Conference included the calling of the roll of delegates, the election of a chief secretary, and the appointment of a Credentials Committee. The latter committee by formal report determined that 85 of the annual conferences had approved the call of the Extra Session and 25 had failed to report, and also that a quorum consisting of two-thirds of the qualified delegates were in attendance, which report was adopted by the Conference.

18.   At said Conference the Episcopal Committee organized. Charges against Bishop Sims were presented to it. The Episcopal Committee appointed a Judicial Committee to hear the charges against Bishop Sims. The Judicial Committee, after attempting to summon Bishop Sims to the hearing without success, and upon notice to his counsel, proceeded to hear evidence in support of the charges against him.

19.   The charges upon which the trial was had were served upon the plaintiff on September 15, together with a notice to appear for trial September 25, which proposed trial was enjoined through legal proceedings instituted by or on behalf of the plaintiffs; and again on October 8, together with notice that the plain-

tiff would be tried at the Extra Session of the General Conference. Bishop Sims acknowledged that he knew of the proposed trial at the Extra Session by his letter to the elders on November 14, advising them that the Extra Session was called illegally for the express purpose of trying him on charges which were heard on September 25, and by his acknowledgment in the answer filed in the District Court of Arkansas to the same effect.

20. Bishop Sims did not attend the trial before the Judicial Committee in person or by his attorney. The Committee at the close of its hearing reported to the Episcopal Committee a finding of guilty against Bishop Sims and recommended his expulsion as a bishop of the Church. The Episcopal Committee considered said report and unanimously approved the recommendation therein. The Episcopal Committee prepared and submitted its report to the Extra Session on November 21, making like recommendation.

21. The members and delegates constituting the Extra Session voted upon the question of approval or disapproval of the recommendation of the Episcopal Committee. A standing vote was taken by districts, counted by the Secretary and reported to Bishop Gregg, who was then presiding. The vote was 999 in favor of expulsion and 35 opposed.

22. Although the plaintiff did not appear before the Conference, the right to appear and to appeal to the Extra Session of the General Conference was available to him. Appeals were made by other bishops similarly tried at said Conference, and consideration was given to such appeals by the Conference.

23. Following the Extra Session of the General Conference, the Bishops' Council assigned the defendant to preside over the Philadelphia, Delaware and Maritime Conferences of the First Episcopal District and Bishop Wright to the remaining Conferences in said District.

In order to complete the record the following answers are made to the requests of the parties for findings of fact.

Plaintiff's requests are affirmed with the exception of Nos. 16, 32, 34, 35, 36, 37, 56 and 58, which are deemed to be immaterial; 25, 26, 39, 52, 55, 57 and 59 are refused as stated and 41-49 are refused as being at variance with the foregoing findings.

Defendant's requests are affirmed with the exception of Nos. 27, 29, 30 and 31, which are refused.

For the reasons stated in our discussion, we reach the following

CONCLUSIONS OF LAW

1. This court has jurisdiction of the issues presented in this case by reason of diversity of citizenship of the parties.

2. The call of the Extra Session of the General Conference of the Church has not been shown to be in violation of the requirements of the Discipline.

3. The meeting of communicants and officials of the Church at Little Rock, Arkansas, on November 20-23, 1946, constituted an Extra Session of the General Conference of the Church.

4. The conduct of the Extra Session was in conformity with the laws of the Church as interpreted and applied by the supreme church authorities, and was not in violation of the laws of Pennsylvania.

5. The actions adopted by said Conference included the expulsion of the plaintiff as a bishop of the Church, and the amendment of the Discipline to permit the election of a president of the Bishops' Council in place of the senior bishop.

6. The conduct of the trial of the plaintiff by the Judiciary Committee and the subsequent approval and adoption of its recommendations by the Episcopal Committee and the General Conference was not in violation of any express provisions of the Discipline.

7. The plaintiff had ample notice and opportunity to appear for trial before the Judiciary Committee and to appeal to the General Conference.

8. The defendant was assigned to the Philadelphia, Delaware and Maritime Conferences of the First Episcopal District by the Bishops' Council.

9. The bill of complaint should be dismissed.

10. No necessity has been shown for the granting of the injunction prayed for by the defendant and the prayer is dismissed.

11. The costs of the respective parties of this proceeding should be borne by them.

12. A decree may be entered in accordance herewith.

The requests of the parties for conclusions of law are disposed of as follows:

Plaintiff's requests are refused. Defendant's requests are affirmed with the exception of Nos. 6, 9, 10, 11, 14, 15, 18, 19, 26, 27, 30, 31, 41, 42, which are refused as to the language used or as being at variance with the conclusions above stated.

Bibliography

A. M. E. Church Review, The (various issues).

Allen, Richard. *The Life, Experience, and Gospel Labors of the Right Reverend Richard Allen.* Philadelphia: A. M. E. Book Concern, 1887.

Anderson, William K. *Methodism.* N.Y.: Methodist Publishing House, 1947.

Arnett, B. W. *The Budget, 1885, 1887, 1888, 1900, 1904.* Philadelphia.

————. *Colored Sunday Schools.* Nashville: A. M. E. Sunday School Union, 1896.

————. *Proceedings, Quarto-Centenary Conference.* Xenia, Ohio, 1890.

Berry, L. L. *A Century of Missions of the A. M. E. Church.* N.Y.: Gutenburg Printing Co., 1942.

Brawley, Benjamin. *A Short History of the American Negro.* N.Y.: Macmillan Co., 1919.

————. *A Social History of the American Negro.* N.Y.: Macmillan Co., 1921.

Brown, Charles Brockden. *Arthur Merwyn.* Philadelphia: David McKay.

Brown, William Wells. *The Rising Son.* Boston: A. G. Brown & Co., 1882.

Buckley, James M. *A History of Methodism in the United States,* 2 vols. N.Y.: Harper & Brothers, 1890.

Butterfield, L. H. (ed.). *Letters of Benjamin Rush.* Princeton: Princeton University Press, 1951.

Carey, Mathew. *The Malignant Fever in Philadelphia,* 2d ed. Philadelphia: issued by author, November 23, 1793.

Cell, George C. *The Rediscovery of John Wesley.* N.Y.: Henry Holt & Co., 1935.

Christian Recorder, The (various issues).

Coan, Josephus R. *Daniel Alexander Payne*. Philadelphia: A. M. E. Book Concern, 1935.

Coleman, Lucretia H. Newman. *Poor Ben: A Story of Real Life*. Nashville: A. M. E. Sunday School Union, 1890.

Cromwell, John Wesley. *The Negro in American History*. Washington, D.C.: The American Negro Academy, 1914.

Davis, M. H. *The Dogmas and Precepts of the Fathers*. Nashville: A. M. E. Sunday School Union, 1948.

Dodd, William E. *The Cotton Kingdom*. New Haven: Yale University Press, 1921.

————. *Expansion and Conflict*. N.Y.: Houghton Mifflin Co., 1915.

————. *The Old South Struggles for Democracy*. N.Y.: MacMillan Co., 1937.

Dow, Lorenzo. *History of a Cosmopolite, a Journal of Life*. Cincinnati: H. S. and J. Applegate & Co.

Du Bois, W. E. B. *Black Reconstruction*. N.Y.: Harcourt, Brace & Co., 1935.

Gaines, Wesley J. *African Methodism in the South*. Atlanta: Franklin Publishing House, 1890.

General Conference Minutes (various years).

Goodman, Nathan G. *Benjamin Rush, Physician and Citizen*. Philadelphia: University of Pennsylvania Press, 1934.

Handy, James A. *Scraps of A. M. E. Church History*. Philadelphia: A. M. E. Book Concern, n.d.

Hart, Albert Bushnell. *Slavery and Abolition*. "American History Series," Vol. 16; N.Y.: Harper & Brothers, 1906.

Helper, Hinton Rowan. *The Impending Crisis*. N.Y.: Burdell Brothers, 1857.

Hill, Charles L. *The Episcopacy: Its Functions, Its Authority, Its Limitations*. Wilberforce, Ohio. An address delivered before the Connections Council of the A. M. E. Church at Birmingham, Alabama, February 17, 1944, and published by order of the Council.

Hockett, Homer C. *Political and Social History of the United States, 1492-1828*. N.Y.: Macmillan Co., 1929.

Hunter, Charles S. *History of the St. Paul A. M. E. Church, St. Louis, Missouri.* St. Louis: Robinson and Blocke Print, 1921.

Jenifer, John T. *History of the A. M. E. Church.* Nashville: A. M. E. Sunday School Union, 1916.

Johnson, James Weldon. *Along This Way.* N.Y.: Viking Press, 1933.

Journal of Religion, The (various issues).

Kealing, H. T. *History of the A. M. E. Church in Texas.* n.p., n.d.

Kennedy, J. P. *Swallow Barn.* N.Y.: George Putnam, 1851.

Lampton, E. W. *Digest of Rulings of the A. M. E. Church.* Washington, D.C.: Record Publishing Co., 1907.

Love, The Rev. W. F. *Forty Years in the Ministry.* Waco, Texas: Paul Quinn Weekly Publishers, 1899.

Luccock, Halford E., and Hutchinson, Paul. *The Story of Methodism.* Philadelphia: Abingdon Press, 1907.

McConnell, F. J. *John Wesley.* N.Y.: Abingdon Press, 1939.

Matlack, L. C. *The Anti-Slavery Struggle and Triumph of the Methodist Episcopal Church.* N.Y.: Phillips and Hunt, 1881.

Mays, Benjamin E. *The Negro's God.* Boston: Mt. Vernon Press, 1938.

Miller, John C. *Triumph of Freedom.* Boston: Brown & Co., 1948.

Missionary Recorder, The (various issues).

Mitchell, S. Weir. *Red City.* N.Y.: Century Co., 1913.

Mixon, W. H. *History of the A. M. E. Church in Alabama.* n.p., n.d.

Morgan, J. H. *History of the New Jersey Conference, 1872-1887.* Camden: S. Chew, Printers, 1887.

Newton, A. H. *Out of the Briars.* Philadelphia: A. M. E. Book Concern, 1916.

Oldroyd, Osborn H. *Words of Lincoln.* Washington, D.C.: Mershom Co. Press, 1895.

Payne, Daniel A. *History of the A. M. E. Church.* Nashville: A. M. E. Sunday School Union, 1891.

Payne, Daniel A. *Recollections of Seventy Years*. Nashville: A. M. E. Sunday School Union, 1888.

————. *Semi-Centenary and Retrospect of the A. M. E. Church, 1818-1866*. Philadelphia: A.M.E. Book Concern, 1866.

Penn, I. Garland. *The Afro-American Press and Its Editors*. Springfield, Mass.: Walter & Co., 1891.

Phillips, Ulrich B. *American Negro Slavery*. N.Y.: D. Appleton & Co., 1928.

Pollard, E. A. *Black Diamonds*. N.Y.: Fudney and Russell, 1860.

Powell, J. H. *Bring Out Your Dead*. Philadelphia: University of Pennsylvania Press, 1949.

Ransom, Reverdy C. *The Pilgrimage of Harriet Ransom's Son*. Nashville: A. M. E. Sunday School Union, 1950.

————. *Preface to the History of the A. M. E. Church*. Nashville: A. M. E. Sunday School Union, 1950.

Repository of Religion and Literature, 1858-60, ed. Daniel A. Payne; from 1861, ed. J. M. Brown. Indianapolis and Philadelphia.

Rhoades, Lillian Jones. *The Story of Philadelphia*. N.Y.: American Book Co., 1900.

Rhodes, James Ford. *History of the United States From the Compromise of 1850*, 9 vols. N.Y.: Harper & Brothers, 1922.

Ridgell, Alfred. *Africa and African Methodism*. Atlanta: Franklin Printing Co., 1896.

Rogers, J. A. *World's Great Men of Color*, 2 vols. N.Y.: F. Hubner & Co., 1947.

Rosenwald Fund. *School Money in Black and White*. Chicago, 1937.

Rush, Benjamin. *The Autobiography of Benjamin Rush*, ed. George W. Corner. Princeton: Princeton University Press, 1948.

Scharf, Thomas, and Wescott, Thompson. *History of Philadelphia*, 3 vols. Philadelphia: L. H. Everts & Co., 1884.

Schlesinger, Arthur Meier. *Political and Social History of the United States, 1829-1925*. N.Y.: Macmillan Co., 1930.

Shorter, James A. *The Life of Bishop James A. Shorter*. Baltimore: J. Lanahan, 1890.

Singleton, George A. "Religious Instruction of the Negro in the United States Before the Rebellion." A Master of Arts thesis in the University of Chicago Library.

Smith, C. S. *History of the A. M. E. Church.* Philadelphia: A. M. E. Book Concern, 1922.

————. *The Life of Daniel A. Payne.* Nashville: A. M. E. Sunday School Union, 1894.

Smith, David. *Autobiography of David Smith.* Zenia, Ohio: *Gazette* Office, 1881.

Southern Christian Recorder, The (various issues).

Stevens, Abel. *History of Methodism,* 4 vols. N.Y.: M. B. Conicete, 1895.

Steward, T. G. *Fifty Years in the Gospel Ministry.* Philadelphia: A. M. E. Book Concern, 1921.

Sweet, William Warren. *The American Churches.* N.Y.: Abingdon-Cokesbury, 1948.

————. *The Story of Religion in America.* N.Y.: Harper & Brothers, 1930.

Tanner, B. T. *Apology for African Methodism.* Baltimore: Methodist Episcopal Book Concern, 1887.

————. *Outline of the History of the A. M. E. Church.* Philadelphia: A. M. E. Book Concern, 1883.

————, ed. *Reprint of the First Edition of the Discipline of the African M. E. Church.* Philadelphia: A. M. E. Book Concern, 1917.

Tolbert, Horace. *The Sons of Allen.* Zenia, Ohio: The Aldine Press, 1906.

Turner, H. M. *Methodist Polity.* Philadelphia: A. M. E. Book Concern, 1888.

Van Doren, Carl. *The Great Rehearsal.* N.Y.: Viking Press, 1948.

Voice of Missions, The (various issues).

Wakeley, J. B. *Lost Chapters of Methodism.* 200 Mulberry St., N.Y.: issued by author, 1858.

Watson, John F. *Annals of Philadelphia.* Philadelphia: Leary, Stuart & Co., 1909.

Wayman, A. W. *Cyclopedia of African Methodism.* Baltimore: Methodist Episcopal Book Depository, 1882.

Wayman, A. W. *Manual or Guide Book of the Discipline of the A. M. E. Church*. Baltimore, 1880.

————. *My Recollections*. Philadelphia: A. M. E. Book Concern, 1881.

Welch, Elaine. *William Paul Quinn*. 3508 South Parkway, Chicago, 1933.

Wesley, Charles H. *Richard Allen, Apostle of Freedom*. Washington, D.C.: Associated Publishers, 1935.

Western Christian Recorder, The (various issues).

Wightman, William H. *The Life of William Capers*. Nashville, 1858.

Wilson, Joseph T. *The Black Phalanx*. Hartford, Conn.: American Publishing Co., 1890.

Wilson, Woodrow. *Division and Reunion: Epochs of American History*. N.Y.: Longmans, Green & Co., 1921.

Winchester. *John Wesley*. N.Y.: Macmillan Co., 1916.

Woodson, Carter G. *Education of the Negro Prior to 1861*. Washington, D.C.: Negro Life and History, 1919.

————. *History of the Negro Church*. Washington, D.C.: Associated Publishers, 1921.

Index

A

Abington, C. W., 171
Abolition writers, 81
Adams, Eugene A., 163
Adams, Samuel, 20
A. M. E. Book Concern, 30, 37
African M. E. Church, xix
A. M. E. Church Review, 81, 84
Alabama Annual Conference, 106
Alexander, John A., 181
Alexander, Sadie T. M., 174
Allen, Alexander Joseph, 2, 85, 173
Allen, Flora, 112
Allen, G. W., 85
Allen, Mayor William, xvii
Allen, Richard, xiv, xviii, 7, 12, 15, 20-22, 29, 42, 112
Allen, Sarah, 112, 135
Allen Building, 83, 158
Allen Temple, 28, 60
Allen University, 134
Anti-slavery Resolution, 58
Armstrong, J. H., 140
Arnett, B. W., 129, 137
Athanasius, 10
Attucks, Crispus, xvi
"Aunt Annie," 21
Avery, A. D., 163

B

Baber, George W., 96, 109, 174, 176, 181
Baltimore, Priscilla, 72
Baltimore Annual Conference, 31
Baltimore Associates, 135
Baxter, D. M., 83
Beans, Scipio, 70

Bethel Church, Baltimore, 69
Bethel Church, Philadelphia, 18
Bias, Dr. J. G., 42
Blacksmith shop, xix
Boggs, John, 28, 69, 115
Bonaparte, Napoleon, 3
Bonner, I. H., 76, 111
Book of Discipline, 23
Boston Massacre, 8
Bradwell, C. L., 85, 102
Broadie, Philip, 38
Brooks, Phillips, 62
Brooks, W. S., 97, 143
Brown, Governor Joe, Appendix B, 12, 13
Brown, Morris, 1, 26, 33, 35, 71, 90, 108, 114
Brownlow, W. G., 62
Bryant, Ira T., 168, 170
Bryant, M. E., 85
Buchanan, James, 41
Buckley, James M., 13

C

Cain, R. H., 129, 134
Calhoun, John C., 66
Campbell, Anthony, 116
Campbell, Jabez P., 32, 69, 73, 116
Campbell College, 95
Canady, H. D., 163
Cannon, Noah W. C., 28, 108, 115
Carey, A. J., 143
Cell, George C., 5
Chappelle, Wm. D., 85
Charleston, John, 28, 69, 115
Cheeks, R. M., 85
Christian Herald, 37
Christian Recorder, 37

247

Church attorneys: Fred A. Isgrig; J.
A. Hibler; J. R. Booker; the Rev-
erends V. M. Townsend and John
Adams, 175
Clark, M. M. 128
Clarkson, Thomas, 8
Clayborne, J. H., 85, 176
Clement, Thomas Jefferson, 159
"Cliveden," xvii
Coburn, Daniel, 130
Committee on General Conference,
175
Conference Course of Studies, 90
Conner, J. M., 142
Constantine, Appendix B, 10
Coulter, E. G., 5
Crusaders, Appendix B, 11
Cuff, Burgoyne, 134
Cuff, Reuben, 134
Cuff, Thomas, 134
Curry, G. E., 174, 176
Cushites, Appendix B, 4

D

Davies, Judge Elmer, 173
Davis, Jefferson, 40, 66
Davis, Monroe H., 176, 190
Davis, Samuel, 47
Dayton, W. L., 41
Delaney, Major Martin R., 81
Department of Pensions, 174, 186
Derrick, William B., 140
Dew, Thomas R., 62
Dickins, John, 18
Disney, R. R., 18
Divorce question, 41
Dorsey, James, 172
Doughty, Charles, 37
Douglas, Stephen A., 40
Dow, Lorenzo, xviii, 108
Dred Scott Decision, 59
Du Bois, W. E. B., xix, 59, 93

E

Earley, J. M., 34
Edward Waters College, 96

Emanuel A. M. E. Church, Charles-
ton, 103
Embry, James C., 85, 140
Episcopal Address, First, 37
"Evergreen Cottage," 38

F

First Extra General Conference, 176
Flipper, Carl F., 76
Flipper, J. S., 144, 164, 167-168,
171
Fountain, Jr., Wm. A., 96
Fountain, Sr., Wm. A., 143, 145,
176
Franklin, Benjamin, xvi, 19
Freeman, Moses, 28, 69
Fremont, J. C., 41
Fugitive Slave Law, 59

G

Gaines, A. L., 139
Gaines, Wesley J., 103
Gaines, William, 103
Garretson, Freeborn, 14, 46
Garrison, William Lloyd, 66
General Conference of 1816, 21
General Conference of 1852, 165
General Conference of 1860, 65
Gomez, Joseph, 165, 181
Green, A. M., 85
Green, Augustus R., 37, 128
Green, Shields, 66
Gregg, John A., 138
Gumbs, S. H. V., 164, 181

H

Hancock, John, xvi, 20
Handy, James A., 38, 103, 138
Harmon, John, 163
Harris, W. L., 53
Hatcher, E. C., 86
Heard, William H., 27, 126
Heath, Anne E., 78
Heck, Barbara, 6
Helper, Hinton Rowan, 51

Hemmingway, L. H., 93, 181
Henderson, T. W., 71
Hill, Charles L., 93, 182
Hill, Stephen, 23, 132
Hogarth, George, 31, 36, 81, 128
Hoosier, Harry, 7
Horace, Appendix B, 11
Howard, Edward J., 157, 173
Hughes, J. H., 160
Hughes, Lucy M., 77, 98
Hurst, John, 73, 142, 163

I

"Indian Queen," 26
Isgrig, Judge Fred A., 176

J

Jack, Gullak, 26
Jackson, Andrew, 30
Jackson, Arthur S., 87, 95, 170, 174, 187
Jackson, G. L., 163
Jackson, Mansfield E., 163
Jefferson, Thomas, xiv
Jerome, Appendix B, 1
Johnson, Henry J., 130
Johnson, James H. A., 103
Johnson, John Albert, 108, 164
Johnson, William D., 143, 160, 172
Jones, Absalom, 22
Jones, E. Stanley, 13
Jones, W. H., 126, 131
Jordan, Frederick D., 181
Judicial Court, 181

K

Kansas and Nebraska Bill, 59
Kant, Immanuel, 8
Kealing, H. T., 85
Kittrell College, 85

L

Lafayette, Appendix B, 8
Lambert, William, 115
Lampton College, 95, 141
Latimer, Appendix B, 15

Lawrence, G. W., 71
Lee, B. F., 138
Lee, Jesse, 7
Legal Redress Committee, 172
Lewis, S. H., 180
Lewis, W. A., 173
Liberator, 66
Lincoln, Abraham, 63
Link, Nora L., 78
Locke, John, 8
Long, C. S., 132
Long, Lutrelle, G., 133
Long, Thomas, 132
Lord, S. E. Churchstone, 108
Louisiana Conference, 106
Lynch, James, 101

M

McDade, J. W., 163
Madison, James, Appendix B, 11, quoted
Marshall, John, 46
Miller, William, 28
Missouri Annual Conference, 39
Mobile, Alabama, 27
Mobile Register, 66
Mohammed, Appendix B, 11
Monk, V. C., 167
Morgan, J. R. V., 70
Morris, Gouverneur, 20
Morris, Robert, xvii, 20
Morris, Sr., S. S., 86
Murray, Jane Ann, 18
Mystery, 81

N

Napper, R. O., 158
Nazrey, Willis, 32, 108
New England Conference, 58
New Era, 167
New York Tribune, 66
Newsome, H. N., 163
Nichols, D. Ward, 83, 84, 144, 174, 181, 186
Nichols, L. Ruffin, 117
Norris, David, 83

O

Oglethorpe, James, 5
Ohio Annual Conference, 30
Old Folks Home, 134
Old St. George Church, xviii
Olmstead, Frederick Law, 61
Otis, James, xvi

P

Paine, Thomas, 8
Parent Home & Foreign Missionary
  Society, 75
Parker, Theodore, 62
Parks, Henry Blanton, 98, 111, 145,
  170
Payne, D. A., 34, 43, 63, 69, 88, 90,
  100-101, 103-104, 122
Payne College, Georgia, 96
Payne Theological Seminary, 96
Pension Department, 174, 186
Perry, W. C., 108
Pinkston, A. L., 173
Polk, Alma, 176
Pope, W. T., 163
Presbyterian Church, 55
Primm, H. Thomas, 78, 176
Protestant Episcopal Church, 54

Q

Queen Elizabeth, Appendix B, 8
Quinn, William Paul, 27, 34, 41, 71,
  78, 108, 115-116

R

Ralston, Robert, 17
Ransom, Reverdy C., 97, 98, 139, 146,
  157, 163, 171, 176, 182
Reid, Elmer, 163
Republican Party, 40
Revels, Hiram, 126
Rhett, Robert B., 66
Rice, David Eugene, 172
Robinson, J. G., 85
Robinson, Richard, 70
Roosevelt, Franklin D., 155-156
Ruffin Nichols Seminary, 96

Rush, Benjamin, M. D., 46, Appendix B, 8

S

Salter, M. B., 138, 140
Scarborough, W. S., 91
Schureman, P. D. W., 115
Schureman, W. D. W., 115
Schurz, Carl, 63
Selby, Eustace A., 159, 187
Seward, W. H., 40
Sharp, Granville, 8, 18
Shorter College, 106
Sims, D. H., 159, 170, 171, 175
Singleton, George A., 145, 163, 167,
  170, 171
Sisson, J. F. A., 111, 125
Slavery, 40
Smith, Adam, 6
Smith, Christine S., 77, 170
Smith, David, 70, 134, 135
Smith, Fannie Kerbo, 181
Smith, Stephen, 134
Standford, A. L., 104
Stephens, Alexander H., 40, Appen-
  dix B, 12-13
Stevens, Thaddeus, 40
Steward, Charles, 117
Steward, T. G., 130
Steward, W. G., 129
Stewart, Benjamin, 108

T

Tacitus, Appendix B, 11
Taney, Roger B., 3
Tanner, B. T., 84, 138
Tapsico, Jacob, 24
Texas Pioneers, 131-132
Thomas, Jeremiah, 115
Tookes, H. Y., 87, 180
Toombs, Robert, 40
Trimble, Judge T. C., 175
Tudas, Jonathan, 128
Turner, H. M., 66, 124, 133, 170,
  Appendix B, 5, 11-12
Turner College, 96

U

Union Seminary, 92
University of Pennsylvania, 124

V

Van Doren, Carl, xix
Vanderhorst, Richard, 104
Vernon, William T., 143, 168
Voice of Missions, 104

W

Walden, Harvey E., 172
Walker, D. O., 93, 163, 165, 179, 181
Walker, J. W., 165
Ward, T. M. D., 36, 106, 117-121
Washington, George, xvii, 20, Appendix B, 8, quoted
Waters, Caesar, 14
Waters, Edward, 30, 33
Watkins, W. R., 77
Wayman, Alexander, 36, 101, 102, 103
Webb, Thomas, 6
Wesley, John, xviii, 4, 5, 12, 45
Wesleyan Church, 54

Western Christian Recorder, 83
Wheatley, Phillis, xvii
Wheddon, D. D., 53
White, William, 15
White slaves, Appendix B, 8
Williams, Bruce H., 133
Williams, Noah W., 171, 182
Williams, P. C., 83
Williams, Roger, 3
Wilson, A. B., 78
Wilson, Woodrow, 162
Wise, Daniel, 53
Witherspoon, Daniel L., 174
Womack, P. E., 171
Women's Mite Missionary Society, 77, 170
Wright, Bishop R. R., 84, 91, 93, 157
Wright, Milton S. J., 91
Wright, Wallace M., 70

Y

Yancey, William Y., 66
Yellow Fever, xix
Young, G. B., 182
Young Allenite, 171

DATE DUE

GAYLORD   PRINTED IN U.S.A.